Musorgsky REMEMBERED

Russian Music Studies

Malcolm Hamrick Brown, founding editor

Musorgsky in 1874. Photograph presented to Rimsky-Korsakov.

Musorgsky REMEMBERED

COMPILED AND EDITED BY
Alexandra Orlova

TRANSLATED BY
Véronique Zaytzeff and Frederick Morrison

INDIANA UNIVERSITY PRESS
Bloomington and Indianapolis

The paper used in this publication meets the minimum requirements of
American National Standard for Information Sciences—Permanence of
Paper for Printed Library Materials, ANSI Z39.48-1984.

™

Manufactured in the United States of America

Library of Congress Cataloging-in-Publication Data

M.P. Musorgskiĭ. English. Selections.
    Musorgsky remembered / compiled and edited by Alexandra Orlova;
translated by Véronique Zaytzeff and Frederick Morrison.
        p.   cm. — (Russian music studies)
    Rev. translation of: M.P. Musorgskiĭ.
    Includes index.
    ISBN 0-253-34264-3
    1. Mussorgsky, Modest Petrovich, 1839–1881.   2. Composers—Russia.
I. Orlova, Aleksandra Anatol'evna, date.   II. Zaytzeff,
Véronique, date.   III. Morrison, Frederick, date.
IV. Title.   V. Series: Russian music studies (Bloomington, Ind.)
ML410.M97M2213   1991
780'.92—dc20
[B]   90-25310

1 2 3 4 5   95 94 93 92 91

C O N T E N T S

viii | Contents

Illustrations appear on pp. iv, 32, 62, 83, 112, and 147.

Many eminent figures share a common fate in that recollections about them are surprisingly insignificant and superficial. Published memoirs are seldom worthy of the person to whom they are devoted, for they usually do not convey the greatness of the genius. For example, reminiscences about Tchaikovsky, except for those of Laroche and Kashkin, and in part those of Glazunov, deal with petty details of his everyday life. Reminiscences about Musorgsky often distort his personality and misinterpret both the man and the music.

One might then ask why publish these recollections about Musorgsky? Although they reveal little about the composer's personality, which is what we are looking for when we read the testimony of contemporaries, they do recreate the psychological atmosphere surrounding Musorgsky and allow us to see the tragedy of the innovator and of the solitary genius. Besides, by examining these reminiscences and by comparing the information provided by the different authors, we can revaluate the legends that have grown about the composer. In comparing the information given by witnesses with that given by the illustrious man himself, the researcher is better able to approach the truth, i.e., the historical truth, and to refute the numerous misrepresentations which have accumulated in the writings of Musorgsky's biographers, many of whom have relied too uncritically upon the veracity of his contemporaries. The compiler's problem in this case (as, incidentally, in any similar work based on documents) resembles the work of a prosecutor conducting a cross-examination.

The first researcher to gather reminiscences about Musorgsky was Vasilii Iakovlev, co-editor with Iiurii Keldysh of the collection *M. P. Musorgskii k piatidesiatiletiiu so dnia smerti, 1881–1931. Stat'i i materialy* [M. P. Musorgsky on the fiftieth anniversary of his death, 1881–1931. Articles and materials] (Moscow: Muzgiz, 1932). Twenty-five of the thirty-six memoirs in the present volume are extracted from this work.

Iakovlev called attention to the "one-sided character of testimonies about Musorgsky," and he underscored the fact that in many of the memoirs by different authors, "we see total agreement and even some kind of deliberate emphasis on the same traits, which at times, perhaps, conveys the impression of definite bias and exaggeration," especially in the information "dealing with the last years of the composer's life" (ibid., p. 166).

Iakovlev was quite right in his observation. Furthermore, the memoirs which were still unavailable to him, such as those by Golenishchev-Kutuzov (for which he and others researching Musorgsky had great hopes) do not alter his criticism. Unfortunately, a great many of the memoirs are prejudiced, they lack objectivity, and, I dare say, are myopic.

In the present volume, in contrast to Iakovlev's collection, references to Musorgsky's letters and those of his contemporaries are quoted only when it seems absolutely necessary. Vladimir Stasov's memoirs, extracted earlier by Iakovlev, have been given in more complete form. Excerpts from Liudmila Shestakova's memoirs, *Moi Vechera* [My evenings], as well as Filaret Musorgsky's are quoted from autographs in the archives of Liudmila Shestakova (archive 857) and of Musorgsky (archive 502), in the Manuscript Section of the State Public Library of Leningrad.

The memoirs in the present collection may be classified, for the sake of discussion, in four general if not precisely parallel categories: those that are verifiable as authentic and essentially objective; those that are authentic but biased; those written by persons who did not witness everything they are reporting; and those by persons who were not themselves acquainted with Musorgsky and who are reporting secondhand information. In every memoir there are undoubtedly elements in more than one category. Thus, while Stasov's memoirs are in essence truthful, they are somewhat biased. Rimsky-Korsakov's are even more biased, with many situations presented in a distorted light. Readers can determine for themselves to which category this or that memoir belongs. Indeed, the purpose of the endnotes is to help establish the truth.

Musorgsky's relationship with the other members of the Balakirev circle has been treated elsewhere.[1] Here I will only point out that although there was much ideological identity within the circle, genuine intimacy was almost totally absent. This was true not just in Musorgsky's case. The members of the circle cherished each other; they valued each other as persons of like mind, giving each other endearing, often facetious nicknames. However, their real emotional life was quite unknown to one another. Furthermore, Borodin, Rimsky-Korsakov, and Cui had families apart from their professional and creative lives; they did not suffer solitude or the misunderstanding of those nearest them. Balakirev and Musorgsky, on the other hand, found themselves tragically alone. The former found solace in religion; the latter, unfortunately for him and for his art, in alcohol.

Oppressed by want and the necessity of seeking employment as a petty official, devoting the best hours of the day not to creativity but to odious bureaucratic duties, infinitely alone, often losing friends, Musorgsky was continually disappointed in the companions who shared his ideas and who, as it seemed to him, ultimately became traitors to their common cause. Rimsky-Korsakov became distracted in his intense study of music theory. Cui wrote an insulting review of *Boris Godunov*. Musorgsky turned to drinking, and this led to his eventual collapse and a premature death.

On meeting the young poet Arsenii Golenishchev-Kutuzov, Musorgsky came to believe in his talent and thought that he had found a true friend. All too soon he was again disappointed. The alleged reason was the poet's marriage (Musorgsky, as well as Stasov, was fiercely opposed to marriage for an artist), but in fact the breach in their friendship began to show earlier. Golenishchev-Kutuzov's memoirs need careful scrutiny, since they run askew of the categories enumerated. They are the notes of an eyewitness. They were not written "third hand." But they are nevertheless biased, not "simply" biased, as are the reminiscences of the Balakirev circle, such as those by Rimsky-Korsakov or Balakirev. Golenishchev-Kutuzov's memoirs are almost totally deceitful. They are calculated to shed light on Musorgsky's work from a particular angle, in order to demonstrate that Musorgsky was not at all the person we know through his music. Indeed, according to Golenishchev-Kutuzov, the artist composed one thing but wrote down something else. Golenishchev-Kutuzov's memoirs are a polemical document, directed against Stasov in particular and the "Mighty Handful" as a whole. The author of the memoirs assigned himself the purpose of demonstrating that Musorgsky was a man without any willpower, who created according to the dictates of the circle and did not follow his own artistic nature. According to Golenishchev-Kutuzov, the works he created were fabricated, labored, and foreign to his nature. In his youth, at the time of his friendship with Musorgsky, Golenishchev-Kutuzov had been an enthusiast of the radical sixties, a supporter of the democratic movement in the era before the reforms; but he very quickly retreated from his enthusiasms. And in his recollections about Musorgsky, he projects his later beliefs onto the composer. By depicting Musorgsky as a refined aesthete, removed from life (more exactly from the prosaic life) and alien to the interests of the Russian people, Golenishchev-Kutuzov demonstrates how far he himself was from understanding the real Musorgsky, how far, indeed, these two former friends were removed from each other both spiritually and artistically.

Musorgsky based many of his compositions on Golenishchev-Kutuzov's texts, which were somewhat primitive and spur-of-the-moment ventures. The composer altered the texts and thereby created highly philosophical works (for example, the *Songs and Dances of Death*). It would be profoundly instructive to examine in detail the composer's transformations of Golenishchev-Kutuzov's original texts!

Soviet musicologists have widely varying views of Golenishchev-Kutuzov's memoirs. The academician B. Asafiev, the professor Iu. Tiulin, and recently, the musicologist M. Rakhmanova have all given them unfailing credence, quoting them as if they were the words of the composer himself, expressing no doubts about their objectivity. Others, among them E. Frid, A. Kandinsky, and S. Shlifshtein, have viewed the memoirs very critically. The present compiler has also pointed out the necessity of viewing these memoirs with care.[2]

The opinion of P. Aravin, musicologist and author of *Vospominaniia Golenishcheva-Kutuzova* [Golenishchev-Kutuzov's memoirs], is worth noting: "In the process of working with this material, I had to study the entire archives relating to the poet. . . . And it then became clear that between Musorgsky and Golenishchev-Kutuzov there was never a complete sympathy of thought."[3] He is entirely correct, although I would like to make a slight change—to substitute the word "spirit" for the word "thought."

Golenishchev-Kutuzov does more than "tailor" Musorgsky's personality to his own ideals: he deliberately distorts the facts. For example, he extends the period of time they lived together, and this creates the illusion of a long-lasting relationship. He quotes some lines from a purported letter written to him by the composer, but such a letter is not to be found anywhere in the poet's archive. And since Golenishchev-Kutuzov carefully kept everything, even short notes from Musorgsky, the suspicion arises that those quoted lines did not belong to the composer, all the more so since their style and content do not correspond to other letters by Musorgsky.

One is tempted to think that it was not by accident that during his lifetime Golenishchev-Kutuzov withheld publications of his notes on Musorgsky. He might well have feared, with reason, his own exposure, and it would have destroyed the fascination he created in his circle for being the great composer's closest friend.

The memoirs in this collection are arranged according to the principle established earlier by Iakovlev. The reminiscences are not segmented and fitted into a common chronological framework. Instead, the chronology *vis-à-vis* each individual memoirist is respected. The sequence of authors follows a general chronological plan, since each memoir tends to focus on a particular time period; therefore, those memoirs dealing with the last years of Musorgsky's life are placed at the end, while those dealing with earlier or broader periods are placed in the beginning (e.g., those by N. Kompaneiskii and V. Stasov). It goes without saying that a certain amount of repetition is unavoidable.

Alexandra Orlova
Jersey City, New Jersey

Notes

1. A. Orlova, "Musorgskii i gruppa 'Piati' " [Musorgsky and the group of 'five'], paper read at the International Congress on Musorgsky, Milan, Italy, May 1981; published in *Musorgskij l'opera, il pensiero* (Milan, 1985). The same issue is dealt with in the Foreword to *M. P. Musorgskii. Literaturnoe nasledie. Pis'ma i avtobiograficheskie materialy* [M. P. Musorgsky. Literary heritage. Letters and autobiographical materials] (Moscow, 1971); and in the Introduction to A. Orlova, *Musorgsky's Days and*

Works: A Biography in Documents, translated and edited by Roy J. Guenther (Ann Arbor: UMI Research Press, 1983). It is again treated in "Pamiati Musorgskogo (k 150-letiiu so dnia rozhdeniia)" [To the memory of Musorgsky (in commemoration of the 150th anniversary of his birth)], *Kontinent* 60 (1989).

2. Introduction to *Musorgsky's Days and Works.*

3. *Sovetskaia muzyka* [Soviet music] 34/3 (March 1970), p. 110.

Most of the selections in the present volume appeared originally in *M. P. Musorgskii k piatidesiatiletiiu so dnia smerti, 1881–1931. Stat'i i materialy* [M. P. Musorgsky on the fiftieth anniversary of his death, 1881–1931. Articles and materials], edited by Iurii Keldysh and Vasilii Iakovlev (Moscow: Muzgiz, 1932). Additional selections, short biographies of the memoirists, and endnotes were added by Alexandra Orlova for this edition.

The composer's name is spelled in a variety of ways in the documents: Musarskii, Musirskoi (as in the entry for his birth in the Register of Births), Muserskoi, Musurskii. None of the spellings include the letter *g*. It was Modest who added it, on the basis of an ancestor whose nickname was Musorga. In the present work we use the spelling "Musorgsky" in the translation but "Musorgskii" in the notes in citations of Russian-language publications.

Names well known to English-language readers, such as Rimsky-Korsakov and Tchaikovsky, are spelled with a *y*. Less-familiar names are spelled according to the Library of Congress transliteration system, with some minor variations.

Musorgsky REMEMBERED

Nikolai Kompaneiskii

Vospominaniia o Musorgskom

Recollections of Musorgsky

Nikolai Kompaneiskii (1848–1910) was a composer, the author of religious music, a singer, and a music critic. He was educated in the same Cadet School of the Imperial Guards as Musorgsky, but at a much later date. In his youth, he associated with A. Serov and Musorgsky; and he took singing lessons from A. Petrov. His recollections of events he actually witnessed are worthy of attention, but the rest is based on hearsay and gossip, and therefore is not trustworthy.

· · · ·

. . . The boy was sent by his parents to the Cadet School of the Imperial Guards,[1] where Musorgsky was still surrounded by the same atmosphere of serfdom. Each ensign had his own lackey, who came from the serfs and was given a flogging by the administration if he failed to please his young master.

The same type of serf-like relationship, with a tinge of petty military tyranny, was established between the older and the younger cadets. The cadets in the advanced class called themselves "Sir Cornets" and behaved haughtily toward their junior counterparts, whom they called "Vandals." Each cornet had a lackey as well as a vandal at his service. The vandal was subject to a number of humiliations from the cornet, since might makes right, such as having to carry his cornet on his back to his morning bath. Messrs. Cornets considered it debasing to do homework. The same attitude was shared by the director of the school, General Sutgof.[2]

All the dreams of the Messrs. Cornets were focused on the grandeur and honor of the uniform of the Imperial Guard. The highest praise at the school was to call someone a "real cornet." The cadets called their beloved priest Cornet Krupskii. When they were through with their military exercises, the cornets devoted their free time to dancing, love making, and drinking. General Sutgof was very determined that the drunken cadets should not come back to school on foot and should not drink common vodka; he championed the honor of the school and was proud when a cadet returned from vacation drunk on champagne and sprawled in a carriage drawn by his own trotters. It was in such an institution . . . that the young Musorgsky received his education. He studied German philosophy enthusiastically, read historical works, and translated foreign books. For such behavior, General Sutgof, who took a great interest in him, would give him a good scolding: "But what kind of an officer are you going to be, *mon cher?*"

During his entire stay at the Cadet School Musorgsky took piano lessons.[3] Herke introduced the young Russian virtuoso to German piano literature exclusively. The young pianist liked to improvise, relying only on his ear and imagination, since he was totally ignorant of ways to put his thoughts on paper and was utterly unaware of the elementary rules of music. While in the Cadet School, he constantly had to thump out dances on the piano for the pleasure of the cadets, varying his repertoire with his own improvisations.[4]

While he was at school, Musorgsky used to sing arias from Italian operas, in a clear baritone voice. This fashionably educated young man had not the faintest notion about the existence of Russian composers, still less about such individuals as Glinka or Dargomyzhsky. He did not even dream of the existence of music theory or musical science. The comment in his autobiography that, while at school, he would often visit the teacher of religion, the priest Krupskii, and that thanks to him, he was able to fathom the essence of ancient Greek and Catholic religious music, only bears witness to the fact that, later on, he was still unfamiliar with this subject. The priest Krupskii was also in the school during my time (1866). Being seriously interested in the study of religious music, I also went to him for clarification of some questions I had; more than once I conversed with him and came to the conclusion that in this specialty his knowledge was almost completely nil; therefore he could have given Musorgsky only the most elementary information on ancient religious music.[5]

[Musorgsky's life in the Preobrazhenskii Regiment consisted of [6]] training, marching, riding drill, social calls, dances, cards, drinking, political amours in search of a rich countess or, if it came to the worst, a merchant's daughter with a fat dowry. Musorgsky mastered the external qualities of an officer of the Preobrazhenskii: his manners were polished, he walked cockily on his tiptoes, dressed like a dandy, spoke excellent French, danced even better, played the piano masterfully, and sang beautifully. He even learned how to drink himself to oblivion; in addition, he abandoned his reprehensible studies of German philosophy; to make a long story short, fortune was smiling upon him. . . .

But . . . he could not afford to spend as much money as his comrades did. . . . He participated in the carousing, and for nights on end he would pound out polkas on the ivories. His comrades appreciated his services, but this was not sufficient to support the honor of the Guards' uniform. One had to spend one's fortune. . . . The unsuitable conditions forced Musorgsky to resign.[7] However, the three years of existence in the milieu of the Guards officers exerted a fatal influence on his whole life and was the reason for his being unable to make proper use of his enormous and original musical talents. This waste of time, day after day, distracted him from useful work, taught him idleness, prevented him from developing discipline of thought, and brought him finally into the milieu of people for whom knowledge was totally alien. He was deprived of exchanging ideas and thoughts, which is so vital for a young artist. Later on, when Musorgsky did not try to conceal the bad influence of the Guards milieu, he would occasionally say: "This is in accordance with the true Preobrazhenskii style."[8]

As a pupil at the same school where I was also perfecting my equestrian skills, Musorgsky was remembered as being an excellent pianist, and also for having had the honor of being invited to the home of the school's director to play duets with his daughter. The interest aroused in our school was quite understandable when the concert given in the Hall of the Assembly of the Nobles featured *Porazhenie Sennakheriba* [Destruction of Sennakherib],[9] a work composed by a former cadet. Everyone was saying, "Look what kind of cadets we have here in the Guards; we are not like the Army." By that time, I had already botched a fair amount of music paper, and for that reason, I rushed to the concert hall. As I remember, I was disappointed with *Destruction of Sennakherib* and its composer. "Come with me, I will introduce you," M., a captain in the household troops of the cuirassiers regiment, said. "He is over there, standing next to the column on the upper step." And I saw a dandy, of medium height, whose appearance, I dare say, was not attractive. He was snub-nosed, with protruding eyes, little red cheeks, and slightly curly hair. A real cockerel, and a provocative one at that. I was all set to refuse to be introduced, but it was too late: my friend was already talking to him. I soon found that I was talking to an extremely refined, smartly dressed aristocrat, with tightly pursed lips, lilac gloves, and elegant manners. His speech came through clenched teeth and was interspersed with many French words. Everything gave the impression that he was a fashionable fop, but at the same time, this aristocrat had something which made him highly likable and not at all banal. His expression changed quickly; at one minute he was stern-faced, the next he was laughing wholeheartedly. His speech was bold in its changes of intonation and rhythm, for his voice had a wide range. His movements were jerky, his attitude challenging, but immediately afterward some sort of shyness and timidity would reveal a very nervous nature and gentle character. Some five years later, at O[sip] A[fanasievich] Petrov's, where Musorgsky was a frequent guest, before the staging of his opera *Boris Godunov,* I got to know Modest Petrovich much better. By that time, I was enthralled with his compositions and would play them as much as I could wherever I went. Our closer relationship convinced me of his phenomenal musical talent. At the time I was seriously studying music theory from the viewpoint of acoustics as well as

how it would apply to art, and consequently I am sure it is quite understandable why I was interested in the opinion on this subject of such an
original composer as Musorgsky. From our conversations, I was soon convinced that the great composer was as innocent as a newborn babe when it
came to music theory and the technique of composition. He did not even
have the broad outlook of a piano virtuoso. I am convinced that he did not
want to undertake a serious study of composing technique, or even think
about it: he did not have time. He would study it sporadically, but as he was
self-educated, he was not prepared for systematic work.[10] Although he talked
extensively about the seriousness of the role of the arts, and assigned them
an instructive rather than a simply diversionary function, he wrote music
only in his spare time, at random. The melody would flow instantly from his
lively conversation, while its accompaniments would appear in masterly figures in Lisztian style. Theoretically, these figures were extraordinarily clear,
artistic, original, and genuine, but technically they were of an inappropriate
complexity and clumsiness. But considering Musorgsky's technical preparation and his attitude about work, he had to be a genius to compose at all.

Musorgsky's memory for music was staggering. He was at O. A. Petrov's
the day Petersburg received Wagner's *Siegfried*. Musorgsky played it
through, singing its score; and when asked to repeat Wotan's scene, he
played it from memory, from beginning to end. He was able to do the same
with Rubinstein's opera *Demon*.[11] Immediately after hearing its premiere
Musorgsky stopped by to visit "Grandfather" Petrov and played all the characteristic passages, from A to Z, heightening them by exaggeration. This
impromptu performance was almost twice as good as his "Rayok" [Peep-
show].[12] Musorgsky was a first-class pianist; he was scarcely inferior to Rubinstein, especially when interpreting the essence of a composer's music. It
is not so difficult to imagine what came from his hands when he played
Slav'sia, Slav'sia [Glory to Thee], when we read that the old keys of the Virt
droned like bells and boomed like a brass orchestra.[13] At the piano, Musorgsky was an inimitable humorous storyteller. He kept a straight face, which
enhanced the comic aspect even more. I recall some hilarious scenes, such as
the one of the young deacon's wife playing sentimentally *La prière d'une
vierge* [A virgin's prayer][14] on a badly tuned piano. I think it quite important
to stress that Musorgsky, most likely, never knew precisely what his
compositions sounded like. He played them from memory, with slight
changes each time. Thus, when he performed them, his rendering never
followed the written score. I also think when somebody was singing and he
was the accompanist, as he always was, he did not really hear the singer's
performance.

What impelled Musorgsky to abandon such a promising subject as
Salammbô?[15] One day I asked Modest Petrovich why he stopped the work he
had begun. He stared at me, then burst out laughing, and making a gesture
with his hand, he said: "It would have been no good. It would have been an

anomalous Carthage." Then, after a moment of silence, he continued seriously: "There is enough of the East in *Iudif* [Judith].[16] Art is no game. Time is valuable." What Modest Petrovich meant was that it was impossible to describe the East without having seen it, without knowing its melodies.

He possessed great dramatic gifts and easily could have become a leading actor. Drama, satire, and comedy were natural for him. . . . Anyone who has ever lived in the midst of the hearty Russian people knows how sharp their tongues are, and how witty their humor can be, and at the same time, how good naturedly they make fun of everything. Modest Petrovich was a true Russian. I do not know whether he ever took singing lessons or whether he had had a good voice,[17] but when I heard him singing in the seventies, his vocal abilities had severely declined. Despite this, however, he was still one of the best singers I ever had the opportunity to hear.

I recall the day I went to Serov to show him "Svetik Savishna" [Darling Savishna]. He glanced at it quickly and with great derision said: "Ah, this is the famous *Destruction of Sennakherib.*[18] Well, show it to us, sing it for us." In my youth I used to be a singer, and as I had paid so much attention to all the vocal literature, I came to be known as the singer with an international repertoire. When I finished singing, Serov remained silent for a long time, as if he were embarrassed or afraid to give an opinion which might shatter his authority as a critic; then, he quickly muttered: "A horrible scene. This is Shakespeare put to music. What a pity he wields such a clumsy pen."

The opera *Boris Godunov* made a strong impression on the public and created a great deal of talk in society although judgments differed. The majority were of the opinion that there was very little music as such in the new opera, and if it was a success it was due to the artists: their wonderful acting, they said, came to the composer's rescue. I recall that after the scene in the inn, I went to see some acquaintances sitting in a box whom I had persuaded to take some interest in the new opera. The mood in the box was extremely animated; they were all talking, laughing, and discussing the different types of tramps. All had been enraptured with the performances by Petrov, Kommissarzhevskii, Leonova, and even Diuzhikov, a very poor artist who played Misail. After the first scene of the fourth act ("Granovitaia Palata" [The palace of facets]), I went to another box; there, an elderly lady was still holding her handkerchief to her eyes.

"I am delighted to see that the opera made such a strong impression on you."

"That's not an opera, there is no music in it. To be honest, I could not take my eyes off the stage. What a wonderful actor Mel'nikov is! His words are still ringing in my ears. He is not just an artist, he is a genius!"

"And how do you like Shuiskii?"

"He is a wonderful actor, too; but Mel'nikov is far better!"

Vasin'ka Vasil'ev the Second, nicknamed The Little One, sang the part of Shuiskii. He had a good voice, but he was a terrible actor. . . . But the public's opinion that the new opera was successful because of the artists, that their wonderful acting had saved the composer, was a delusion. What really happened was that mediocre artists appeared to be brilliant because they performed magnificent recitatives, full of truth and dramatic effect. This is the great merit of Musorgsky's operas. . . . I saw the opera *Boris Godunov* on several occasions and with different casts, but the public kept the same opinion about the incomparable acting.

I would like to say a few words about the real reason for the great Russian artist's untimely death. Musorgsky was a warm-hearted man, but after his mother's death in 1865, he was quite alone and most unfortunate. He did have a wide circle of acquaintances; however, excluding his musical circle (and right at the end) the Petrov family and a few others, the majority of these acquaintances belonged to the aristocracy, where purely social, superficial, and conventional ties were cultivated. Musorgsky's closest friends were bachelors, burning out their lives in endless carousing. For some reason, he was wary of married life. One day, when Liudmila Shestakova began to talk to him about marriage, he answered her most seriously: "If you read in the papers the news that I shot or hanged myself, it will mean that I got married the day before." There is no point in naming those who pushed the weak-willed Musorgsky into the morass which progressively undermined his health.[19] Existence was miserable; it was a continuous dichotomy between the real and the ideal: between being enslaved by his bureaucratic duty or devoting himself to art. He sought oblivion from that life in the company of a few true friends and became accustomed to spending sleepless nights, poisoning himself with alcohol in the [tavern] Malyi Iaroslavets. Unfortunately, in that sympathetic company no one was strong enough to influence the weak-willed Musorgsky constructively. Quite the contrary: in most of the houses opened to him, his hosts indulged him with the poison. The staging of *Boris Godunov* was particularly hard on his health. He sought the patronage and support of powerful people both inside and outside the musical milieu; he could not refuse an invitation for a cup of tea or an invitation to entertain the public with his singing and playing; and then he would indulge himself with drink. With a sigh he would say: "Oh! The road to Parnassus, the one that leads to the top, is steep and tortuous." But when he did ascend it, he was invited into homes which vied for his company, but they were homes with no real love of music. A crowd, dressed to the nines, would be invited for an evening in the company of the renowned composer. Enthralled by his glory and often oblivious to the degree of his humiliation, the celebrated composer would play and sing for the pleasure of the guests; he would wear himself out, wasting precious energy. He would then dine, drinking copiously; then, about three or four o'clock in the morning, he would return to the Malyi Iaroslavets. In addition to these evenings given in honor of the renowned composer, he often had to participate as an accompanist in the concerts of the students, who adored him.[20] The poisoning of his organism exerted an ever-greater influence on his lucidity and on his ability to sustain the intense nervous exertion brought on during the periods of blessed inspiration and creativity. Musorgsky was, more than anyone else, his own worst enemy and, at the same time, he was everyone else's best friend. His good nature knew no limit; one marvels at the meekness and placidity with which he endured all the jokes made about the direction he was taking in his art. He would laugh, saying: "Just imagine what dearest Pyotr Stepanovich told me yesterday during dinner at the Iaroslavets. 'As a professor at the Conservatory, I am prepared to give you some advice on how to compose an opera.' Bravo! He is such a dear. I will have to borrow something from his *Oprichnik.*"[21]

Musorgsky never even insulted those who, indeed, deserved an insult, although he would harmlessly joke about everyone who amused him. Generally speaking, he was endowed with an extraordinary number of those traits of talent and character typically bestowed on a Russian. In addition to his musical talent, he was blessed with great intelligence and a quick mind, but he never applied himself to the systematic study of a subject.

I remember vividly the shock created by Musorgsky's death. I was devastated when I read the obituary.[22] On my way to the Nikolaev Hospital, I asked myself if it were possible that everything was over and that there was no return. Just the other day I had seen his twinkling eyes and heard him say: "Everything is fine now. I have completely recovered, and soon we will start working again." Was it possible that that fiery soul, who grieved over his famished, benighted people, was no more? When I entered the hospital chapel, all my doubts and hopes vanished. There lay the lifeless, cold body of Musorgsky, the great composer. He had died, broken down by fate, victim of a nervous disorder, before his enormous, unexhaustible talent had run dry. . . . Now, everything was over. A bright ray of the springtime sun infused the colorless face with tints of rose; the pursed lips gave him that expression he used to have when lost in thought. I remembered this expression from three years ago, when we both sat on a small green sofa in front of the casket of his dearly beloved "grandfather" Petrov, whispering about the great sorrow that befell his friends and its consequences.[23] It was only then that I understood how wonderful, tender, and loving Musorgsky was, how dearly he loved Osip Afanasievich, and how much he was distressed by his death. He stood by the coffin and sobbed as disconsolately and loudly as a child. After drinking a glass of water, and having overcome his hysterical fit, he sat down on the small green sofa and began to talk, his voice breaking: "With grandfather's death, I've lost everything. I've lost the support of my bitter life. Lately, when I was in this house, I felt as if I belonged to it. I've lost an irreplaceable mentor. He brought me up on the truth, and he gave me the inspiration to create. Just when it started to bloom, Russian opera was nipped in the bud. Now, in its place there will be a rank growth of foreign imitations that will stifle true Russian opera for years ahead."

Vladimir Stasov

Vospominaniia o Musorgskom

Recollections of Musorgsky

Vladimir Stasov (1824–1906), an art and music critic, was the ideological leader of the Balakirev circle.

. . .   .   .   .

. . . Musorgsky soon reached the conclusion that if, indeed, his life's true calling was to be a musician and a composer, and he did not want to fall behind his elder and more advanced friends, he had to work very hard. Therefore, it was no longer advisable to stay on in the army, for which at any rate, he had little inclination. He decided to resign his commission in the Preobrazhenskii Regiment. I vividly recall how I met him in 1857, through M[ilii] A[lekseevich] Balakirev, and how we immediately became close friends. I remember that during the summer and fall of 1858,[1] during our walks, I diligently tried to talk him out of resigning. I used to tell him that Lermontov himself was able to be an officer in the hussars and at the same time a great poet,[2] in spite of the expenses and the parades. Musorgsky would reply: "That was Lermontov, but I am not like him; may be he was able to cope with it but I cannot. Military service keeps me from working as I ought to!"

For the new Russian school of music the second half of the sixties was not only a time of unusually brisk activity; it was also a most exhilarating time of creativity. On one hand there was the fifty-year-old Dargomyzhsky, who had suddenly flared anew with unexpected force, fearlessly moving toward the completion of his brilliant last work.[3] On the other hand, a number of twenty-year-olds were just emerging: endowed with strong, original, highly diverse talents, they were beginning to compose a number of really important works. It was a time of truly lively and exuberant activity.

At the beginning of their careers, Balakirev was his fellow composers' most reliable critic, their mentor when it came to musical forms and orchestration. Balakirev had been the earliest among them to master the form and achieve eminence, and now he was stretching out a trustworthy hand to his comrades. He provided the young composers with the majority of the themes for their most important compositions. He was the one who suggested that C[esar] A[ntonovich] Cui write an opera about Ratcliff, that N[ikolai] A[ndreevich] Rimsky-Korsakov write *Pskovitianka* [The maid of Pskov] as well as *Antar*, and that A[leksandr] P[orfirievich] Borodin write his *Tsarskaia Nevesta* [The tsar's bride] (which, by the way, Borodin never completed). Balakirev had an unusually powerful influence on his musical circle: none of his comrades matched his passion for research. He discovered and immediately performed the as yet unknown works of the masters of the post-Beethoven period, such as F[ranz] Schubert, Schumann, Berlioz, and Listz. A newly discovered composition would make him radiantly happy. With his ardent passion he would infect all of his followers, he was such a powerful leader.[4]

Balakirev was surrounded by a phalanx of young composers with the most varied natures and interests, but with an identical talent: passionate, powerful, and deep-rooted. They all developed and achieved their first successes at practically the same time. By the middle of the sixties each of them had composed many original and important works which were to play a significant role not only in the course of their own creativity but also in the history of Russian music. Cui was the composer of the overture to *Kavkazskii plennik* [The prisoner of the Caucasus], a beautiful scherzo for orchestra, and several songs in which all his passionate, nervous, and graceful nature found expression. At times his work is reminiscent of Schumann. He was also capable of striking soulful notes of an emotional depth well beyond the reach of any other composer. One of his best songs of that period is the one based on the words "V dushe gorit ogon' liubvi" [My soul is aflame with love].[5] Cui had also started to work on his marvelous first opera, *Ratcliff*.[6] N[ikolai] A[ndreevich] Rimsky-Korsakov had already met Balakirev and started to compose talented works while still a cadet in the Naval School.[7] In 1865, having barely returned from a world cruise, he composed a symphony which immediately attracted the attention of even such a demanding public as ours was then.[8] He was soon to compose a whole series of strikingly beautiful and poetic songs: "Evreiskaia pesn'" [Hebrew song], "Plenivshis' rozoi, solovei" [Enslaved by a rose, the nightingale], "Iz slyoz moikh" [From my tears], "Sosna" [The pine tree], "Iuzhnaia noch'" [Southern night], "V temnoi roshche" [In the dark grove]. And he was already thinking about *Sadko* and *Antar*.[9] Finally, Borodin, the last one of the group to publish although he was somewhat older than the others, produced his magnificent and original symphony in 1862. It made a strong impression on Balakirev from its very first measures; and he immediately recognized the enormous originality of the new composer. At that time, Borodin had already written the first of his wonderful songs: "Falshivaia nota" [The false note] and "Spiashchaia kniazhna" [The sleeping princess].[10] These very talented young men were not only fellow musicians but also friends. They met constantly, would spend whole nights together playing music, and, naturally, had a strong effect on each other since they lifted one another's spirits and fanned each other's poetical fire. In that circle, Musorgsky was one of the most important and one of the most gifted.

During those years Musorgsky produced some of his most perfect compositions—a whole series of songs.[11] The group gathered in several friendly neighboring homes, either at Dargomyzhsky's or Cui's, or Shestakova's (Glinka's sister), or, finally, sometimes, at my place. Nothing can compare with the marvelous artistry that prevailed in these intimate gatherings. Each man in the group was such a talented composer. Each brought with him that wonderful poetic atmosphere intrinsic to the artist deeply involved in his work and seized with inspiration. They rarely came empty-handed to the meetings: one would bring either one of his new works, barely finished, or he would bring excerpts of what was being composed at the moment; another would show a new scherzo; a third, a new song; a fourth, part of a symphony or an overture; a fifth, a chorus; and yet another one, an operatic ensemble. What a freedom of creative forces it was! What a luxurious triumph of fantasy, inspiration, and musical innovation! They would crowd around the piano, where the accompanist was either Balakirev or Musorgsky, the best pianists of the group. The reading of the piece would begin immediately, followed by the criticism, the weighing of the merits and shortcomings, the attack and the defense. Then they would sing and play the best-loved previous compositions by the members. During these meetings, where talent, vivacity, exacting criticism, and gaiety were all in full swing, Musorgsky's songs always made a great impression. The tragic character of some and the comical character and humor of others had a profound effect on this highly talented and therefore highly susceptible audience. These songs were, almost without exception, performed by unanimous request. No wonder! The talent of the composition was constantly paralleled by the talent of the execution. Musorgsky was a magnificent pianist, and he got better every day (naturally, we are not talking about the concert pieces). He would accompany the singing—mainly his own—with peerless perfection. What was a mere listeners' enthusiasm in the face of that exceptional honesty, wit, grace, and simplicity, pouring forth from Musorgsky!

The song "Savishna" was composed before any of the others.[12] As Musorgsky himself told me later, he got the idea for the piece while in the country at his brother's (at the Minkino estate), during the summer of 1865. One day, standing by the window he was startled by the sight of the commotion that was taking place before his eyes. The unfortunate village idiot was pouring out his love to a young peasant girl. He begged her to love him, but he felt ashamed of himself, his ugliness, and his miserable condition. He realized that nothing on earth, especially the happiness of love, existed for him. Musorgsky was deeply affected, for both the subject and the scene strongly impressed him. In a trice he had both the original forms and sounds to embody the shattering images. But he did not finish the song at that time. First he wrote his "Kolybel'naia pesnia" [Lullaby] ("Spi, usni, krestianskii syn") [Sleep, sleep, peasant's son], which is full of painful, anguished sorrow. It was only several months later that he completed "Savishna." Musorgsky wrote his own text for this song, as he was to do for all his best songs.

I have already mentioned what a great master Musorgsky was as an accompanist and as a singer. Quite often at the time, as well as later on, during our little get-togethers and meetings and among ourselves, we would say that in this field he was definitely unique and incomparable. Even such an utterly outstanding pianist as A[nton] Rubinstein[13] was only half the equal of Musorgsky. With equal perfection both could accompany the brilliant songs of Schumann, Schubert, and other great Western composers. But Musorgsky had another talent which was unattainable by Rubinstein or any Western musician: this was the talent for performing national music, especially these truly popular, completely new, realistic scenes and pictures *à la* Gogol' I just mentioned. Here, Musorgsky was in his own special, novel, and original kingdom, where no purely Western musician could follow him. But, fortunately for him (and also for his entire group of fellow composers), two others joined them, around the mid-sixties, in performing the entirely native compositions of this new Russian music. They became his close followers, comrades, and helpers. Aleksandra and Nadezhda Purgold were two young ladies of unusual talent.[14] The first was a singer, the second a pianist. Both Glinka and Dargomyzhsky were always surrounded by a whole retinue of amateur singers and pianists. The latter would usually perform these composers' songs and arias for their immediate circle, but sometimes they would also perform them in public. No doubt, more than one had real talent, an attractive manner, and great enthusiasm. But none of them (I have every right to say this, since I heard all of them, at either Glinka's or Dargomyzhsky's) even closely matched the talent and deep musical feeling of the Purgold sisters.

The elder sister, the singer, had little talent for performing formal operatic arias. On the other hand, she was inimitable in the realistic and lively performance of those musical works whose principal feature was their genuine, true-to-life realism, the passion of the soul, or the human comedy. Because of this gift, Dargomyzhsky's and Musorgsky's music was prominent in her repertoire. How she could perform Musorgsky's best works! She would very faithfully reproduce his realistic recitative, so close and dear to her own heart, but she did not copy him blindly. She would freely interpret the work she performed, following her own instincts, and would add something of her own, more often than not a note of subtle and beautiful femininity. And according to the composers themselves, she would often add such expression that even they saw their own works anew. Her younger sister also came very close to Musorgsky's accomplishments when she accompanied the singers and her sister. She would add her own inflection and character, her own audacious and subtle expression (this was not surprising in that she was herself a gifted composer and a powerful musician). In his conversation and letters Musorgsky often called her "our dear orchestra." The presence of the two sisters in the circle of the "comrade composers" added enormously to the general harmony. When Dargomyzhsky was rehearsing *Kamennyi Gost'* [The stone guest] toward the end of 1868, both sisters played an important part: the elder one was magnificent and unusually poetic in her rendering of Anna and Laura; and the younger one played the role of the orchestra.[15] Dargomyzhsky himself played the part of Don Juan, Musorgsky that of Leporello and Don Carlos. No audience today will ever have the opportunity to hear Dargomyzhsky's work in such a perfect performance. Even at that time only Petrov[16] was their equal; his rendition of Leporello's part was one of the wonders of his already amazing repertoire.

In the fall, when Musorgsky returned to Petersburg, the first act of *Zhenit'ba* [The marriage] was performed by the circle of comrade musicians.[17] Dargomyzhsky, who, at the beginning of the summer had been so deeply moved by the first rehearsals of the opera, was now playing the role of Kochkaryov, Musorgsky himself that of Podkolesin; Aleksandra Nikolaevna Purgold was playing the matchmaker Fyokla; and her sister, Nadezhda Nikolaevna, was the accompanist. Both the rehearsals and the performance were accompanied by bursts of laughter because the exact tone of Gogol's brilliant comedy was so carefully preserved at every turn. Several years later, Musorgsky gave me the original piano score of his *Marriage* and wrote to me (January 2, 1873):

> Today is a special day for me and you too. It's your birthday. I have been thinking about you all day, and I have been asking myself what I would do for you. The answer came in a flash. And as it often happens with truly impudent fellows: I have decided to give myself as the gift. So that is what I am doing. Take my early work based on Gogol's *Marriage,* have a look at my attempts at recitative, compare them with *Boris,* compare the years 1868 and 1871, and you will see that I irrevocably send you myself. I have included the part of Kochkaryov copied by Dargomyzhsky, as a precious memorial to him from his last days: he copied it out, notwithstanding his grave illness and his own work on *The Stone Guest.* I cannot stand confusion and I think that for the one who is interested, *Marriage* will clarify a lot of my musical daring. You know how dearly I value this *Marriage,* and to set the record straight, you know that it was suggested to me by Dargomyzhsky (as a joke) and by Cui (for whom it was not a joke). The time and the period of the work are clear; the location is also given. To make a long story short, everything is done openly, without any concealment. Take me, my dear friend, and do with me whatever you wish.[18]

And now, after Musorgsky's death, I shall do not what I wish to do, but what I must do: I will give the piano score, along with the musical autographs, papers, and letters of my dear deceased friend to our public library.

While composing his new opera [*Boris Godunov*], just as he did when writing *Salammbô*, Musorgsky was totally engrossed not only in the characters' dialogues but also in the setting of the entire staging: all the external and internal details of the drama, the mimicry, the grouping, the postures, and so on. I will give one absolutely characteristic example. In the autograph libretto, the first scene of the opera bears the following directions:

> The walls of the Novodevichii Monastery near Moscow; close to the middle are the prominent gates of the monastery and they have an awning over them. The people, in small groups, start gathering in the monastery's courtyard; their movements are slack, their walking desultory. Boyars cross the stage, exchanging bows with the people, and make their way toward the monastery gates. When they disappear through the gates, the people start to wander about the stage. Some of them (mainly women) peek through the gates, others whisper to each other or simply scratch the backs of their heads. The Police Officer enters. At his sight, people gather into a compact crowd and stand motionless; the women—with their hands to their cheeks, the men hold their caps, or cross their arms on their chests, their heads lowered.

One can give many such examples in the opera.

Initially, the opera *Boris Godunov* was to have had only four acts and almost no female roles. All of us closest to Musorgsky, myself included, while we greatly admired the dramatic effect and the realism of the opera, we nevertheless continued to point out that the opera was not perfect. We felt that many essential details were missing, and that however great the beauty of the parts we heard, the opera still appeared unfinished. Musorgsky (as would any author) persistently defended what he had done; the opera was the result of his considered reflection and inspiration. For a long time he would not agree with us. Finally, he yielded, but only to force. In the fall of 1870, the theatrical directors refused to put *Boris* on stage, because they found too many choruses and ensembles and a noticeable absence of individual parts.[19] This rejection was a blessing. Musorgsky decided to rework the opera. At last he yielded to his friends' requests, especially mine and that of the talented architect Victor Hartmann,[20] who passionately loved Musorgsky's compositions. Hartmann particularly liked the excerpts from the "Scene by the Fountain," which Musorgsky now reworked. The work on this scene had previously been almost completed, but, God knows why, Musorgsky had abandoned it. I also advised him to compose a short song for the hostess of the inn, whose part, as it stood, was too small and insignificant: she had only a few words to say. We decided together that it would be good to give her more "character," namely, to make her a former *débauchée,* who has gone through fire and water (she is after all meant to be an innkeeper on a major thoroughfare). Musorgsky took the text for this little song "Ia poimala siza seleznia" [I have caught a dove-grey drake] from Shein's[21] collection, which I had recently discovered. That same collection provided the text for the mother's short song "Kak komar drova rubil" [The mosquito chopped wood] and the tsarevich's "Turu-turu"

[Little rooster]. Musorgsky himself wrote the text for the tsarevich Fyodor's story "Popin'ka nash sidel s mamkami v svetlitse" [Our Popin'ka was with the nurses in the women's quarters]. He based it on our discovery of Karamzin's account that parrots had been first brought to Russia, as a gift for the tsar, during Boris's reign. The scene with the clock was also based on a detailed description we had discovered in Karamzin. We decided to use yet another of his accounts: of the people's rebellion and of the Jesuits Czernikovskii and Lavitskii. This provided the theme for the magnificent scene in which people jeer the boyar Khrushchev, the Kromy's *voevode* [commander], as well as for the scene of the people's reprisal of the Jesuits,[22] the moment of the victorious Pretender's approach with his army.* The text for the people's chorus "Gaida! Raskhodilas', razgulialas' sila molodetskaia!'" [Forward! Our valiant ardor has become unharnessed and has broken loose!] was based on a robber's song, suggested by D[aniil] L[ukich] Mordovtsev.[23] As for Varlaam's song, which had been included in the first version of the opera, we searched out the song "Kak vo gorode [bylo] vo Kazani" [So it was in the city of Kazan'], based on a short note by Pushkin. The text of this song is included in the *Drevnie russkie stikhotvoreniia* [Ancient Russian poems] and elsewhere.** It was during this time too that much was added to Pimen's scene, chiefly the chorus of the "night-bird," which is heard from afar, offstage. In all likelihood, none of these important songs of Musorgsky's would have been written if his opera had been accepted immediately by the directors and put on stage. As for the music itself, after the rejection of the opera, new music was composed, supplemented with parts borrowed from previous material. As I have mentioned before, the major part had been borrowed from *Salammbô,* although it was significantly changed and developed. The melody for Varlaam's and Misail's sermon to the people, "Solntse, luna pomerknuli" [The sun and the moon have grown dark], was borrowed by Musorgsky from the melody of a *bylina* by Riabinin, a popular singer of tales who came from Olonets to Petersburg in 1868. Musorgsky had heard him during a public meeting of the Geographical Society and later at A[leksandr] F[yodorovich] Gilferding's.[25] Along with all these changes, during the winter of 1870 Musorgsky made another important modification: he decided to conclude the opera, not with Boris's death, but with the scene of the people's rebellion, the Pretender's triumph, and the Holy Fool's weeping for wretched Mother Russia. This conclusion certainly enhanced the tragic, shattering force and the menacing intent of the opera. V[ladimir] V[asilievich] Nikol'skii, Musorgsky's friend, suggested this crucial

---

*I remember how, at Musorgsky's request, I was to search for Latin exclamations for the Jesuits which had a prevalence of the letters *i* and *u* (so that the low and cowardly fright of the Jesuits would be expressed more accurately and closely); with this purpose in mind, I suggested the exclamation "Sanctis-si-ma Vir-go Ju-va ser-vos tu-os."

**I recall Musorgsky's joy when I brought him the text I had finally discovered during the winter of 1868–1869. He was at one of the concerts of the Free School, in the Hall of the Assembly of the Nobles. He started to read it avidly, right there, in the hall, during the concert. He was carried away by it.[24]

transposition. Musorgsky was enthusiastic and, in a couple of days, he had reworked the ending. I must confess that I was devastated and extremely envious of Nikol'skii for having been the one to suggest such a brilliant, magnificent idea.[26]

From that very winter of 1868 up to the beginnings of 1874 (when *Boris* was put on stage), first excerpts, and then the entire opera, were performed dozens of times in the circle of the comrade composers. The rejoicing, rapture, and admiration were general; each of these talented men, although he might find flaws in the opera, was aware that an important new work had been created right here, before his eyes. Prior to his death, Dargomyzhsky also heard some of the principal excerpts of the opera: the first scene, and the scene in the inn. And although he was busy at the time, working on the conclusion of his great and brilliant masterpiece *Kamennyi Gost'* [The stone guest], which was the apex of his artistic life, with great generosity and enthusiasm, he kept repeating to all that Musorgsky "is going even further than I."[27] Musorgsky would usually perform everything himself at the musical gatherings of the comrades: the choruses, the recitatives, the ensembles, and the arias. Aleksandra Nikolaevna Purgold was his superb assistant. She performed the female roles—the nurse Kseniia and Marina—as well as the tsarevich and the small boys pestering the Holy Fool. She sang with ardor, passion, grace, youthful energy, and playfulness, but mainly with a simplicity and naturalness that came close to the incomparable renditions of Musorgsky himself. The rehearsals for *Boris* took place at L[iudmila] I[vanovna] Shestakova's, at V[ladimir] F[yodorovich] Purgold's, at A[lina] A[leksandrovna] Khvostova's.[28] Khvostova, too, sang superbly both romances and opera, with true excellence, simplicity, faithfulness, and artistic feeling. She performed the female roles in *Ratcliff* [William Ratcliff] and *Pskovitianka* [The maid of Pskov] and the best songs of Balakirev, Cui, Rimsky-Korsakov, Borodin, and Musorgsky; perhaps, best of all, she sang the marvelous nurse's fairy tale in *The Maid of Pskov*.[29] *Boris Godunov* was constantly being changed each time these friends got together. When the opera was completely finished at last, during the winter of 1871–1872, excerpts were performed on several occasions by Iu[liia] F[yodorovna] Platonova and F[yodor] P[etrovich] Kommissarzhevskii[30] at the home of Mr. Lukashevich,[31] the head of wardrobe and set design, who at that time, was still very much interested in the fortunes of the new Russian opera. In February 1873, in the Mariinskii Theater, at a benefit performance for the producer G[ennadii] P[etrovich] Kondratiev, three excerpts of the opera were performed: the scenes "At the Inn," "In Marina's Boudoir," and "By the Fountain." Shortly after that Musorgsky had written me (January 2, 1873).

Soon we will be brought to trial! Gleefully we dream of how we will stand before the executioner, fully preoccupied now by *Khovanshchina* (the new opera that Musorgsky was already working on) judged for *Boris*. With courage bordering on audacity, we look toward the far musical distance that beckons us. The verdict does not frighten us. We shall be told: "You have violated the laws of God and man!" We shall answer: "Yes!," and we shall think: "This is only the beginning!" They shall caw: "Soon you shall be forgotten forever!"* We shall answer: *"Non, non, et non, Madame!"* [Madam!]

The three scenes sung at the benefit were an enormous success. Petrov, who performed Varlaam brilliantly, outshone them all. I would say that in his repertoire, there were no other parts that he performed with greater talent and creative power than that of Leporello in *The Stone Guest* and Varlaam in *Boris*. This role best showed the maturity, force, and breadth of his talent. The singularity, humor, historical accuracy, and plenitude of the national character that Petrov put into the part have never been equaled. The other performers were also excellent, and D[ar'ia] M[ikhailovna] Leonova was superb in her role as the hostess of the inn. The next morning, one friend sent Musorgsky his "hurrah!" and another his congratulations and warm wishes. On the night of the performance, a lady admirer had sent him his first garland.[32] Several months later, the rehearsals for the complete opera were under way. After the first one, on January 9, 1874, an extremely lively and happy Musorgsky, all "excited" (as he wrote me at the time), had his best photograph taken by Lorens. According to our agreement, he offered me the first print.[33]

At long last, on January 27, 1874, the full opera was performed. It was Musorgsky's great triumph. On one hand the old people, those who were indifferent, the conservatives, and the worshippers of the banal operatic music of the period sulked and were angry (this was also, in its way, a triumph!); the pedants of the conservatory and the critics protested furiously. Some sort of stupid plot was hatched to deprive Musorgsky of the four garlands from his female supporters with the inscriptions: "Slava tebe za Borisa, slava" [Glory to Thee for Boris!], "Podnialas' sila pododonnaia" [A force has arisen from the "bosom of the deep," which was a quotation from the people's chorus in Act V], "K novym beregam!" [Toward new shores!], and so forth. The garlands were to have been presented after the first performance, but his unfortunate admirers were forced to send them to Musorgsky's home. On the other hand, the young generation rejoiced and immediately lauded Musorgsky to the skies. What did it matter to them if the critics competed with each other in tearing Musorgsky to pieces? One critic talked about his illiteracy; another about his crudeness and lack of taste; a third one about the violation of traditions; a fourth one about the unsuitability of starting the chorus straight from the pedal; a fifth one saw a kind of melodramatics in the Jesuit Rangoni's part: a sixth one said that the

*An allusion to a letter from our well-known I[van] S[ergeevich] Turgenev, who, shortly before this, wrote to me that the entire new Russian school was worthless, and that it would soon be as forgotten as the Egyptian Rampsinites XLIV.

best parts were the "rounded off" scenes of the opera—according to the usual prescription for an opera (such as the cute but in no way original child's story "Popin'ka nash sidel" [Our Popin'ka was . . .], or the trio at the end of the "Scene by the Fountain"). Someone said that the author was too "satisfied with himself" (!), that his music was "immature and hasty" (!), and so they continued.³⁴ What did the young care about all this pettiness, boorishness, misinterpretation, and scholasticism, which were nothing but ingrained habits of envy and malice! The young people with their fresh and unprejudiced vision saw that a great artistic force had created and given our people a new, marvelous, national opera, and they rejoiced and celebrated. Twenty performances were given to very full houses.³⁵ Often at night a crowd of young people, as they approached the Liteinyi Bridge to cross to the Vyborg side, would sing "velichanie boiarina narodom" [the people honor the boyar] and other choruses. The younger generation overlooked what was weak and unsatisfactory in the opera (such as Marina's scene with the maids and the girls from Sandomir, and a few others) and hailed everything else with the same enthusiasm that their fathers had hailed the best of Pushkin, Gogol', and Ostrovskii. They understood, and therefore they applauded Musorgsky for being one of their own and dear to their hearts.

Throughout 1871 Musorgsky was busy with the new scenes to be added to *Boris*.³⁶ He was living with his loyal friend N[ikolai] A[ndreevich] Rimsky-Korsakov, and toward the end of the year was working particularly hard. It was an unprecedented event in the history of music: in the same apartment, in the same room, and at the same time, two operatic masterpieces, *Boris* and *Pskovitianka* [The maid of Pskov] were being composed. Two friends sat, each at his own desk, silently writing his opera. Later, when a particular excerpt, scene, chorus, or ensemble was ready, each would play his new piece on the piano for the other, and then for the rest of their comrades and friends. When had anything like this ever been seen or heard before?

I shall never forget how, when they were still young men living together in one room, I would go there early in the morning and find them both still asleep. I would wake them up; get them out of bed; give them whatever was necessary for their morning toilet; hand them stockings, pants, robes or jackets, and shoes. We would drink tea together and eat the Swiss cheese sandwiches, which we liked so much that Rimsky-Korsakov and I were often called "Russulas" [A play on words. "Cheese eater" and the mushroom Russula are homonyms.—Trans.]. And immediately after morning tea we would start working at what we most loved and was so vital to us—music. The piano could be heard and the singing would start, and with great excitement and bustle they would show me what they had composed the previous day, or the day before, or the day before that. How wonderful it was, but how long ago.³⁷

In 1875 Musorgsky composed a series of songs with the general heading *Pliaska smerti* [Dance of death].³⁸ I was the one who had suggested the subject. Count A[rsenii] A[rkadievich] Golenishchev-Kutuzov, Musorgsky's friend, who shared his apartment from 1874 to 1875, wrote the text and Musorgsky composed the music. The series included: (a) "Trepak." During a snowstorm, the Grim Reaper meets an old drunken and hapless peasant in the forest and freezes him to death. This tragic song, one of the most beautiful written by Musorgsky, was performed many times when our group met at L[iudmila] I[vanovna] Shestakova's by O[sip] A[fanasievich] Petrov. He sang it with the same uncompromising realism and sense of tragedy with which he sang "Savishna." The song is dated February 17, 1875. (b) "Kolybel'nia" [Lullaby]. Death snatches a sick child from her mother's embrace. This song, gloriously beautiful and deeply dramatic, once made such a strong impression on one of the listeners, a young mother, that she fainted. It was usually performed by Anna Iakovlevna Petrova (Petrov's wife) with inimitable perfection, despite the fact that she no longer had that wonderful contralto that drove Petersburg out of its mind in the thirties and forties, when she sang the parts of Vania and Ratmir.[39] Even in her old age her singing retained so much talent, passion, and dramatic expression that nobody could ever equal her. At those same meetings at Shestakova's, meetings which were truly unforgettable for the lucky ones who frequented them, A[nna] I[akovlevna] Petrova sometimes would sing "Sirotka" [The orphan][40] by Musorgsky and "Pesnia raskol'nitsy Marfy" [The song of Marfa the Old Believer] from *Khovanshchina,* with a truly incomparable sense of the tragedy and emotion that the songs arouse. "Lullaby" is dated April 14, 1875. (c) "Serenada" [Serenade]. Death in the guise of a knight-troubadour strangles a beautiful young girl while singing a love song to her. This song is dated May 11, 1875. (d) "Polkovodets" [The field marshal]. Death, portrayed as a general, destroys a whole crowd of people in the midst of the stormy riot of battle. This is a magnificent song, one of Musorgsky's best works. The song is dated June 1877. Along with these four themes, I had suggested several others: the death of a stern, fanatic monk in his cell while the distant ringing of a bell is heard; a political exile on his way back home perishes at sea, which represents his homeland; the death of a young woman while dreaming about love and her last, treasured ball. I had also suggested other themes.[41] But Musorgsky, although very pleased with them, had no time to complete a song; he would just play excerpts for me and the others. Even the four songs he did complete, mentioned above, remained unpublished at that time.

During his last five or six years, Musorgsky was totally engrossed in two operas written simultaneously: *Khovanshchina* and *Sorochinskaia Iarmarka* [The fair at Sorochintsy]. I had suggested the first subject in the spring of 1872, when *Boris Godunov* had not yet been put on stage. It was my belief that the struggle of the Old and the New Russia, the falling of the former and the rising of the latter, was a rich field for drama and opera, and Musorgsky shared my views. I thought that the majestic figure of Dosifei—

the head of the Old Believers—should be at the heart of the work. He was a strong, energetic man of great intelligence, who had suffered greatly. Like a commanding and powerful force he directed all the movements of the two princes—Khovanskii representing the old, dark, fanatic, and impenetrable Russia, and Golitsyn representing Europe, which was now beginning to be understood and appreciated even among Tsarevna Sof'ia's followers. There were to be various characters and events taking place in the German and the Streltsy settlements. There would be a pastor and his elderly sister, their young German niece, and two Old Believers: Marfa, the picture of youth and passion (somewhat similar to Potiphar's wife), and Susanna, the dry, sallow, wicked old fanatic. These two women constantly clashed with each other. There would be a youthful ten-year-old Peter with his Poteshnyi Regiment; and the intelligent and energetic Sof'ia with her wild Streltsy. One would see the Old Believers' monastery and the suicide by fire of the wild fanatics at the end of the opera, when Dosifei realized that "Old Russia was dying and a New Russia was born." It all seemed to be a worthwhile enterprise. Musorgsky eagerly began work on the opera. His research of the Old Believers, of Old Russian historical sources, as well as his general research of the sources from the eighteenth century, was extremely thorough. Numerous, often long letters written to me at that time were filled with the details of that research and with our discussions about the composition of the opera, its characters, and its scenes. His best work was composed between 1872 and 1875, and that work was magnificent and showed enormous talent.[42] But after that period, affected by his failing health and his shattered physique, his talent began to weaken and, apparently, to change. His compositions became confused, bizarre, and even, at times, incoherent and tasteless.[43] In order to finish the opera more quickly, since it had become too much for him, he greatly changed the libretto, leaving out many scenes, details, and even characters; quite often this was done at great detriment to the opera.[44] In the summer of 1880, he finally finished *Khovanshchina*[45] while living at the *dacha* of his close friend D[ar'ia] M[ikhailovna] Leonova, the very talented artist who was the "hostess of the inn" (in *Boris*) and Marfa the Old Believer (in *Khovanshchina*), and who sang many of his best songs.

The idea of another opera, *Sorochinskaia Iarmarka* [The fair at Sorochintsy], came to Musorgsky in 1875, as a result of his desire to create a Ukranian role for O[sip] A[fanasievich] Petrov, whose unusual talent he greatly admired and to whom he became very close during the staging of *Boris* in the years 1873 and 1874. He also became close friends with Petrov's wife, A[nna] Ia[kovlevna], who, as we said above, was a remarkable singer even in her old age. The opera was to remain far from completed,[46] but the second act (the scene with Khivria and the reader, and other passages) presents some comic moments which are as good as those that Musorgsky wrote in better times.

Two series of songs written at that time, one entitled *Bez solntsa* [Sunless]

(1874), based on the words by his friend Count Kutuzov, and another based on verses by Count A[leksei] Tolstoi (1877), are far less representative of the earlier Musorgsky's works.[47]

His very last compositions were "Pesn' Mefistofelia v Auerbakhovom pogrebe o blokhe" [Mephistopheles' song about the flea in Auerbach's cellar], composed during a trip in 1879; and as a result of an impression from the same trip, two capriccios, "Baidarki" and "Gurzuf"; and a big piece, "Buria na Chyornom more" [Storm on the Black Sea]. All three are piano pieces.[48] He then thought about writing a long "suite for orchestra, harps, and piano" on themes he had gathered (as he wrote to me on August 5, 1880) "from various helpful wayfarers of this world. Its program is to include themes from Bulgarian shores, a Black Sea crossing, the Caucasus, the Caspian Sea, and Fergana up to Burma. The suite is unfinished." The 1866 romance "Pesn' Eryomy" [The song of Eryoma] was reworked by Musorgsky into the romance entitled "Dniepr." However, except for the "Pesnia o blokhe" [The song of the flea], none of these late compositions reflect Musorgsky's earlier talent, force, and originality.

His dissatisfaction with his official duties, mentioned to me more than once in his letters,[49] his lack of means, his forced withdrawal from the Ministry of State Properties in 1879 (and the following year, his departure from the Government Control, where he had been given a job thanks to the efforts of T[ertii] I[vanovich] Filippov[50]), his failing health, and more than anything else the castration of *Boris* by the directors of the theater and its subsequent removal from the repertoire for an unknown cause:[51] all of this had a fatal effect on his mood, on his entire moral constitution, and at the same time deeply affected his creativity and his talent itself. Both the talent and the creativity began to weaken. The only thing that could still lift his spirits and console him was his constant participation in the countless concerts to which he was invited as the splendid accompanist for the singers. The majority of these concerts were given in order to raise money for students and for young people. Musorgsky never declined an invitation. He always had such enormous success that, at one time, he seriously considered earning his living as a pianist and accompanist. On June 15, 1876, he wrote to me: "Since I am so active on the keys, I am starting to reach the conclusion that if it is my fate to earn my daily bread by clanging,—I will be able to manage it. . . . " But this did not happen. The piano and concerts never brought him any money. He had to continue to earn his living through his official duties, for which he was criticized and ridiculed by Rostislav and other worthless critics. His trip through southern Russia with D[ar'ia] M[ikhailovna] Leonova in the summer of 1879 and the series of triumphs they both achieved in concerts in Poltava, Kherson', Odessa, etc., revived him for a short while.[52] But very shortly after that his health definitely declined, and he passed away on March 16, 1881, in the Nikolaev Military Hospital. The concern and care of friends and admirers had been insufficient to help him.

Musorgsky died far from fulfilling all that his rich nature had promised, but also far from having been fully appreciated by his homeland. This last task will be the responsibility of future generations.

iz *Nekrologa Musorgskogo*

FROM *Musorgsky's Obituary*

Once again Russia has lost a great man! Today, Monday, March 16, at five o'clock in the morning, in Nikolaev Military Hospital, near Smol'nyi, Modest Petrovich Musorgsky passed away from paralysis of the heart and of the spinal cord. The disease which had been developing over the years in the greatly ruined and now shattered physique climaxed on February 12, with three nervous shocks succeeding each other in a matter of only a few hours. The following day, thanks to the efforts of his friends and those closest to him, Musorgsky was placed in the military hospital, and soon he started to improve under the care of Dr. L[ev] B[ernardovich] Bertenson, who showed the suffering invalid the warmest concern and the most loving solicitude. During the next two weeks, Musorgsky suddenly improved so much that he frequently repeated to the numerous friends who visited him: "Never in my life did I feel so well as I do now." The people close to him could not stop marveling at this happy change; they found in his appearance an unexpected change for the better; they noticed that his strength, good spirits, and healthy complexion were returning. And hope began to revive among Musorgsky's sincere admirers. But he was suddenly overcome by an unexpected relapse:[53] new and frightening symptoms began to appear, his arms and legs were paralyzed, and in a very few days he was no more. Total consciousness and memory did not leave him until his last minutes. He died without pain or suffering; the agony lasted only a couple of seconds. Who among the many friends, who only yesterday had spent several hours with him during the day or evening, could have imagined that they were seeing him for the last time and that in a few hours he would be no more?

Musorgsky died on his 42nd birthday in the very prime of life and talent. (He was born on March 16, 1839.[54]) How distant the years of old age should have been, and how much one could have expected of him, in view of his powerful talent and dynamic nature! But he was stricken by the cast-iron, implacable hand of that very bitter fate which hangs, practically without exception, over the greatest talents in our fatherland: almost none of them lives long, lives as long as he could and should live; almost none of them accomplishes everything he obviously was called to and for which he was born. Almost everyone is mown down halfway.

IZ *Perov i Musorgskii*

FROM *Perov and Musorgsky*

Did Musorgsky (who, incidentally, had never heard of Perov's painting) intend to write the opera "Pugachevtsy" after completing *Khovanshchina*? We had many a talk on this topic, and the traces of his intentions can be found in our correspondence.[55] Musorgsky, just like Perov, thought about basing his plot to a large extent on Pushkin's *Captain's Daughter*; however, he was planning to add many other, new elements. In one of the acts of the opera, the very scene painted by Perov was to be used: Pugachyov stands on the porch, surrounded by his comrades, assistants, and a whole crowd of wild, unruly, Russian and Asiatic free-booters, and Father Gerasim stands close by (according to Pushkin).

IZ *Pamiati Musorgskogo*

FROM *In Honor of the Memory of Musorgsky*

His biography is short, sad, and full of woe, as is the case for almost all of our most talented men. He died young. He was still a long way from having accomplished everything he had surely been destined to achieve, endowed as he was with such great powers and talent. He was forced to spend the best years of his life at work behind a government desk. And when, notwithstanding the merciless distractions of day-to-day life, he created great and important works, which will be the pride of Russia in years to come, those in power in the musical world made every effort to suppress those works and to prevent them from ever being known.

IZ *Dvadtsat' pisem Turgeneva i moyo znakomstvo s nim*

FROM *Twenty Letters of Turgenev and Our Acquaintanceship*

[On March 6, 1867, Stasov met Turgenev at a concert given by the Free Music School, in the Hall of the Assembly of the Nobles.] At first, we discussed Briullov. But when we started talking about *Dym* [Smoke] I quickly changed the subject to Glinka, and I asked Turgenev if he really agreed with what his character Potugin[56] said about him.

"But that's horrible!" I said.

"Well, it's really not a question of what Potugin thinks . . . ," retorted Turgenev. "It's a bit of a caricature. I wanted to show a consummate *Westerner*; however, I basically agree with Potugin . . . "

"What? You mean Glinka had only a natural gift for music, and nothing more?"

"Well, of course, Glinka was talented, but he was never what all of you here in Petersburg assumed and now preach in all our papers. . . . "

But we did not spend much time on Glinka. Turgenev changed the subject to the latest Russian composers, whom he utterly disliked and of whom he spoke with the greatest contempt.

"You know my opinion of all of them from what you have read in *Smoke,*" he said, now quite exasperated with me.

"But, Ivan Sergeevich," I said, "how many times did you have a chance to listen to them in Paris?"

"When I come back to Petersburg, I make a point of hearing everything new that is being played here . . . It's terrible . . . By the way, you needn't look far for an example: just listen to what was performed here, tonight. In the first part, they sang some sort of 'magic chorus' by Mr. Dargomyzhsky . . ."

"From *Rogdana?*"[57]

"Well, yes, from *Rogdana,* or wherever else it comes from . . . Magic chorus! Ha, ha, ha! Some wonderful magic! And what horrible music! Truly insignificant, really most ordinary. It's not worth coming to Russia to hear such a 'Russian School'! This type of music will be performed for you wherever you wish, in Germany, or France, at any concert . . . and nobody will pay any attention to it. But, here, it is hailed at once as a great creation, as the original Russian school! Russian! Original! And then, there is *Korol' Lir* [King Lear] by Mr. Balakirev.[58] Balakirev and Shakespeare, what do they have in common? A colossus in poetry and a pygmy in music, who is not even a real musician . . . And then there was this *Khor Sennakheriba* [Chorus of Sennacherib] by Mr. Musorgsky.[59] What self-delusion, what blindness, what benightedness, what a slight to Europe. . . . "

And until that day, or more exactly, until *Dym,* I was unaware of the degree to which Turgenev despised the new Russian music and how little he understood it.

[In the spring of 1870, Stasov met Turgenev at an exhibition in Solianyi and told him] about the big party we were planning for Balakirev on May 30, and how we were to present him with a big silver garland and an address, in the Hall of the Duma, on Whitsunday. This was meant to be a protest by us, the supporters of the new school of Russian music, against the retrogrades in the Russian Musical Society, which had recently happily ousted Balakirev from its bosom and revoked his right to conduct the concerts of that society.[60] But Turgenev had little sympathy with the new Russian music, nor the events which, at that time, were taking place in the bitter battles between the two camps.

[In the spring of 1871 Turgenev] asked me, on his very first trip back to Russia, to make arrangements for him to hear the new Russian music, not only songs but also operas and symphonies.

I had told him that our musical circle met frequently and that during the meetings whole acts or scenes from the new Russian operas were performed to piano accompaniment: *The Stone Guest, The Maid of Pskov, Boris Godunov, William Ratcliff.* We also heard complete symphonies, overtures, and other instrumental creations by our new school on piano, four hands. But for quite a while the comrade composers refused to perform anything for Turgenev. Everyone admired his novels and short stories, everyone sincerely venerated his talent; but nobody appreciated the contempt he had for our new school of music. We all considered it useless to bother with enlightening a man whose musical nature was almost nonexistent. Besides, while living abroad he had become too settled in the old classical prejudices. Consequently, we emphatically refused to perform *The Stone Guest* for Turgenev, which we played quite often at our small gatherings in the early seventies. Musorgsky was the most adamantly opposed to performing for Turgenev.[61] Thus, Turgenev never heard *The Stone Guest*: our circle never played it for him. And when it was performed on stage during the winter, Turgenev was not in Petersburg. How this composition so novel in its use of musical forms was performed at Mme. Viardot's house, one can only guess. One wonders if it was performed according to the score, or according to the way it was performed in our circle when we followed Dargomyzhsky's instructions. The French singers, brought up on Glück and Mozart, in the tradition of the classical and Italian schools, surely were unable to sing it.

As for the new Russian orchestral music, except for Rimsky-Korsakov's *Sadko,* it seems unlikely that Turgenev heard any of it. Nonetheless, he never changed his opposition to this musical trend, which he really did not understand.

But in May 1874, when Turgenev was once more back in Petersburg and asked again for the opportunity to hear the new Russian music, I succeeded in arranging a musical gathering of all the members of our circle at my house. Rubinstein, who sometimes paid us a visit, came too. The entire first half of the evening was filled with Rubinstein's playing. . . . All of us were in seventh heaven, Turgenev included. He was overwhelmed with an inexpressible enthusiasm and rapture. But when Rubinstein left around ten, hurrying to catch the train to Peterhof, and we were left alone, i.e., Turgenev and our musical *company,* whom he had just come to know, Turgenev had an attack which scared us all. . . .

The consequence of this painful attack of gout, along with everything else, was that we never had an occasion to introduce Turgenev to the new Russian operas or symphonies. Nor did he have a chance to hear *Detskaia* [The nursery] by Musorgsky, which was an especially original composition. And there was never another opportunity to acquaint Turgenev with this music.[62]

Turgenev was a great writer. His novels and short stories were realistic and truthful, in accord with the Russian tradition; nonetheless, his tastes and judgment in art made him, as is often the case with many European artists in the West, an enemy of realism and truth about life.

[From Turgenev's letter no. 5. Paris, March 27/15, 1872.] "And now, you can behead me, if you want to. There are only two really talented 'young' Russian musicians: Tchaikovsky and Rimsky-Korsakov.[63] As for all the rest—not as people, of course (as people they are wonderful), but as artists: put them in a bag and drown them! The Egyptian King Rampsinat XLIV is not as forgotten now as they will be in fifteen to twenty years. That is my sole comfort."

IZ PIS'MA K *N. Findeizenu*

FROM A LETTER TO *N[ikolai] Findeizen*

Nobody, myself included, even heard that Musorgsky had ever been in love. . . . Nevertheless, he showed something that could be called "amorousness" to (1) Nad[ezhda] Petr[ovna] Opochinina (I think she is still alive),[64] to whom (if I am not mistaken) the song "Noch' " [Night] was dedicated, (2) Mariia Vas[ilievna] Shilovskaia . . .[65] and particularly (3) the young singer Latysheva, who sang in the early sixties, among other things, Serov's opera *Iudif'* [Judith]. Musorianin and I always admired her *very much*. Surely, one can say Musorgsky was in love with her. As for Leonova, she *never* appealed to him in the least.

Filaret Musorgsky

Rasskaz o brate

My Brother's Story

Filaret Musorgsky (1836–1889) was the composer's brother and the father of Taniushka and Goga Musorgsky. They are the dedicates of the song "S kukloi" ("Tiapa, bai") [With the doll, (Sleep, Tiapa)], from *Detskaia* [The nursery]. These recollections are in the form of letters written to Stasov at his request when Stasov was preparing Musorgsky's biography.

.   .   .

While at the Cadet School, he continued to take lessons with Herke until 1854; however, in his last two years, i.e., in 1852 and 1853, he went for his lessons only once a week, on Saturdays.[1] In school, he played the piano a lot, and he was constantly present at the lessons that Herke gave to the daughter of the Director of the Cadet School, General Sutgof. He often performed in the Director's home; however, at that time, his only composition was the polka *Porte-enseigne*.

He was a very good student at the Cadet School: always among the top ten; he was very close to many of his comrades and was well liked by them. He would visit the homes of his comrades' parents, such as the Evreinovs, the Kruglikovs, and the Smel'skiis.

He was an avid reader of history. He also enthusiastically read German philosophy and translated Lavater,[2] but I do not know the location of that translation.

If my memory serves me well, Modest made the acquaintance of Dargomyzhsky through Vladimir Petrovich Opochinin, in 1860[3] I think, and through Dargomyzhsky he met the Shilovskiis. He often paid visits to the Shilovskiis, at their estate near Moscow, in Glebov. He was their guest for the summers of 1860 and 1861.

In boyhood and adolescence, and also when he was an adult, he always regarded everything that had to do with the people and the peasants with a special love; he considered the Russian peasant a real man (in this he was sadly mistaken). As a result of this attitude, he suffered material losses and hardship. It was precisely this love for the peasants that forced him to go to

work, in 1863, for the Engineering Department, and because of a staff re-
duction, in 1868 he began to work for the Forestry Department of the State
Ministry of Properties.[4]

During the years 1858 to 1863, he lived with different members of his
family; until 1862 he lived with mother and me, and in the latter part of
1862 and 1863, with me and my wife.[5] In 1864 and 1865 he lived in an artel
with Levashev, the Loginovs and the Lobkovskiis,[6] during this period he
translated famous French and German criminal cases. In the fall of 1865, he
fell seriously ill. It was the onset of a frightening disease *(delirium tremens)*.
As a result, my wife made Modest leave the artel and brought him home
(against his will, at first). He lived with our family from 1865 through a part
of 1868, at which date we left Petersburg for good. After 1868, I am unable
to provide exact information on where and how Modest lived.

In general, Modest began to compose more-serious works when he took
lessons with Balakirev. As for Herke, he had only taught him piano, nothing
more. He taught him no musical theory; and Modest composed his first
polka while he was still unaware of theory.

Aleksandr Borodin

Vospominaniia o Musorgskom (pervye vstrechi)

Recollections about Musorgsky (Our First Encounters)

Aleksandr Borodin (1833–1887) wrote these recollections at Stasov's request when Stasov was preparing Musorgsky's biography.

·   ·   ·

My first meeting with Modest Petrovich Musorgsky took place in 1856 (I think it was the fall, September or October). I had just completed my training as a military physician and was doing my internship in the Second Military Hospital; M[odest] P[etrovich] was a very young officer in the Pre-obrazhenskii Regiment (he was seventeen at the time). We met in the hospital duty room. I was the doctor on call, and he was the officer of the day. We were in the day room, the duty was boring; and as we were both outgoing people, it is easy to see how we got into conversation and very quickly became friends. That evening we were both invited to the house of the head physician, Popov, who had a grown daughter. The Popovs held many soirées for her to which, as a rule, they invited the physicians and the officers on duty. This was a special kindness from the head physician. M[odest] P[etrovich] at that time was just a very graceful little boy; he looked like an officer in a picture: his little closely fitted uniform was neat as a pin; his short legs slightly bowed; his hair sleek and pomaded; his fingernails manicured; and his carefully tended hands were those of a gentleman. He had graceful and aristocratic manners; his conversation, spoken slightly through his teeth and interspersed with French sentences, which was somewhat artificial, was nonetheless aristocratic. There was a hint of foppishness, although a very moderate one. He was unusually courteous and well brought up. The ladies paid him court. He would sit down at the piano and, affectedly throwing up his hands, would begin to play, very sweetly, graciously, etc., excerpts from *Trovatore*, or *Traviata*, and so on, while all around him, people were buzzing in a chorus *"Charmant, délicieux!"* etc. In such circumstances I met M[odest] P[etrovich] about three or four times at Popov's during my duty at the hospital. After that, for a long time I did not see M[odest] P[etrovich]. Popov had resigned from the hospital, the soirées had come to an end, and I was no longer on duty at the hospital, as I had become a lecturer in the Chemistry Department.

In the fall of 1859, I saw him again at S[tepan] A[lekseevich] Ivanovskii's, an adjunct professor at the Academy and a physician in the Artillery School. Musorgsky had already resigned.[1] He had matured considerably, and had started to put on weight; he no longer had an officer's mannerisms. He was still elegantly dressed, his manners were still refined, *but that hint of foppishness* had totally vanished. We were introduced; we, of course, immediately recognized each other and recalled our first meeting at Popov's. Musorgsky stated that he had resigned from the army because he was "seriously study-ing music, and that combining military duties with art was difficult," and so on. The conversation involuntarily turned to music. I was still an ardent admirer of Mendelssohn but, at that time, barely knew Schumann. Musorg-sky was already acquainted with Balakirev, and he had had a taste of many musical novelties which I did not even suspect. The Ivanovskiis, seeing that we had found a common ground for conversation, i.e., music, suggested we play a piano duet version of Mendelssohn's Symphony in A minor.[2] M[odest] P[etrovich] frowned a little bit and said that he would be very happy to comply, but requested that he be allowed "to omit the Andante, which is not really symphonic, but more like the *Lieder ohne Worte* or some-thing comparable, that has been orchestrated." We played the first part and the scherzo. Then Musorgsky started to talk enthusiastically about Schu-mann's symphonies, but, at that time, they were totally unknown to me. He started sketching in excerpts of Schumann's Symphony [No. 3] in E-flat major. When he reached the middle movement, he stopped playing and said: "Well, now musical mathematics begin." It was new and very attrac-tive to me. Seeing that I was so interested, he played more of the new music for me. I then learned that he also wrote music. Understandably I showed great interest in that news. He began to play one of his scherzos very softly (that probably was the one in B-flat major[3]); at the Trio he said with set teeth: "Well, that's oriental." I was extremely affected by what were for me unprecedented new elements in music. I cannot say that they particularly appealed to me at first: rather, they somewhat puzzled me by their novelty. But in listening more attentively, I soon began to appreciate them and revel in them. I must admit I did not take his declaration very seriously when he said that he wanted to devote himself wholeheartedly to music. I thought it was rather pretentious, and I condescended to him a bit over that. But, after getting to know his scherzo, I no longer knew if I should believe him or not.

On my return from abroad, in the fall of 1862, I met Balakirev (at S[ergei] P[etrovich] Botkin's house[4]); and it was at Balakirev's, when he lived on Ofitserskaia Street in Khil'kevich's house, that I met Musorgsky the third time. We recognized each other immediately, and both of us recalled the first two occasions on which we had met. Musorgsky had by now developed his musical talent substantially. Balakirev wanted to introduce me to the music of his own circle and, above all, show me the symphony of the "absent one" (meaning Rimsky-Korsakov, who was at the time still a naval officer; he had just left on a long voyage⁵ to North America). Musorgsky and Balakirev sat down at the piano (Musorgsky on *primo,* and Balakirev on *secondo*). Musorgsky's playing was quite different from what I had heard during our first two meetings. I was dazzled by the brilliance, expressiveness, and energy of the performance, as well as by the beauty of the piece. They played the finale from the symphony. Then, learning that I had a latent impulse to write music, Musorgsky asked me to show them something. I was extremely abashed and categorically refused to comply.

M[ilii] A[lekseevich] Balakirev

IZ *Pisem M. Calcovoressi, V.V. Stasovu, i V. Kalenskomu*

FROM *Letters to M[ichel] D. Calcovoressi, V[ladimir] V[asilievich] Stasov, and V. Kalenski*

Milii Balakirev (1836–1910) had a complex relationship with Musorgsky. Balakirev underestimated his student and was always ill disposed toward his works. All this is reflected in this short memoir, written at Stasov's request.

. . .

[My collaboration with Musorgsky] rests on the following: we played piano duet versions (he was a superb pianist) of all the musical repertoire that existed at the time—classical, ancient, modern. Principally we performed Bach, Handel, Mozart, Haydn, Beethoven, Schubert, Schumann, Berlioz, and Liszt. Due, in part, to my own efforts, he was already well acquainted with the music of Glinka and Dargomyzhsky. Furthermore, I showed him the forms in composition.[1]

Since I had not been trained in musical theory, I could not teach Musorgsky harmony . . . but I could explain *the form of a composition*. With that in mind, we played Beethoven's symphonies and many pieces by Schumann, Schubert, Glinka . . . concentrating on the analysis of the form.[2] If my memory serves me well, he paid for very few lessons. Somehow, for reasons I no longer remember, the lessons always turned into friendly discussions. His first works did not escape my critical hand. Thus, I helped him and explained orchestration to him, when he was composing the B-flat scherzo. . . . Since I was unable to explain the principles of voice leading to him, i.e., harmony, I simply made corrections here and there when I felt that something was amiss. And such was the situation up to the time he composed *Boris*.[3]

After 1870, I had every reason for losing my ties with our circle,[4] but as long as Musorgsky and Borodin were alive, the separation was not obvious; however, when they died, the break became definite. As far as who was right and who was wrong, let time be the judge.

Musorgsky in 1876

A[leksandra] Unkovskaia

Vospominaniia

Recollections

Aleksandra Unkovskaia, née Zakhar'ina (d. 1920s) was a violinist and a conductor.

.   .   .

Balakirev, Musorgsky, and their friends, the young musician pioneers of the new music, were frequently at my father's home[1] in Petersburg. Almost every day and evening we had music. As a child I would fall asleep to music around nine o'clock. After a good night's sleep, I would awake at about four o'clock in the morning to more music. I knew Glinka's opera *Zhizn' za tsaria* [A life for the tsar], *Ruslan i Liudmila* [Ruslan and Ludmila], and Dargomyzhsky's opera *Rusalka* by heart, since they were performed almost every day in our house. *Maman*[2]—an excellent pianist and a student of Henselt—was the orchestra; the operatic arias were shared by my father and his friends. However, as quite often there were not enough friends for all the parts, one person would perform several roles, and everybody would sing the chorus. The men sang the female parts, and Uncle Mitia, *Maman*'s brother, even found a way to sing Liudmila's part in *Ruslan,* in a woman's voice, in the proper register, perfectly performing all the *fioritturas.* . . . Sometimes they even dressed in costumes—everyone had a good time, studying the music of the Russian classics in an atmosphere of carefree delight.

The foreign classics were also played in our house, and when Beethoven's fugues were played, the young composer Borozdin[3] would start *dancing* to them.

V. U.

V. U. has not been identified.

.　　.　　.

The talented composer and musician M[odest] P[etrovich] Musorgsky was endowed with innumerable qualities which made him such a special member in our society. In the early sixties, I was still young and I had recently finished a class for beginners. I liked to frequent Kumanina's home, near the Kokushkin Bridge, where the musical world of Russian opera, the performers and their loyal audience, would so often meet in the Gumbins'[1] apartment. I was pleased to be able to see the artists, not on the stage, but in this friendly company; I liked to listen to them while standing near them instead of hearing them across the orchestra pit. Needless to say, such a polished accompanist as Musorgsky was always a favorite guest with the singers; but he seldom limited himself to the humble role of accompanist. Not only did he give enormous pleasure to his audience with his skillful playing, but he could, when he wanted, make all those present laugh. One such comic concert is still vivid in my memory. Musorgsky was in a particularly good mood and had not left the piano all evening. What didn't he play! It could be a well-known aria played with such a change in tempo and rhythm that to listen without laughing was impossible; or he could play a different piece with each hand: the left one "Lieber Augustin" and the right one Faust's waltz. Later, there was a *pot pourri* of various gay polkas and waltzes, solemn hymns, funeral marches, organ music, and so on. And all the time either in the bass notes or in the treble the dashing sounds of *Kamarinskaia*[2] were constantly to be heard, but always conforming to the mood of the piece into whose structure it intruded.

The vocal part of the concert was about to begin. At first, there was an imitation of the women in Italian opera, and, strange as it may seem, Musorgsky's high falsetto rendering of *Adio del pisati* [*sic*] was reminiscent of the never-to-be-forgotten Bosio.[3] Suddenly the soprano aria broke off, and completely unexpectedly Petrov's bass resounded, singing his last aria from *A Life for the Tsar*[4] in a very nasal tone of voice. On hearing it Osip Afanas'evich, who was playing *préférence*[5] in the adjoining room, stopped the game and came running into the hall. With a good-natured smile he said that he ought to teach a good lesson to the small boy who dared to mimic his elders. There was a lot of laughter. It seems that all this happened just yesterday, but already so many of the people are no longer with us.

Nadezhda Rimskaia-Korsakova

Moyo znakomstvo s Musorgskim

My Acquaintance with Musorgsky

Nadezhda Rimskaia-Korsakova, née Purgold (1848–1919), a pianist and a composer, was the wife of N. Rimsky-Korsakov. Her recollections are true, but they tend to disparage Musorgsky.

.　.　.

I was introduced to Musorgsky at Dargomyzhsky's. At the time Dargomyzhsky was in the fervor of creative inspiration, writing with amazing celerity the scenes in *The Stone Guest*. He created the scenes one after the other, as if they had been written already and he suddenly started to throw them at us, out of a hat, as would a magician. The second scene had just been completed. My sister A[leksandra] N[ikolaevna] was studying Laura's part, and I accompanied her. Dargomyzhsky set the day for the rehearsal and told us that Don Juan's part would be sung by Musorgsky—a composer and a singer. At the time, neither my sister nor I had met him, nor did we know anything about him.

On the appointed day, at the given hour,[1] we were at Dargomyzhsky's, curious to meet him and excited about performing Laura's difficult scene in front of so knowledgeable an audience.

Musorgsky had such an original personality that having met him once, it was impossible to forget him. I shall start by describing his appearance. He was of medium height, well proportioned; his hands were elegant; his hair wavy and nicely shaped; his light-grey eyes somewhat protruding and rather big. However, his face was very unattractive, especially the nose, which was always reddish blue because it had been frostbitten at a parade, according to the explanation given by Musorgsky. Musorgsky's eyes were not at all expressive: one would say that they were almost like cassiterite.[2] In general, his face was languid and unexpressive, as if it were hiding some sort of enigma. While conversing Musorgsky never raised his voice: on the contrary, he would lower his speech almost to a whisper.* But his manners were polished

---

*I vividly recall how he talked, as if he were murmuring to himself under his breath some sort of witty or piquant sally. I remember how, deliberately and laughing softly, he would abuse one of his friends when it was obvious that he was praising him.

and aristocratic. It was obvious that this was a man of the world with a good education.

Musorgsky's personality impressed both my sister and me. No wonder: he was so interesting, so original, talented, and mysterious. We were carried away by his singing. He had a pleasant although not powerful baritone voice, but it was very expressive. His subtle understanding of all the nuances of the soul coupled with his artlessness, sincerity, and total lack of affectation or exaggeration—all had a charming effect. Afterwards, I realized how versatile he was as a performer; he played lyrical, dramatic, comic, and humorous pieces equally well. Moreover, he was an excellent pianist: his playing had brilliance, force, enthusiasm, and stylishness combined with humor. He could sing such pieces as "Rayok" [Peepshow], "Ozornik" [The mischievous one], "Kozyol" [The he-goat], "Klassik" [The classicist], and others with inimitable humor. On the other hand, his renditions of the parts of Ivan the Terrible and Tsar Boris were profound and performed with great dramatic effect.[3]

Musorgsky was an enemy of the routine or the prosaic not only in music but in all aspects of life, even in minor details. Simple, ordinary words repelled him. He even contrived to change and mangle surnames. His letters were unusually original and piquant; the wittiness, humor, and accuracy of his adjectives caused sparks. But toward the end of his life, this originality became artificial; it is particularly noticeable in his letters to V[ladimir] V[asilievich] Stasov. Incidentally, this artificiality and pretentiousness were manifest not only in his letters but in his whole manner.[4]

Moi vospominaniia o A[leksandr] S[ergeeviche] Dargomyzhskom

My Reminiscences of A[leksandr] S[ergeevich] Dargomyzhsky

The music for *The Stone Guest* evolved at incredible speed before our very eyes.

We waited impatiently for each new page, and immediately performed them at A[leksandr] S[ergeevich]'s. He would go over the part with my sister while I accompanied them at the piano. . . . In addition to the three of us, there was Musorgsky, who sang the parts of Leporello and Don Juan incomparably, and General Veliaminov, who conscientiously performed the parts of the monk, the commodore, and the "foolish guest," as Dargomyzhsky called him.

That surge of creativity which overwhelmed Dargomyzhsky while writing *The Stone Guest* came to influence his whole character. He warmed up to the musicians around him and began to show a greater interest in their compositions. This was most apparent in his relation with Musorgsky, with whose work he had such an affinity. I remember how Musorgsky showed Dargomyzhsky the first song from *Detskaia* [The nursery] at our home. This was "Rasskazhi mne naniushka" [Tell me, dear Nanny]; after listening to the piece, A[leksandr] S[ergeevich] Dargomyzhsky said: "Well, that has outdone me." And in regard to the two scenes from *Boris*—the first scene with all the people and the scene in the inn—Dargomyzhsky said: "Musorgsky is going further than I am." When we performed *Zhenit'ba* [The marriage] in our home, A[leksandr] S[ergeevich] sang Kochkaryov's part and laughed himself to tears, marveling at the wit and the expressiveness of its music. When Kochkaryov says: "Ekspeditorchenki, etakie kanal'chenki" [the little filing clerks, such little rascals], A[leksandr] S[ergeevich] would always go amiss; he would laugh so hard, he could not keep singing, and he would tell me: "You are playing some sort of symphony here. You are interfering with my singing" (in the accompaniment in that passage, Musorgsky had amusing musical flourishes).

Zapisano so slov N[adezhdy] Rimskoi-Korsakovoi Vasiliem Iastrebtsevym

Vasilii Iastrebtsev Reports N[adezhda] Rimskaia-Korsakova's Words

Pliaski Persidok [The Persian dance][5] was already in the program, but there was still no trace of its score. What was one to do? Musorgsky did not have time to write it. Nikolai Andreevich, without further delay, decided to orchestrate this number himself. The piece was a great success at the concert.[6] Musorgsky took many curtain calls; he was extremely happy, and coming back behind the stage, he repeated more than once, with a plain childish naivete that *he himself wanted to orchestrate the piece "exactly" the way Korsakov had done it;* that he was utterly amazed at Rimsky's *clairvoyance* of his own intentions. But Musorgsky had not *even seen* the changes in the harmonics that Nikolai Andreevich had made in the orchestration.[7]

Sofiia Fortunato

Moi dalyokie vospominaniia o M[odeste]
P[etroviche] Musorgskom

My Distant Recollections of M[odest]
P[etrovich] Musorgsky

Sofiia Fortunato, née Serbina (1851–1929), was actually Vladimir Stasov's daughter. Her first husband was Vasilii Prokof'evich Medvedev (1844–1878), a lawyer. More than any other recollections of Musorgsky, Fortunato's memoirs attract the reader with their unbiased character, her respect and love for Musorgsky, and her desire to understand and appreciate him.

.   .   .

One of the most vivid impressions in my life was made by dear Modest Petrovich Musorgsky. I was still a little girl when I saw him for the first time. Nevertheless, this man was so unique that, having seen him once, it was impossible to forget him. He was such a graceful, such an elegant man. Our acquaintance dates from the late fifties of the last century, when he had just left a military career and donned his civilian clothes. At that time he was still very thin, of medium height, with small hands and feet. He was always, as one says, smartly dressed, and he was exceptionally elegant. His head was slightly peculiar: it was fairly large with a rather big face and dark wavy hair. His eyes were somewhat protruding, large and light colored; they seemed to be particularly luminous in contrast to his quite swarthy complexion, his dark beard and moustache. His manners were very mild and graceful; his speech, often interspersed with fluent French phrases, testified to good breeding. All these characteristics gave him the appearance of being particularly graceful and elegant. If I repeat these two words so often, it is because they suited him so well; they were so appropriate for him.

Life in my father's family was rather original. The apartment was spacious, divided in two by a big corridor. This hallway made a turn, and at its end there were several rooms belonging to my father's old aunt; beyond those were the rooms occupied by people who had come to live with my father's family and who now served it.

The first part of this corridor divided the apartment in two. The female realm was on the left; the large reception room held a grand piano; this area also served as a dining room. Then there were the drawing rooms and the ladies' bedrooms. On the right side of the corridor were the gentlemen's rooms, mainly used by the male guests. On Sundays, a big company would usually gather for lunch. The gentlemen would sit at one end of the table, and my father sat in the middle of their company. The result of such a division was that we, the women and the little girls, were very seldom able to hear the discussions and the conversations held at the gentlemen's end of the table; we were even less able to participate in their subsequent conversations, since after lunch they would retire to the gentlemen's half and would, in clouds of smoke, continue their conversations without restraint. They would usually come back to the reception room at tea time. As children, and later as adolescents, we were always sent back to the dining room, and there we lived our own life. It is for that reason that it is almost impossible for me to repeat *verbatim* what was overheard of Musorgsky's conversations. Another reason is the remoteness of that life. The general impression was that Musorgsky always shared the opinions of those who were the most progressive, humanitarian, and enlightened. The obscurants, as a rule, did not stay long with our family. Those closest to us, such as V[ladimir] V[asilievich],[1] as well as his brothers, in particular Dm[itrii] Vas[ilievich], were the heart of the lively cultural society in those times. As is now well known, the late fifties and the whole decade of the sixties witnessed the cultural Golden Age of Russia. Almost all of those who got together with our family took a very active part in this cultural renewal. It was therefore quite understandable that such a company, for the young, lively, and adventuresome Musorgsky, was like water for the millstone. Thus, notwithstanding his youth, at first shyly, but later on more and more boldly, he entered this circle and soon became a full-fledged member. Before long they began to gather for purely musical purposes. And it was then that M[odest] P[etrovich] clearly assumed a very active role.

Although I was extremely young, I was nevertheless astonished by his nature. Outwardly, he was such a man of the world, so elegant, and, it seemed, somewhat superficial. But with his music and his unforgettable, penetrating performances, he began to stir deeply felt reflections and feelings. How strange it all was! Really quite a marvel! Here, at the piano, where all this highly talented company brought their new creations, which sometimes sparked strong arguments, he, without ever offending anyone's self-esteem or being rude or abrupt, managed to withstand the pressure and hold his own course. His extraordinary good breeding balanced both his confirmed belief that he was right and his inflexibility in refusing to accept opinions which were foreign to him and unsuitable for him. How adept he was at defending his convictions while respecting the point of view of other people! A rare virtue!

Here, in a nutshell I have given the whole cast of his mind, his talent, his ability to play and sing his own creations and those of the others. And this image of him will never leave my soul until the day I die.

I already had the opportunity, in my reminiscences about N[ikolai] A[ndreevich] Rimsky-Korsakov, to state the degree to which the members of this young musical company were inseparable. Those who were then close to them could not mention one of them without mentioning the others. What was amazing was the fact that the general comportment of this circle was so highly spiritual that base elements of jealousy did not affect them. Each of them contributed something of his own, according to his nature, but at the same time each was equally interested in the compositions of the others. This trait seemed to be ingrained in M[odest] P[etrovich] more deeply and more strongly than in the others, if that were at all possible. It compelled everyone who knew him to love and value him even more.

As for me, I consider that this time was for us, mere children, a time of exceptional moral instruction which influenced our whole lives.

Such musical and ethical associations with these extraordinary people were not simply pleasures or pleasant pastimes, but were vital, avidly sought-out spiritual necessities. That is the reason why one recalls this period with such a feeling of pure joy.

Our ecstasies were endless when the musical gatherings became regular. Many things have been written about these soirées, and they became the center of many a talk. We were as enthusiastic about those meetings in private houses, such as my father's, or my uncle's,[2] or L[iudmila] I[vanovna] Shestakova's, as we were about assiduously attending the public concerts. M[odest] P[etrovich] always played a very big role in both. One should also point out that in conversation as well as in music, he was a great humorist and a great comic, which meant that he was always a conspicuous member of any gathering.

In the early seventies, my personal fortune was such that I had to leave Petersburg for many years. I came back only once in a while, but never for more than a short period of time. Of course, I invariably took the opportunity to pay a call on this company of beloved musicians so dear to my heart, and I would again store up, alas, for long periods, the impressions left by their glorious art. Musorgsky was always true to himself, always unique and unforgettable.

In 1879, Musorgsky, in the company of Leonova, took a trip to the southern cities of Russia, with the purpose not only of giving concerts but also of visiting Odessa and the Crimea. At that time, I lived in Yalta and I managed the then important Hotel Rossiia, which had a very large reception hall and quite a good grand piano. When one remembers my deep love for music in general and for Musorgsky's in particular, for his lovely and absolutely characteristic performances, it would be easy to imagine my bliss when I saw the announcement of Musorgsky's and Leonova's concert. Yalta, at that time, was a very small city; there was no city map or directory; consequently, the posters that had been made in other cities were pasted up, as printed, in Yalta, which meant that I was unable to find out where the musicians had found lodgings. I had to wait for the scheduled day. The concert was to be given in the building of the old club, on the seafront where the Hotel Dzhalita was built, and in whose interior, even today, the old club is preserved; in M[odest] P[etrovich]'s time the building had a small concert hall where concerts as well as other performances were given.

When I arrived at the concert, I was distressed to see a very small number of concert-goers, although at the time, one could say that high society from foreign capitals as well as major cities converged on Yalta. For a long time, I kept the posters from the two concerts Musorgsky gave in Yalta, but after numerous moves they are now lost. I remember that Leonova sang Chopin's mazurka "Esli b ia solnyshkom" [If like a sun I were . . .] and other songs; Musorgsky also played Chopin. Which pieces he played, I no longer remember. I know for sure that he played *Utro na Moskve-reke* [Morning on the Moscow River] and *Marsh strel'tsov* [The Streltsy march] from *Khovanshchina.*3

During the first intermission I ran to the green room. M[odest] P[etrovich] was sitting in an armchair, his arms hanging at his sides, looking like a wounded bird. The absence of any real audience and the failure of the concert had obviously depressed him very much. It turned out that having arrived in Yalta the previous evening and finding the hotels overbooked (since it was already August and almost the height of the season), Musorgsky and Leonova had no place to stay. They were forced to find lodging at a private house, which was thoroughly uncomfortable, dirty, and repulsive. And our dearest Musorianin had no alternative but to put up with such accommodations! Naturally, I made arrangements for them to move the following day to the Rossiia, a hotel furnished with great comfort. It had a magnificent, large hall with a decent grand piano, and, moreover, the hotel was full of people whom it would be possible to interest in the forthcoming concert. This time, the concert was a great success.

Musorgsky and Leonova spent about a week in Yalta.4 Of course, we asked them to entertain us with their music outside the concert hall, and they complied graciously and repeatedly. Thus, we had the opportunity to listen to many of Musorgsky's beautiful songs played by the composer himself and sung by Leonova. But most significant of all, we heard several scenes from *Boris* and *Khovanshchina*. Is it necessary to say how powerful and intense the emotional experience was for these listeners, young and old, who had almost never listened to music? They were stirred to the depths of their hearts.

We made several trips with Musorgsky and Leonova to the area surrounding Yalta. Musorgsky was deeply moved by the natural beauty of the sea and the mountains, also by the glorious moonlight and the sweetness in the air.

He usually climbed into the back of those comfortable basket carriages (then so much in use in the Crimea), to avoid having to participate in the conversation and thus spoil his mood. One of the most successful trips was to Gurzuf.

That was my last meeting with the unforgettable M[odest] P[etrovich]. He was still as charming and attractive as he used to be, when I first knew him.

IZ *Vospominanii o vstrechakh s Rimskim-Korsakovym*

FROM *Recollections of Meetings with Rimsky-Korsakov*

At the time, a group called the "Balakirev circle" used to meet quite often at my father's. Of course, Nikolai Andreevich was always present. At these gatherings, the members would show what they had composed since the last meeting. Usually Musorgsky, the best pianist in the group, played; and as he was also a singer, he sang the romances and, at times, almost the complete operas.

For those who had never heard such performers as Glinka, Serov, Dargomyzhsky, and Musorgsky (people who incidentally did not have exceptional voices), it might seem strange when I say that I never heard or never would hear again such remarkable executions as they could give. I doubt that anybody else has had such an opportunity to hear anything like it. Strictly speaking, I only understood Glinka and Serov by instinct, for I was still very young. But when it came to Dargomyzhsky's and Musorgsky's performances, regardless of any personal impressions, I can testify that not only musically educated people but totally uneducated people would sob violently while listening to them, such was the force of their talent, such was their ability to bring to life the character they played, with so enormous a dramatic effect for humor and comedy. The impression they made was fascinating. N[ikolai] A[ndreevich] would usually sit at the piano and assist Musorgsky, since, despite all his virtuosity, even Musorgsky did not have enough fingers to play an entire orchestra.

It was in such circumstances that we heard *Pskovitianka* [The maid of Pskov], *Boris Godunov, Igor'* [Prince Igor], *Ratcliff,*[5] as they were being written, as we did with everything else which was then being composed by the new Russian school.

Varvara Komarova-Stasova

Varvara Komarova-Stasova (1862–1942), musicologist and writer under the pen name Vladimir Karenin, was the daughter of the lawyer Dmitrii Stasov (1828–1918), a musical and public figure. She was the author of monographs about George Sand and about her uncle Vladimir Stasov. Her memoirs, as well as those of her cousin Sofiia Fortunato, are attractive because of their sincerity and the authenticity of Musorgsky's portrait, and her recollections of Musorgsky's singing are valuable.

·   ·   ·

I remember Musorgsky from the time I was seven years old.[1] More exactly, I was seven when I paid attention to his coming to our house, since undoubtedly he must have come to my parents' house before that time, but I do not remember that, not having given it any importance. And here, all of a sudden, he entered the circle of our childhood as "Musorianin," as all the adults called him, and we children immediately started to address him this way too, having come to the conclusion that it was his real name. He would often come to our house, either in town, or the *dacha,* in Zamanilovka, near Pargolov. Since he did not strike a pose with us and did not speak to us in that artificial language ordinarily used by adults in a house where there are children with whose parents they are on friendly terms, we children not only quickly became attached to him but also began to consider him as one of us. My sister Zinochka and I were particularly thrilled because when he greeted us, he would always kiss our hands, as if we were grown-up ladies and would say: "Good day, *boyarishna*," or "Your hand, *boyarishna*," and this seemed to us incredibly surprising and amusing. But in return we would chat freely with him, as if he were our equal. My brothers were not shy with him either. They would tell him all about everything they were doing; my younger brother was not even able to pronounce his name correctly; he called him "Musolianin," so when Musorgsky would come to see us and my brother caught sight of him, he would shout "Here comes Musolianin!" The musical scenes "Kot Matros" [The sailor cat], "V Iukki verkhom na palochke"

[In Iukk', riding on a stick] and "Son" [Dream] [based on Zinochka's story, which it seems, was not published, and may not exist in manuscript], and a fourth small scene taken from our childhood life, were performed by Musorgsky on the piano. They were said to represent stories from our childhood.[2]

With me, since I was the eldest, Musorgsky often talked about "serious matters." Thus, he was the first to explain to me that the stars were divided into various constellations and that many single stars, as well as constellations, had their own names. He taught me how to find the Big and the Little Dipper, Cassiopea, Orion, and Canis Major with the Dog Star. I still remember our conversation one New Year's Eve. He explained to me—until then, somehow, I had not paid any attention to it—that tomorrow there was to be a "new year," and he told me what it meant and why it was celebrated in the middle of the winter and not in the fall (when everyone comes to town from the *dacha* and when, according to a child's viewpoint, the new year begins, which ends the next spring; and as for the summer—it is something special, extraneous to the year).

Musorgsky was often a guest at our *dacha* in Zamanilovka, and we became accustomed to the fact that he took part in all the events of our life: he watched my two-year-old brother being bathed outside, in the sun: my little brother would scream and run away, on the sand, naked, and he could only be enticed to come back when promised strawberries. Later on, Musorgsky would reenact this amusing scene, and he would mimic the way my brother requested the promised "bellies-bellies."

I do not clearly remember when and how it happened that we children began to be present when Musorgsky performed his own compositions or those of the others. To be more precise, I cannot remember a time, when from very early childhood, I would not be nearby (hiding in a corner, or behind an armchair, or even under the table) when the famous musicians, who so often came to our house—Balakirev, Borodin, Rimsky-Korsakov, Cui, Musorgsky, Rubinstein—were playing the great works of the world's musical literature or their own compositions, often not yet finished but still works in progress. Listening to them, we children, little by little, were able to memorize almost the whole piece so that in our nursery we would sing "Kak v gorode bylo vo Kazani" [So it was in the City of Kazan'], "Popin'ka," "O, tsarevich, u-umoliaiu, ne-e kliani menia za re-echi moi" [Oh, tsarevich, I beg of you, do not damn me for my evil words], or:

> Ratklif, Ratklif, ty krov'iu istekaesh'.
> Poidi siuda, pereviazhu ia ranu. . . . [3]
>
> [Ratcliff, Ratcliff, thou art bleeding to death,
> Come here, I will dress thy wound. . . .]

and for the sake of the beat, in order not to miss the eighth, we sang this pause on the letter "m": "M m ... podi siuda" [Mm ... come here]. Or we would scream: "Domine, Domine, salvum fac!" as it was sung by the frightened Jesuits in the last act of *Boris*; or we would sing Borodin's "Ia khrabr, ia smel, strakha ia-a ne zna-a-iu"[4] [I am courageous, I am audacious, I know no fear].

This is why I said I cannot remember a time when I did not know these operas. And when, for the first time, excerpts from *Boris* were performed and then the entire *Boris*,[5] we children categorically demanded to be taken to the theater. I remember how deeply hurt we were by an old friend of our parents, E. A. Shakeev. He teased us by telling us a fairy tale which went thus: "Once upon a time there were parents who were too kind. Father Dmitrii and Mother Pavlina had wicked children—Varia and Zina—who insisted on being taken to the theater. But in punishment, they were not taken to the theater, and in their place Uncle Zhenia went," and so on. From that day on we nicknamed Uncle Zhenia "Pavlina," and in spite of him we were taken to the theater. How could it have been otherwise? After all, it was, in a way, our own opera.

I can vividly remember these two performances as if it were yesterday. I can even picture the singers' costumes and hear the nuances in the performances by Palechek, Platonova, Petrov, Mel'nikov, Kommissarzhevskii, and Krutikova.* The night excerpts from *Boris* were performed was the same evening that one act of *Lohengrin* was given, with Raab as the singer; it was a benefit performance for someone. . . . [7]

The same thing happened with *Igor'* [Prince Igor]. We were slowly introduced to it and knew all the changes and alterations the opera underwent as it was being written. For instance, the chorus now sung in the prologue was originally intended for the finale, where it had different words; and the actual finale was later performed during the concerts of the Free School; I still have the poster for that concert.

We children, listening to the separate numbers and scenes of these operas, already had chosen parts that we particularly liked; and sometimes we would even dare to ask "Musorianin" or Aleksandr Porfirievich to play this or that scene for us. Thus, I remember how Borodin, on my humble request—I was about thirteen then—once played the Polovetskii chorus and the dances of the Second Act of *Prince Igor,* which I have adored ever since. Musorgsky kept on saying: "Now, allow me to play it for you, *professore!* You can't do it with your fat little pullets." (This expression referred to Borodin's hands, which were white and pudgy. But one had to recognize that they were by no means clumsy, and therefore this friendly joke provoked only laughter.) And then, Musorgsky sang Konchak's aria. He sang it absolutely incomparably, with his unique underscoring of certain sentences or words. For instance, in a particularly original way he exaggerated the pronunciation of "Ia tebe pod-dariu" [I shall offer thee], while making a wide gesture with his hand.

---

*I wish to point out that, in the first performance, the part of the hostess of the inn was not sung by Leonova but by Abarinova, who later went on to the Aleksandrin Theater.[6]

Even now the way he sang the following verses in an astonishing, purely oriental sublimity, resounds in my ears:

> Vsyo khanu zdes' podvlastno,
> Vsyo boitsia menia,
> Vsyo trrrepeshchet krugom. . . .
>
> [Here, everything is under the khan's ruling
> Everything fears me
> Everything here is trrrembling. . . .]

And then, with an inimitable gentleness, he could do:

> No ty menia ne boialsia,
> Poshchady ty ne prosil kniaz'
>
> [But thou, Prince, thou wert not afraid of me,
> Thou didst not ask for mercy, Prince.]

And with a kind of passionate anguish:

> Akh, ne vragom by tvoim. . . .
> [Oh, If I were not thy enemy. . . .]

After hearing Musorgsky, any other performance of *Prince Igor* which I heard on stage, even by Kariakin[8]—he sang that part remarkably—seemed inferior to me, and I still hear Musorgsky's voice singing: "Esli khochesh', liubuiu iz nikh vybirai" [If thou wish, choose anyone of them].

I also remember how, as little children, we laughed to see a grown-up at the piano singing such "songs" as were usually sung by our nannies; for example, the one about "Selezen'" [The drake] or "Kak komar drova rubil, klopik vodu nosil" [The mosquito chopped wood, and the little bedbug carried water].[9] But it was only later that we realized the difference between "the songs a child invents" and art songs. Naturally without putting this difference into words, we also understood the comic character of "Rayok" [Peepshow]. I recall very clearly how Musorgsky deliberately distorted the "vocalization," when Patti's admirer was indignant at her wearing a "parik-rik-rik belokokkury" [blo-blo-blond wi-wi-wig], and we, on our own, would sing: "O Patti, Patti, Papapatti."

But I also remember how Musorgsky sang "Sirotka" [The orphan], "Zabytyi" [Forgotten], and "Trepak"[10] for the first time in our home and how we, huddled in a corner, silently cried and were ashamed of our tears in front of the adults.

When in 1872 my aunts went abroad for several years and my uncles moved to a new apartment on Nadezhdin Street, all these friend-composers, if I remember correctly, met every Wednesday at Vladimir Vasilievich

Stasov's to make music, or, as it was said in their circle (it was, it seems, Glinka's expression), "to produce music." But at our house, these meetings were still held on Thursdays, and we would, as before, listen in. We heard both scenes from *Khovanshchina,* as Musorgsky was writing it at that time,* and the readings of scenes from the drama "Shuiskii" by Count A[rsenii] A[rkadievich] Golenishchev-Kutuzov, who was working on it at that time.[12] Toward the end of that period, I would occasionally be taken to these "Wednesdays" at Vl[adimir] Vas[ilievich]'s, and I recall seeing a charming young girl there, who soon became the Countess Kutuzova.[13]

At this period, during the summer, Musorgsky came even more often than before to our *dacha.* He would come either by himself or with Vl[adimir] Vas[ilievich], usually on a Saturday evening and stayed until Monday morning; sometimes, he would stay even longer if there was a party on Friday or Tuesday. As a rule, during the summer we never saw Borodin, Cui, or Rimsky-Korsakov; although Rimsky-Korsakov did live somewhere nearby for one or two summers, and would walk or drive to pay us a visit as a *dacha* neighbor. When I was a child, for some reason, I was terribly afraid of him. It was only much later, in my last year in the *gymnasium,* when I was taking lessons with him, that I "discovered" how exceptionally nice, gentle, witty, and gay this great man and great musician was. As for Musorgsky, I repeat, we children were not in the least afraid of him and would often run to him with any kind of nonsense and even ask him to act as a judge during some of our "dramatic conflicts." I remember the hot summer of 1875 (mother left us for a while to go to Revel' to visit an acquaintance of hers, and we stayed with father), and Musorgsky and Vl[adimir] Vas[ilievich] visited us particularly often. They had decided to reread Gogol'. In the horrible midday heat, after lunch, everybody gathered in the study and took a seat on the sofas; then, taking turns, my father, Vl[adimir] Vas[ilievich], and Musorgsky read aloud "Maiskaia noch' " [May night], "Koliaska" [The carriage], "Nos" [The nose], and "Myortvye Dushi" [Dead souls]. Everyone would laugh boisterously.

This lasted until I entered the *gymnasium.* Apparently, Musorgsky started to visit us less frequently at that time, and I had become involved in other activities and was participating less in what was happening at home. At first Musorgsky came about twice a week, but later on, only once a month. He came in the evening or at lunchtime. Usually right after dinner (and sometimes immediately after coming) he sat down in the rocking chair and either dozed or daydreamed with his eyes closed and his hands waving in front of his face, as if he were fanning himself. He was already quite changed from the way he had been with us as children; he talked much less and, in general,

---

*I remember many scenes and separate musical episodes which were deleted later: for example, Emma's scene with her uncle-pastor, and the little German waltz she sang; or Peter's scene with the Poteshny Regiment; or the now significantly shortened Tararui's exit, as well as Loter's arrival and the destruction of the clerk's booth.[11]

told fewer stories than before. Often he would utter some isolated sentences or even single words which were, at times, rather obscure. He gave me the impression, at that time, of being someone important and rather mysterious.

In his last years, I saw him at Leonova's concerts, where he was the accompanist, but by that time he had already become quite a stranger to me. At the beginning of 1881, Uncle Vladimir Vasilievich came running to our house to tell us of Musorgsky's illness. And very soon after, we learned of his death. That sad news of his illness and then of his death, this death of a man who had been so dear to us when we were children, our Musorianin, made no shattering impression on me, an already grown-up young lady, then finishing school. I do not even remember his funeral. I am extremely ashamed to confess that I absolutely failed to realize the great weight of this loss for Russia, my whole family, or me personally. I am ashamed to admit it, but it is the truth. I am not interested in justifying whether this indifference was due to my youthful egotism, wrapped up in my own life as I was at the time, or whether it was due to Musorgsky's progressive estrangement from us, the little ones. Only now do I fully realize how kind fate was in bestowing on me the joy of having known, in very early youth, one of the greatest geniuses of Russia. I was able to see him and listen to him as one does with a close friend of the family, in the natural way a child accepts things, which allowed me unwittingly to see reflected in everyday life the soul that had created *Boris* and *Khovanshchina*.

Liudmila Shestakova

Moi vechera

My Evenings

Liudmila Shestakova, née Glinka (1816–1906) was a musical and public figure who did many things to perpetuate the memory of her brother, Mikhail Glinka. She was a friend of the Balakirev circle and diligently participated in it. Musorgsky treated her with a filial tenderness and thought very highly of her activities.

.   .   .

After the death of my little girl in 1863,[1] I was unable to listen to music for a long time, although V[ladimir] V[asilievich] Stasov, more than once, invited me to his evenings; it was only in 1866 that I was able to bring myself to accept his invitation;[2] it was precisely that evening that the circle I wish to talk about came into existence. Stasov had invited Dargomyzhsky and Balakirev, whom I had known for a long time, but there were also unknown faces: Cui, Musorgsky, and Rimsky-Korsakov. Balakirev introduced us. I invited Musorgsky and Rimsky-Korsakov to my home, and they began to pay me visits, at first rather infrequently, but later on more and more often. They chose a day that was convenient for themselves and came along with Balakirev, who supervised their musical education.

Later, Dargomyzhsky, Stasov, Cui, and Borodin joined us. We would all get together twice a week, and once in a while three times a week. This lasted until 1870, the year Dargomyzhsky died,[3] when there were some changes in the composition of the circle.

Modest Petrovich Musorgsky and Nikolai Andreevich Rimsky-Korsakov were very close friends; they would almost always come to my place a little earlier than the others, so that they would have time to talk about their new compositions. Now and then there were some amusing incidents. Korsakov would sit at the piano and perform what he had composed since he had last seen Musorgsky. Musorgsky would listen attentively and then make some remark. On hearing it, Korsakov would jump up and start pacing the room, while Musorgsky peacefully sat at the piano playing something. Then, having calmed down, Nikolai Andreevich would approach Modest Petrovich, listen more carefully to his remark, and often end up agreeing with him.

From 1866 to 1870, Dargomyzhsky was in the midst of composing *The Stone Guest,* and Balakirev was writing an overture and songs. Musorgsky gave us such songs as "Svetik Savishna" [Darling Savishna], among others, and he started to work on his opera *Boris Godunov.*[4] Each of these new works met with our great enthusiasm.

These four years (1866–1869) were marked by ardent activity; total unanimity reigned in the circle, with work and life in full swing. The day was not long enough to perform what had been composed or fully discuss the music, so after leaving me, they would see each other home, taking their time, and parting reluctantly.

I used to retire rather early, at about ten thirty in the evening. I would fold up my work: Musorgsky would notice it and loudly announce that "the first warning has been given." When, after a little while, I would get up to look at the clock, he would declare: "Second warning—we must not wait for the third one," and he would say jokingly that finally they would be told "Get out of here, imbeciles."* But often, seeing that they were so happy together, I would allow them to stay longer. I will not deny that these meetings were a great joy to me.

Early in 1870, Musorgsky gave the Directors his opera *Boris Godunov;*[5] it had only three acts and roles only for men.

Soon after, there was a luncheon at Iu[liia] F[yodorovna] Platonova's,[6] on the occasion of her benefit performance. She asked me to come and added that on the morning of the luncheon, the fate of Musorgsky's opera was going to be decided and that Napravnik and Kondratiev would be there.[7] I went and waited for these men to arrive with great impatience. It is easy to understand why I met them with: "Is *Boris* accepted?" "No," they answered. "Impossible! What kind of opera has no female roles! Surely Musorgsky is very talented, so let him add one scene, and *Boris* will be accepted."

I knew that Musorgsky would not want to hear this news, and I did not want to tell him right away. I just wrote a note to him and V[ladimir] V[asilievich] Stasov, asking them to come around six o'clock in the evening. A deeply interested Stasov started to talk to Musorgsky about the inclusion of new parts in the opera, and Musorgsky himself began to play various motives, so the evening was very lively.[8] Musorgsky began to work without delay.

At that time (May 1870),[9] I[van] S[ergeevich] Turgenev was in Petersburg and had promised the Makovskiis that he would spend an evening with them. The Makovskiis, for some reason, decided to invite our musical circle for the evening. Everyone flatly declined the invitation. Elena Timofeevna was really angry and, with the help, naturally, of Konstantin Egorovich, drew in pastel a caricature of all the members of the circle, which she gave me as a gift; I later gave it to V[ladimir] V[asilievich] Stasov.[10] In the carica-

---

*This is a quote from Gogol's *The Marriage,* which he adored and for which he was even starting to compose music.

ture everybody was shown as an animal except V[ladimir] V[asilievich] Stasov; he was pictured as a peasant with a horn, leading all of them to the temple of glory visible in the distance.[11] Musorgsky was a rooster, Cui a fox; Borodin was inside a retort, and Korsakov was a lobster; both Purgold sisters were also represented. The trouble was that the resemblance was too striking. I foresaw that there would be grudges and tried to convince Elena Timofeevna, when she brought me the picture, to include me also—as a chicken or some other bird or animal, whatever she wished to draw so that there would be no ill feelings. She refused to comply, saying: "I am mad at them, and not at you!" As expected, this brought trouble; but she was very pleased with her fancy. . . .

These meetings, [the musical gatherings at the house of Vladimir Purgold, who shared his home with his two nieces, Aleksandra and Nadezhda Purgold] did not last very long: in 1872, first with the marriage of the younger niece of V[ladimir] F[yodorovich]—Nadezhda Nikolaevna—the "circle's orchestra," as Musorgsky called her, and then with the marriage of the elder one—Aleksandra Nikolaevna, the singer—the evenings at the Purgolds' came to an end.

During the 1872–1873 season, excerpts of *Boris Godunov*, newly revised by Musorgsky, were performed on stage: the [scene] "at the Inn" and the "Scene by the Fountain."[12] Almost simultaneously *Pskovitianka* [The maid of Pskov] by Rimsky-Korsakov was performed for the first time.[13] Despite my poor health, I was extremely interested in learning what success these works would have, as well as the public's reaction. My interest was quite natural: many of the works had been composed at my home. All of them had been played and sung there as well. My whole soul was impregnated with this music, and I was unable to go to sleep until I had heard news of the outcome of both performances. Later, when I was told that *Boris* had enthralled the public and that there was no end to the applause and ovations, but the *The Maid of Pskov* had been received with more reservation, I was surprised, since the performance of *The Maid of Pskov* at my house had been so beautiful! But I was told that it had less theatrical effect than *Boris Godunov*.

1873 to 1875

I must not fail to mention what happened to me when I heard Musorgsky's "Sirotka" [The orphan] performed by Anna Iakovlevna (Petrova) for the first time. At first, I was thunderstruck; then I burst into such sobs that, for a long while, I was unable to calm down. After that Anna Iakovlevna sang Marfa's aria from *Khovanshchina* by Musorgsky—and how she sang it! She also performed other works of his.

More than once Musorgsky and I went to Petrov's *dacha* in Novaia Derevnia. Musorgsky would compose a vocal work, and come to me, perform it, and then he would say: "It should be shown to our Petrovs. 'Grandfather' (as he called Petrov) will sing it magnificently!"

I also remember how Osip Afanasievich performed Musorgsky's songs "Seminarist" [The seminarian],¹⁴ "Trepak," and others, as well as "Kapral" [The field marshal] by Dargomyzhsky.

Incidentally, it was not surprising that the Petrovs wanted to sing Musorgsky's songs: Musorgsky had more talent than anybody else in the circle, and the Petrovs with their great gifts understood that. Besides, seeing his sincere affection for them, they liked him as if he were their own son.

I shall never forget those wonderful evenings when the Petrovs came to my house. The company which gathered was not a big one: Musorgsky, Borodin, and V[ladimir] V[asilievich] Stasov were my constant guests. Sometimes Stasov's brother—Dmitrii Vasilievich, V[ladimir] V[asilievich] Nikol'skii, A[leksandra] N[ikolaevna] Molas, and A[lina] A[leksandrovna] Khvostova would also come, but nobody else.

Our dear A[leksandra] N[ikolaevna] Molas sang many songs by Musorgsky, Rimsky-Korsakov, Borodin, and others. Then, Osip Afanasievich sang two or three pieces. But when Anna Nikolaevna approached the piano and decided with Musorgsky what she was going to sing, for he always accompanied her (as well as the others), then Osip Afanasievich would go to the dining room, sit at the table—the grand piano was visible from there—and, eating grapes, he would listen with delight to his wife's singing. When Anna Iakovlevna was finished he would applaud, saying: "Young talents must be encouraged!"

On January 27, 1874 the entire opera *Boris Godunov* was performed for the first time. The theater was sold out. The artists, E[duard] F[rantsevich] Napravnik, and the orchestra—everybody loved Musorgsky, and they performed his opera with great zeal. I was in the wings in order to see Iu[liia] F[yodorovna] Platonova, at whose request the opera had been staged. I overheard how one high-ranking person rebuked her for having chosen such an ill-made work for a benefit performance.¹⁵ Yes, they needed something sickly sweet: some Italian rubbish! But a realistic Russian work was, in their opinion, a monstrosity! And these people dare to claim that they are Russians. . . . You do not have any concept of what it is to be Russian! For you, anything foreign is bound to be good!

[In the preparations for the fiftieth jubilee of O(sip) A(fanasievich) Petrov's debut] Musorgsky was my faithful and diligent assistant. [The jubilee, held on April 21, 1876, in the Mariinskii Theater, featured Glinka's opera *Zhizn' za tsaria* (A life for the tsar), in which Petrov had permanently performed the role of Ivan Susanin.] Upon returning to his apartment from the jubilee, he was met by a band of trumpeters playing the polonaise from *A Life for the Tsar*. In addition to a brightly lit apartment, he found the entire staircase and all the rooms decorated with flowers, greens, and sparkling lights; and in one of the rooms there was a new, beautiful concert grand, which had been chosen by M[odest] P[etrovich] Musorgsky.

1876 to 1878

During these years, my evenings were as successful as before. The Petrovs, Musorgsky, Borodin, V[ladimir] V[asilievich] Stasov, Molas, and others would gather at my home. A perfect harmony reigned as usual. Not only I, but all those who came to these gatherings thought that they were unmatched. Some of the evenings went on until one or two o'clock in the morning. Other people also came—among them L[iubov] I[vanovna] Karmalina, Count Arsenii Arkadievich Golenishchev-Kutuzov, a friend of Musorgsky's, and others.

With O[sip] A[fanasievich] Petrov's death, my evenings came to an end.[16] We did meet once in a while, but it was not the same anymore. Musorgsky, having lost Petrov, whom he so much respected and loved, now felt lonely and bored. And Rimsky-Korsakov as a family man was terribly busy, so he distanced himself. True, now and then, Borodin and Musorgsky came together to visit me. They were such good friends. At that time, both were composing operas: Borodin—*Kniaz' Igor'* [Prince Igor], and Musorgsky—*Khovanshchina* and *Sorochinskaia Iarmarka* [The fair at Sorochintsy]. . . .

The one who was unfailingly faithful to the circle was V[ladimir] V[asilievich] Stasov, who from the very beginning up to the present moment,[17] has not changed.

1878 to 1881

During these years, Borodin, Musorgsky, Stasov, and sometimes Rimsky-Korsakov came to my home. But the previous spirit was gone; although Stasov made every effort to revive it, it was no longer the same.

Musorgsky was already quite different, and then in 1881, on March 16, he died. Through Stasov's efforts an elaborate monument in the Russian style was erected on Musorgsky's grave,[18] which is located in the Aleksandr Nevskii Monastery in the Tikhvin Cemetery. . . .

When I saw Modest Petrovich for the first time, he was already a twenty-seven-year-old gentleman and a brilliant officer of the Preobrazhenskii Regiment. From our first meeting I was impressed by his unusual tactfulness and his mild manners. He was a surprisingly well-educated and self-restrained young man. I knew him for fifteen years, and during the whole period I never saw him give vent to an outburst of anger or lose his self-control, or say one single unpleasant word to anyone. More than once, in answer to my question about how he could be so self-controlled, he would say: "For that I am indebted to my mother; she was a saintly woman." Musorgsky's relationship with Balakirev was always a smooth one; Musorgsky respected him totally and marveled at his great talent and inimitable musical memory; they constantly met on very friendly terms. Stasov, with his upright nature, his great love for art, and his amazing energy, was actually the one that Musorgsky respected the most among the members of the circle. Musorgsky always turned to Stasov for advice whenever he had a question about music, literature, or anything else, and it was known that Stasov never refused to be helpful to anyone, especially not to Musorgsky, whose talent and personality he loved so sincerely. As for Musorgsky's relationship with Rimsky-Korsakov, I have already talked about that.

Many often tried to persuade Musorgsky to get married, but his disinclination for marriage reached the point of absurdity: more than once, he seriously assured me that if I were to read in the papers the news that he had shot or hanged himself, it meant that he had gotten married the day before.

After 1872, Modest Petrovich was on most friendly terms with Borodin, who, at that time, was writing his opera *Prince Igor,* while Musorgsky was composing *Khovanshchina.* Quite often, they would come together to see me; at times, Stasov would join them. If Musorgsky had not seen Borodin for a long time, he would send me the following message:

> Dear Liudmila Ivanovna, here is what I beg of you: Borodin and I would like to drop in on you on Thursday, January 22nd, at eight o'clock in the evening. We wish to see you and have a look at Borodin's *heroic* symphony. If it is not too inconvenient for you, my dear, allow us to see you: after all, all the good musical works were begun and created in your home. As for me, I am like a cat: I become attached to a house. Borodin will come with his petition to you.[19]

And these evenings, with the two or three of us, were the most interesting and pleasant ones.

Musorgsky was on the most friendly terms with E[duard] F[rantsevich] Napravnik, G[ennadii] P[etrovich] Kondratiev, I[van] A[leksandrovich] Mel'nikov, F[yodor] P[etrovich] Kommissarzhevskii, and other artists. I do not mention the Petrovs, because in their family he was quite at home; I have already talked about that.

PIS'MO V. STASOVU

LETTER TO V[LADIMIR] STASOV

March 20, 1881

Vladimir Vasilievich, I am sending you the letter from our dear Musin'ka.[20] You cannot imagine how sad I am for not having paid him a visit while he was ailing. I was just going to see him when I received a letter from him informing me that he felt so good that in a couple of days he intended to leave the hospital and come to see me.[21] My only solace is that during all the years we were friends, he never heard from me, in word or deed, the slightest hint of displeasure; yes, I can say that we were friends because he never hid from me his feelings about my brother or other people. Musorgsky's death is an irreplaceable loss to his friends and to art. But having succumbed to the patronage of D[ar'ia] M[ikhailovna] Leonova and of her companion (whose surname I do not recall),[22] there was no future for him—not with his pride, upbringing, and education. Wouldn't you agree that that was difficult? Although I read everything and hear many things, I would like very much to hear more from you; Bakh,[23] you are not just a man, you are a superior man, or to be more exact, everything good that can be found in everybody else, has been all put together in you. I will say that as far as I am concerned, Musorgsky will live forever not only as the author of *Boris,* but as a rare, good, honest, and sincere man.

Yours, L[iudmila] Shestakova

P.S. I am unwell, and I am not going out, but you can be sure that my first outing will be to Musorgsky's grave.

Nikolai Rimsky-Korsakov

IZ *Letopis[i] moei muzykal'noi zhizni*

EXCERPTS FROM *My Musical Life*

Nikolai Rimsky-Korsakov (1844–1908) edited and published Musorgsky's works.

.   .   .

Every Saturday evening, during the months of November and December 1861, I could be found at Balakirev's, where I often met Musorgsky and Cui. It was also at Balakirev's that I got to know V[ladimir] V[asilievich] Stasov.

On one occasion Musorgsky read *Kniaz' Kholmskii*[1] [Prince Kholmsky], and the painter Miasoedov read *Vii* by Gogol'. On other occasions, Balakirev would play either by himself or with Musorgsky four-hand piano arrangements of Schumann's symphonies and Beethoven's quartets. At times, Musorgsky sang something from *Ruslan,* such as the scene between Farlaf and Naina with A[leksandr] P[etrovich] Arsen'ev[2] singing the role of Naina.

The circle's taste leaned strongly toward Glinka, Schumann, and Beethoven's last quartets. The group was rather indifferent toward eight of Beethoven's symphonies and had little respect for Mendelssohn, except for the Overture to *A Midsummer Night's Dream,* the *Hebrides* Overture, and the finale of the Octet.

Musorgsky's symphonic endeavors, apparently composed in conformity to Balakirev's directions and requests, never resulted in much of anything. At the time, Musorgsky's only composition acknowledged by the circle was his chorus from *Oedipus.*[3]

In the winter of 1861–1862 the Balakirev circle was composed of Cui, Musorgsky, and myself. Beyond any question Balakirev was indispensable as an adviser, critic, editor, and teacher to Cui and Musorgsky. Without him they were unable to take one step forward.

For Musorgsky, although he was an excellent pianist [1861–1862], did not possess the remotest technical preparation to be a composer.[4]

During that spring [1862], I went to Balakirev's every Saturday. I waited for those evenings as if they were specially festive occasions. I also visited Cui frequently that spring. At the time he lived on Voskresenskii Prospect and was the head of a boarding school that prepared boys for military schools. Cui had two pianos, and each time I went, we played eight-hand arrangements. The pianists would be either Balakirev, Musorgsky, Musorgsky's brother (Filaret Petrovich, who for some reason was usually addressed as Evgenii Petrovich[5]), Cui, or at times, Dmitrii Vasilievich Stasov. V[ladimir] V[asilievich] Stasov was also usually present. We played eight-hand piano arrangements of the scherzo *Mab* and *The Feast at the Capulets* by Berlioz,[6] in Musorgsky's arrangement, as well as the procession from *King Lear* by Balakirev in his own arrangement. We would play four-hand arrangements of the overtures to *Kavkazskii Plennik* [The prisoner of the Caucasus] and *Syn Mandarina* [The mandarin's son], and also excerpts from my symphony as soon as they were finished.[7] Musorgsky often joined Cui in singing excerpts from the latter's operas. Musorgsky had a rather good baritone voice and he sang beautifully.

As for Musorgsky and Borodin, I considered them comrades rather than teachers like Balakirev and Cui.

To return to Musorgsky, although he was a beautiful pianist and an excellent singer (true, his voice had gotten weaker by that time), and even though two of his short pieces—a scherzo in B-flat major and the chorus from *Oedipus*—had already been publicly performed under A[nton] G[rigorievich] Rubinstein's direction,[8] he had little knowledge of orchestration; the compositions which had been performed had gone through Balakirev's hands. Besides, he was a dilettante in music, and as he was working in some sort of ministry, he could only devote himself to music in his leisure.

I want to point out that in the sixties, Balakirev and Cui, even though they were very close to Musorgsky and sincerely loved him, treated him as a younger friend with little promise, in spite of his obvious talent. They felt that he lacked something, and in their opinion he needed their advice and criticism more than any of the others. Quite often Balakirev would say that Musorgsky "had no head" or that "his brains were weak."[9]

Balakirev and Cui complemented each other, yet each in his own way felt himself mature and *fully adult*. As for Borodin, Musorgsky, and me, they thought we were immature and *juvenile*. Obviously our relation to Balakirev and Cui was somewhat that of subordinates. We unconditionally paid heed to their opinions, we would "put it in our pipes and smoke it," and then put it into execution. On the other hand, realistically, Balakirev and Cui did not need our opinions.

During the 1866–1867 season I drew closer to Musorgsky and would visit him at his house, where he lived with his married brother, Filaret, near the Kashin Bridge. He played many excerpts of his *Salammbô* for me, and I was very much carried away by them. I am fairly sure that he played his fantasy "Ivanova noch' " [St. John's night] for piano and orchestra, which had been inspired by *Danse macabre*. Later, the music of this fantasy, having undergone numerous metamorphoses, was utilized as the material for *Noch' na Lysoi gore* [Night on bald mountain].[10] He also played the charming Jewish choruses: *Porazhenie Sennakheriba* [The destruction of Sennakherib] and *Iisus Navin* [Jesus Navin or Joshua] for me. He took the music for the latter piece from his opera *Salammbô*. The theme for the chorus was based on a song sung by Jews living in the same courtyard as he did and whom he had heard celebrating the Feast of the Tabernacle.[11] Musorgsky also played for me songs which had not been successful with Balakirev and Cui. Among them were "Kalistrat" and the beautiful fantasy "Noch' " [Night], based on the Pushkin poem. The song "Kalistrat" was a precursor of his later realistic direction; and "Noch' " was more representative of the idealistic side of his talent, which he himself later vilified, though still occasionally drawing on its reserve of themes and motifs. He had accumulated this reserve in *Salammbô* and the Jewish choruses written at a time when he was not so concerned with the drab Russian peasant. I would like to point out that the greater part of his works in this idealistic style, for instance, Tsar Boris's arias, the Pretender's words while standing by the fountain, the chorus in the Boyars' *Duma*, Boris's death, and so forth, were all borrowed from *Salammbô*. This idealistic style lacked a proper crystal-clear finish and elegant form; the deficiency was the result of Musorgsky's ignorance of harmony and counterpoint. Balakirev's followers at first ridiculed these unnecessary sciences and then declared that they were beyond Musorgsky's grasp. Consequently, he spent his life without that vital preparation, but to give him proper credit, he elevated that lack of knowledge into a heroic distinction, and as for the technique of the others, he changed that into routine conservatism. When he did succeed in creating a beautiful, liquid sequence that defied all preconceived opinions, he was very happy! I witnessed this more than once.[12]

When I would visit Musorgsky we could converse without restraint, free from Balakirev's or Cui's supervision. I was enthusiastic about the things he played for me and he was delighted, and would freely talk to me about his plans. He had more of them than I did.[13]

I saw him often. . . . We talked a lot about art, and he would play excerpts from his *Salammbô* for me or sing his most recently completed songs. . . .

Starting with the second half of the season, in the spring of 1868, the majority of the members of our circle began to meet almost every week, in the evening, at the home of A[leksandr] S[ergeevich] Dargomyzhsky, who had opened his doors to us. The progress on *The Stone Guest* was going very well. . . .

With each evening at A[leksandr] S[ergeevich]'s the work on *The Stone Guest* moved forward in an orderly fashion. It was immediately performed in the following manner: the author, who had an elderly and husky tenor voice, nevertheless sang the part of Don Juan himself, and he sang it beautifully. Musorgsky was Leporello and Don Carlos, Veliaminov was the monk and the Commendatore, A[leksandra] N[ikolaevna] Purgold was Laura and Donna Anna, and N[adezhda] N[ikolaevna] accompanied everyone on the piano. Often Musorgsky's songs would be performed too (by the author and A[leksandra] N[ikolaevna] Purgold), as well as Balakirev's songs, and Cui's and mine. We would play my *Sadko* and *Chukhonskaia fantaziia* [Fantasy on Finnish themes] by Dargomyzhsky in four-hand piano versions, both rearranged by Nadezhda Nikolaevna. The evenings were highly captivating. . . .

At Balakirev's and Musorgsky's suggestion I set aside the composition of the Symphony in B minor for an indefinite period and turned to *Antar,* the beautiful fairy tale by Senkovskii (Baron Brambeus).

It was about the same time that the initial idea for an opera on Mey's drama *Pskovitianka* [The maid of Pskov] was brought up. Once again it was Balakirev and Musorgsky who called it to my attention: they had a better knowledge of Russian literature than I did.[14]

As far as instrumentation was concerned, there were innovations as well as a delightful use of already proven devices: the low register for flutes and clarinets and so forth; the main theme of *Antar* had been given to the violas, if my memory serves me, in order to please Musorgsky, who was particularly fond of them.

In the beginning of the [1868–1869] season the evenings at Dargomyzhsky's resumed. *The Stone Guest* was performed in its entirety. *The Marriage*[15] also aroused a great deal of interest. Everyone was thunderstruck by Musorgsky's subject, as well as ravished with the characters and his numerous recitative passages, and all were bewildered by some of the chords and the harmonic successions. During the performance, Musorgsky himself, with his unique and inimitable talent, sang Podkolesin, Aleksandra Nikolaevna sang Fyokla, and Veliaminov sang Stepan. Nadezhda Nikolaevna accompanied; and Dargomyzhsky, who was deeply interested in the work and had copied out the part of Kochkaryov in his own hand, performed it with enthusiasm.

I do not remember what Serov and Famintsyn wrote about *Antar*. After *Sadko*'s performance, Famintsyn lashed out at me with a censuring article, accusing me of having imitated *Kamarinskaia* (!!!) This gave Musorgsky the incentive to create his "Klassik" [The classicist], which ridiculed the critic of the sad countenance, and which was based on the words "Ia vrag noveishikh ukhishchrenii" [I am the enemy of the newest devices], in which a musical motif reminiscent of the sea in *Sadko* appeared.[16] The performance of Musorgsky's "The Classicist" was a solace for all of us and for Stasov in particular.

During the summer of 1871 Musorgsky either did not leave Petersburg at all, or if he did leave, it was only for a short period.[17] I saw him very often, usually at my place. During one of his visits, I introduced him to my brother, who came to Petersburg for a short visit while on a sea voyage. Although my brother had been raised on the music of the brilliant epoch of Petersburg's Italian opera, he listened with keen interest to excerpts from *Boris Godunov*, which Modest readily played for him, at his request.[18] We often went to the Purgolds', who at that time lived at No. 1 Pargolov, by the lake.

My life with Musorgsky [1871–1872] was, I assume, a singular example of two composers sharing quarters.[19] How were we able to avoid disturbing one another? In the following way. In the morning, until noon, Musorgsky had the use of the piano while I either recopied or orchestrated something I had already worked out. About noon he went to his work at the ministry, and I had the use of the piano. In the evenings, things were worked out by mutual consent. Moreover, twice a week from nine o'clock in the morning I would be at the conservatory, while Musorgsky quite often had lunch at the Opochinins';[20] thus, everything turned out very well indeed. During that fall and winter, we both worked a lot and constantly exchanged ideas and plans. Musorgsky was in the midst of composing and orchestrating the Polish act for *Boris Godunov* and the folk scene "Pod Kromami" [At Kromy]. As for me I was orchestrating and completing *The Maid of Pskov*.

Napravnik was introduced to *The Maid of Pskov* one evening at Lukashevich's,[21] whither Musorgsky and I had been invited. Modest, who sang all the parts beautifully, helped me present the opera to those who were on hand. Of course, Napravnik did not voice his opinion but just congratulated us for our brilliant performance. Generally, at Krabbe's[22] and often at the Purgolds', *The Maid of Pskov*, with piano accompaniment, would be performed by Musorgsky, who sang [Ivan] the Terrible, Tokmakov, and other male parts, depending on the need. . . .

Toward the end of the theater season [February 5, 1873], two scenes from *Boris Godunov*, the Scene at the Inn and the Scene by the Fountain, were put on stage for some sort of benefit performance.[23] Petrov (Varlaam) was excellent; Platonova (Marina) and Kommissarzhevskii (Dmitrii) were also good. The scenes were enormously successful. Musorgsky and the rest of us were delighted, and it was suggested that the entire *Boris* should be staged in the coming year. After this performance, Musorgsky, Stasov, Aleksandra Nikolaevna, my wife's sister (who in the fall of 1872, had married N[ikolai] P[avlovich] Molas), and others related to the world of music, gathered at our place.[24] During dinner, champagne was drunk and wishes were expressed for the immediate production and success of the entire *Boris*.

Musorgsky, Borodin, and Stasov often met at our house. At that time, Musorgsky was already thinking about *Khovanshchina*.[25]

[At the concert for the benefit of the famine victims, held on February 18, 1874], the chorus from *The Destruction of Sennakherib* was performed partly with my orchestration. Musorgsky had composed a new trio for the chorus, one, by the way, that was much admired by Stasov, but since he did not have enough free time, he had asked me to do the instrumentation.

Musorgsky was already working on *Khovanshchina*. From the excerpts he played for our group of friends we particularly liked "Pliaski persidok" [The Persian dance], which he played beautifully.[26]

None of us knew the real subject and outline of *Khovanshchina;* and from Musorgsky's stories, it was rather difficult to understand the plot as something complete and consistent. This was due to the fact that Musorgsky was then in the habit of expressing himself in a very florid, ornate, and intricate manner. Generally speaking, starting with the production of *Boris*, Musorgsky began to meet less frequently with our group; some sort of change had come over him: a certain secrecy and I would even say a certain haughtiness. His self-esteem had soared, and that obscure and abstruse way of speaking, which was already inherent in him, was greatly magnified. It was often impossible to understand his stories, his reasoning, or the pranks which were supposed to be witty. It is around this time that he started to stay at Malyi Iaroslavets and other restaurants until dawn, with a glass of brandy in his hand. He would either be by himself or in the company of new acquaintances and friends, who at the time were unknown to us. At lunchtime, either at our place or at the homes of mutual friends, Musorgsky almost completely refused alcohol, but later in the evening, he was drawn to Malyi

Musorgsky in 1865

Iaroslavets. Afterwards, one of his companions from those times, a man named V–ky, whom I had known since Tervaioki, told me that their group had a special saying: "prokon'iachitsa" [to "brandify" oneself] and that they put it into practice. The gradual decline of this highly talented author began about the time of the production of *Boris*. Gleams of powerful creativity lasted for a long time, but his mental ability to think logically slowly and gradually declined. Having retired from the ministry, he became a professional composer. Musorgsky began to write more slowly, in a fragmented way, losing the connection between the separate moments of creativity and scattering himself, at that, in too many directions.[27]

What was the reason for Musorgsky's moral and intellectual collapse? To a great extent, at first, it was the influence of the success of *Boris*, which resulted in the blooming of its author's pride and self-esteem; and then it was the opera's plight. It was truncated, and the excellent scene at Kromy was deleted. About two years later, for God only knows what reason, the performances were totally discontinued, although the opera had always been successful and the performances by Petrov (and after his death by F[yodor] I[gnatievich] Stravinskii), Platonova, and Kommissarzhevskii were always beautiful. It was rumored that it was not to the liking of the imperial family; it was said that the censors did not like the subject. The outcome was that the opera, which had been performed for two or three years, was now taken out of the repertoire.[28] On one hand, V[ladimir] Stasov's admiration of Musorgsky's brilliant outbursts of creativity and improvisations heightened Musorgsky's self-importance; on the other hand, being worshipped by people who stood well below him but who were part of his friendly group of boon companions, and being so admired by others who were carried away by his talent as a performer but unable to distinguish a real gleam from a finely played phrase, he was pleased and his vanity was tickled. Even the bartender of the tavern knew *Boris* and *Khovanshchina* almost by heart and worshipped Musorgsky's talent.[29] But the Russian Musical Society did not give Musorgsky any recognition; in the theater they betrayed him, although externally they were civil to him. His friends Borodin, Cui, and I, loving him as before and delighted with what was good, were yet critical of many a thing. The press—with Laroche, Rostislav, and others—abused him. Under such conditions, his passion for cognac and sitting until dawn in the tavern grew and grew. For his new friends "to brandify oneself" was of no consequence, but for his highly strung nature it was pure poison. Although remaining friendly to me, as well as to Cui and Borodin, Musorgsky began to look at me with some suspicion. My studies in harmony and counterpoint, which had begun to interest me, were not to his liking. I had the impression that he suspected me of being a retarded scholastic professor who was still capable of exposing him in parallel fifths—quite an unpleasant idea for him.[30] As for the Conservatory, he could not stand it.[31] His feelings for Balakirev had long cooled down. At the time, Balakirev no longer appeared on our horizon; but earlier he used to say that Modest had a great talent, but that his "brains were weak." And he, having suspected Musorgsky of a penchant toward alcohol, had already distanced himself from him.[32]

The year 1874 could be considered the beginning of Musorgsky's decline, a slow process which continued until the day of his death.[33]

[In 1876] I began reworking *The Maid of Pskov*. My first thought was to reintroduce the prologue, which had been completely deleted even though it played a very important part in Mey's drama.

I began work on it and within a year and half, i.e., in approximately January 1878, the whole task was completed.

The prologue, played entirely on the piano, was performed at our place, with Vera's part sung by A[leksandra] N[ikolaevna] Molas, Nadezhda's by O. I. Veselevoskaia (one of the active members of the Free Music School), and the part of the boyar Sheloga by Musorgsky. Cui, Musorgsky, and Stasov praised the prologue but with reservations. Balakirev was indifferent to it as well as to the entire opera in its new version, except for the pilgrims' chorus, the storm, and the final chorus. Musorgsky, Cui, and Stasov approved the other changes and additions to *The Maid of Pskov*, although they responded to the opera in its new form with restraint and coolness.[34]

We invited Musorgsky to participate in our joint writing. He tried and even composed some sort of galop or something similar and played it for us. But he had diverged from the original plan and had changed the recurring motif, so the result was different. We pointed that out to him. His answer was that he did not have any intention of fatiguing his brains. Therefore, his participation in our joint composition came to nought.[35]

At a rehearsal of a scene from *Boris Godunov* Musorgsky behaved in an odd way.[36] Was it due to the influence of alcohol, or was it on account of striking a pose, an inclination to which he was more and more given? In those times he would often act in an eccentric way and would frequently use unclear and confusing language. At this rehearsal, he pretentiously listened to the playing, for the most part admiring the execution by individual instruments, often while they were playing the tritest and most insignificant musical phrases. He would pensively lower his head or proudly raise it, or shake it; or he would raise his hand in a theatrical gesture, a gesture which had become usual with him. At the end of the scene, when the tomtom representing the ringing of a monastery bell rang pianissimo, Musorgsky bowed deeply, respectfully crossing his arms on his chest. This dress rehearsal took place before the choir practice held at the home of V[ladimir] I[vanovich] Vasil'ev the First, the artist who sang Pimen's part. I was studying my part while I accompanied them. After the practice, there was a dinner during which the master of the house got very intoxicated and talked non-sense. Musorgsky was fine.

The first stage performance of my opera *Maiskaia Noch'* [May night],[37] had an indifferent success in our circle.

At that time Musorgsky began to show his indifference toward everyone else's music, and his reaction to the ring dance was colder than usual. He made wry faces in general and said that there was something wrong with *May Night*. Apparently, my tendency to create a more melodious and rounded form was not very pleasant for the circle; besides I truly scared them with my studies in counterpoint and they became somewhat preju-diced toward me.

During 1879–1880, I again made arrangements for a season of four con-certs to be held by the Free Music School in the Kononov Hall.

The excerpts from *Khovanshchina* which were performed during the sec-ond concert[38] had not all been orchestrated by their author. The Streltsy chorus and Marfa's song belonged entirely to Musorgsky's pen; but I had orchestrated the "Persian Dance." Musorgsky had promised to have this number ready for the concert but had procrastinated; in the end, I offered to orchestrate it. He immediately gave his approval, and when it was per-formed, he was very satisfied with my work, although I had made many changes in his harmony and voice leading.

Among the soloists who participated in the School's concerts that year, in addition to several operatic artists, we had Shostakovskii, who played Liszt's concerto in E-flat major (which went rather well), and D[ar'ia] M[ikhailovna] Leonova, who sang excerpts from *Khovanshchina*.[39]

It had been several years since Leonova had left the imperial stage, and after a trip to Japan, she was now living in Petersburg, giving singing les-sons. She had established these lessons on a grand scale, having founded something like a small school of music. Leonova was a talented artist who formerly had a good contralto voice, but as she virtually never had any formal musical education, she hardly possessed the skills to teach the tech-niques of singing.[40] In her own singing, once in a while there would be something of the gypsy. But in dramatic and comic parts she was often inimitable. And with that aspect of her talent, she was naturally able to be of use to her students. But for the beginners this was not enough; therefore, among her many students, only one, the tenor Donskoi, became an artist at the Moscow Opera. She mainly worked with songs and excerpts from op-eras. She needed an accompanist, a musician who could supervise the proper study of a piece, something that she herself was unable to do. Musorgsky became her maestro.[41] In those years, as he had been long retired, he needed money. Leonova's classes provided him with a certain financial support. He spent quite a lot of time teaching those classes, even giving lessons in elementary theory; and he composed exercises for Leonova's students in the form of trios and quartets, with terrible voice leading.

Leonova was an artist who liked to talk a lot about herself, her qualities and merits. Although her voice had aged significantly, she did not realize it; and she would proudly tell how this artist, or that one, or someone famous had marveled at her voice, which, according to her, had become stronger and wider in range with the passing years. She said that a plaster mold of her throat had been sent to Paris and that everybody there was awed by it. According to her, the only true school of singing was her own. She said that contemporary artists did not know how to sing, and that earlier times were better, and so on, i.e., the usual statement by an aging artist. Her lover, someone named Gridnin, author of some kind of dramatic play, was her business manager and was in charge of her publicity.[42]

Musorgsky's association with her was, to a certain extent, important to her as publicity. Naturally, his duties in her classes were mediocre, but he did not realize it, or at least tried not to be aware of it.

During the summer of 1880, Leonova made a concert tour of southern Russia.[43] Musorgsky was not only the accompanist but also piano soloist in the concerts. Although since his youth Musorgsky had been an excellent pianist, he did not practice seriously and he did not possess a real repertoire. In his later years, he very often appeared as an accompanist to singers in Petersburg's concerts. The singers liked him very much and highly valued his accompaniment. He followed the voice beautifully, sight-reading the music, without any rehearsal. But on his trip with Leonova, he was to appear as a piano soloist. For this occasion he had a rather strange repertoire: for example, during his provincial concerts, he performed the introduction to *Ruslan and Ludmila* in an improvised arrangement or he played the ringing of the bells from his *Boris*.[44] Musorgsky and Leonova toured many of the cities of southern Russia; they even had the opportunity to go to Crimea. Influenced by the landscape of the southern shores, he wrote two short pieces for piano "Gurzuf" and "Na iuzhnom beregu" [On the southern shore], which were published by Bernard on his return. Both pieces were far from being fully successful. In addition I remember how, in our house, he played a rather long and quite confusing fantasy supposed to represent a storm on the Black Sea. This fantasy remained unwritten and has now disappeared forever.

Anatoly Liadov was delighted with my opera *Snegurochka* [The snow maiden]. Musorgsky listened to only a couple excerpts, and for some reason, he was not interested in hearing the entire work; he did praise some passages but all in all he remained totally indifferent to my composition. I really should not have expected otherwise: on the one hand, there was his proud self-conceit and the conviction that the path he had chosen in art was the only true one; and on the other, there was his near-total collapse, his alcoholism, and, as a result of that, a constantly befuddled mind.

For the 1880–1881 season, four concerts were advertised by the Free Music School and were to be held in the Hall of the Municipal Credit Society. Only the first one took place, on February 3, 1881, and Cross and Stravinsky took part in it. Among the choral pieces, Musorgsky's chorus from *The Destruction of Sennakherib* was performed. He was present at the concert and came out to acknowledge the audience's applause.

This concert was Musorgsky's last occasion to hear his work performed in public. About a month later, Musorgsky was placed in the hospital following an attack of *delirium tremens*. Dr. L[ev] B[ernardovich] Bertenson had him admitted and took care of him. On hearing about Musorgsky's misfortune, we—Borodin, Stasov, I, and many others—began visiting the patient. My wife and her sister A[leksandra] N[ikolaevna] Molas also visited him. He had changed, he was terribly weak, and his hair was greying. He was very happy with our visits and sometimes conversed with us in a completely normal way, but then suddenly he would lapse into insane gibberish. This state of affairs lasted for a few weeks; finally, on March 16, he died during the night, apparently of cardiac arrest. His strong constitution turned out to have been completely shattered by alcohol. On the eve of his death, we—all his close friends—had visited him during the day and had stayed rather a long time talking with him. He was buried, as is known, in the Aleksandr Nevskii Monastery. V[ladimir] V[asilievich] Stasov and I arranged the funeral.[45]

After Musorgsky's death, all his remaining manuscripts and drafts were given to me so that they could be put in order, finished, and readied for publication. . . . All of the material was in a very unpolished state; there were absurd, incoherent harmonies, hideous voice leading, sometimes strikingly illogical modulations, sometimes no modulation at all, or unfortunate instrumentation of orchestrated pieces. Generally, it was all a kind of insolent, self-conceited dilettantism; at times, there were moments of real technical dexterity and skill, but more often than not there was a total absence of technical mastery. Notwithstanding all these drawbacks, in the majority of cases, the compositions were so talented and original and they contributed so much that was new and lively that their publication was a must.

The Balakirev circle was composed of technically weak musicians, almost amateurs, who carved the road to the future exclusively by the force of their creative talent, a force which at times was a substitute for technique, and, as was sometimes the case with Musorgsky, the force was not powerful enough to conceal its defects.

Poliksena [Polina] Stasova

Moi vospominaniia

My Memoirs

Polina Stasova, née Kuznetsova (1839–1918), a well-known public figure, was married to Dmitrii Stasov.

. . .

[During winter of 1870 or 1871 Dmitrii Stasov organized a musical event with the participation of Anton Rubinstein.] All our musicians, i.e., Musorgsky, Borodin, Cui, Rimsky-Korsakov, and of course, Voldemar and Meyer were present.[1] When they began talking about Russian music, the atmosphere between Rubinstein and the whole Russian group immediately became strained. Gathering some courage, I said: "All the arguments, all the contradictions fade away when Anton Grigorievich enthralls us with his magical playing! Let's go to the drawing room, Anton Grigorievich." Everybody applauded my suggestion, and marvelous sounds soon began to flow, entrancing everyone. The evening ended with a dinner, as was the custom.

[In the Purgolds' house] an entire opera was set up. Musorgsky's *Boris* was performed in its entirety. The orchestra was in the hands of the talented Nadezhda Nikolaevna, while the female solo was sung by Aleksandra Nikolaevna, who also performed all the male parts; and when she could not handle one of those parts, then Musorgsky and Vel'iaminov[2] would join in, Musorgsky singing the part of Boris himself, as well as those of Pimen, the Pretender, and the two tramps—Varlaam and Misail. These treasured evenings left wonderful impressions on one's soul. Many visitors would come, led by Vl[adimir] Vas[ilievich] Stasov. Hartmann the painter and Antokol'sky also came.[3]

[During the years 1870–1872 at Dmitrii Stasov's] there were some really special evenings to which the two talented Purgold sisters were invited.

[During the winter of 1873–1874] we never missed the Thursdays at Dmitrii Stasov's. Their constant guests included . . . A[leksandr] P[orfirievich] Borodin; our beloved Musorgsky; the dear Stasov brothers, Aleksandr and Vladimir; the deeply loved Nikolai Vasilievich, and his niece Natasha Pivarova. Once in a while Vasilii Matveevich Clark[4] would also come; but our most assiduous visitor was our beloved A[leksandr] V[asilievich] Meyer, who was always witty, and always original in his judgments. We had interesting conversations and music. Musorgsky shared the novelties of his work with us. Once in a while Il'inskii[5] would come and sing for us. A[nton] A[ugustovich] Herke would also come.[6] Then they would play eight-hand piano versions.

Elizaveta Dianina

Zapis' s eyo slov Sergeia Dianina

As Recorded by Sergei Dianin

Elizaveta Dianina, née Balaneva (1862–1927), was one of Borodin's many pupils.

. . .

In those years M[odest] P[etrovich] Musorgsky was a frequent visitor at the Borodins',[1] where he performed his musical compositions. In particular, he quite often played the entire *Boris Godunov*; usually, after this performance one or sometimes several hammers on the piano would be broken. Once Borodin's mother, generally not very sensitive to music, was so touched by the brilliant composer's rendering of *Boris,* that she embraced him and began to kiss M[odest] P[etrovich] after he finished playing.

Il'ia Repin

iz *Dalyokoe Blizkoe*

EXCERPTS FROM *Distant, yet Familiar*

Il'ia Repin (1844–1930), a painter, was affiliated with the group "Peredvizhniki" [Wanderers].

.   .   .

In the winter of 1871–1872, I was commissioned by A. A. Porokhovshchikov, the builder of the Slavianskii Bazar [The Slavic bazaar, a Moscow restaurant], to do a painting representing groups of Slavic composers: Russians, Poles, and Czechs. V[ladimir] V[asilievich] Stasov, whom I had just met, was very enthusiastic about the project and completely selflessly rejoiced at my progress. At great personal sacrifice, wherever he could, he obtained the indispensable portraits of those who had died as well as portraits of those who had long ago abandoned the stage; and he introduced me to all the musicians on my list who were still alive, so that I could paint them from life. . . . Stasov and I both fell in love with the painting, and we made every effort to make it artistic and significant. . . .

Often Stasov, having scarcely stepped across the threshold to my studio at the Academy, in consonance with his exuberant personality, without even closing the door, would shout his sincere and loud praise from the entryway. His powerful enthusiasm would pull me from my chair, and I would rush over to search his briefcase, where—I was certain—I would find portraits I had not yet seen, or get a new perspective on a portrait from some ancient photograph, daguerreotype, or old lithograph, etc., that he had dug up somewhere.

"But, you know, you must also include two of our young aces in the picture. I mean, Musorgsky and Borodin, who belong to 'Moguchaia Kuchka' [The Mighty Handful]," said Vladimir Vasilievich.

I was in total agreement with him.

Everyone liked A[leksandr] P[orfirievich] Borodin: he was a new face and strikingly handsome; as for M[odest] P[etrovich] Musorgsky, although not everybody appreciated him, he astonished everyone with his audacity and vitality; nobody could resist his exuberant laughter, especially in his performance of comic types and his unexpectedly lively and characteristic recitatives. Oh! it is impossible even now to remember without deep sadness how Vladimir Vasilievich did not have the chance to live long enough to see that all Europe has acknowledged that native genius of Russian music—Musorgsky! While he was alive, the guardians of our musical tastes, all sternly educated in the narcotic, sweet sound of Romanticism, would not even deign to retain in their memories the name of an already fully mature national genius. Even such a beloved and popular writer as Saltykov-Shchedrin, when asked his opinion by Musorgsky's admirers, who assumed that the sound of the new comic music would be very much to his liking, had answered with a satirical pen in a vitriolic caricature.[1] All of Petersburg, dying of laughter, read this libel of the young talent. It is amusing to tell how this loud aesthete crucified Musorgsky in the eyes of the connoisseurs, when the same Saltykov-Shchedrin, this newly blooming talent, mooed his own aria on a folk theme—about a coachman who had lost his whip.

Nonetheless, I asked Porokhovshchikov to let me add Musorgsky and Borodin to the group of Russian musicians.

"Good heavens! Are you going to sweep any kind of trash into this painting? Nikolai Rubinstein[2] himself selected the names on the list, and I don't dare either add or subtract any name from the list given to me. . . . I am disappointed by one omission: he did not include Tchaikovsky. You know how we adore Tchaikovsky, here, in Moscow. There is something suspicious here. . . . But what can we do? As for Borodin, I know him; but in music he is just a dilettante: he is a chemistry professor at the Surgico-Medical Academy. . . . No, don't you litter this painting with all kinds of trash! Fewer portraits will make it easier for you, anyway. Hurry up! Hurry up! Finish the painting, the people are waiting for it."

I copied most of the faces from portraits. The only ones that I painted from life were M[ilii] A[lekseevich] Balakirev; Rimsky-Korsakov, who was then still a naval officer; and Napravnik. . . . The painting was successful, but Turgenev rejected it, principally because of its subject.

I happened to have closely watched the process of creating *Khovanshchina* and other masterpieces by this inspired artist, and I heard him sing and perform these compositions himself. They were unexpectedly bright and always original.

Vladimir Vasilievich loudly and cheerfully welcomes him; the lively, chubby little "Modestius" begins a loud and graceful report. Without our pleading, he quickly goes over to the piano, and immediately gives his audience that somersaulting character of unexpected ringing sounds in amusing recitatives, accompanied by his own slightly hoarse and lively singing. Within minutes, the audience can no longer hold its laughter.

[In the summer of 1875] I waited for Vladimir Vasilievich [in Paris]. For a long time he was held up in Petersburg helping Musorgsky with the gems he was then writing.³ Stasov's presence was indispensable: the "Russia of unfathomed depths—the bedrock of all our epics" was on the rise.

Throughout our stay in Paris, Vladimir Vasilievich was of a particularly joyful disposition. But a thought gnawed at his heart: he could not stop thinking about Musorgsky! "Oh, what is happening to our poor Musorianin?!" More than once Vladimir Vasilievich had to go to the rescue of his genius friend, who, in his absence, sank to the very bottom. It was truly unbelievable how this officer of the Guards, with his excellent education and beautiful social graces, this witty conversationalist in ladies' company, that inveterate punster, as soon as he found himself alone, without Vladimir Vasilievich, would quickly sell his furniture and his elegant clothes. Soon after, he would be found in some cheap tavern, all his buoyancy lost, no better than the other habitués, a "has-been" in whom one could no longer recognize that childishly happy, chubby little fellow with his little red potato-shaped nose. Was it really Musorgsky? Musorgsky who was always dressed in a brand-new suit, clicking his heels: the perfect man of the world, perfumed, refined, and fastidious. . . . Oh, how many times, upon his return from abroad, would Vladimir Vasilievich, after great difficulty, finally find him in some basement establishment, nearly in rags. . . . Musorgsky would stay until two o'clock in the morning, sometimes until dawn, with dubious companions. While still abroad, Vladimir Vasilievich would continually bombard all his close friends with letters, asking for news about Musorgsky, about the mysterious stranger he had now become, for nobody knew where Musorgsky had hidden himself.⁴

What profound love Vladimir Vasilievich had for chronicles and manuscripts and what a deep knowledge of them. From his published correspondence with Musorgsky, one quickly becomes aware of the great service he rendered the brilliant musician in his libretto to *Khovanshchina*.⁵

From boyhood Stasov was interested in the musical world: particularly in the Russian musical world of Balakirev, Cui, Borodin, Rimsky-Korsakov, and the others. Of them all, he attached himself most especially to Modest Petrovich. In the very first lines dedicated to his memory, Vladimir Vasilievich wrote: "Musorgsky belongs to the type of people to whom future generations will raise monuments."⁶

I must quote here some lines by Musorgsky himself from a letter addressed to a friend (I think it was to Stasov): "Soon we will be brought to trial! With courage bordering on audacity we look on the remote musical distance that beckons us onward. And the verdict does not frighten us. We shall be told: 'You have violated the laws of God and man.' We shall answer: 'Yes!' and we shall think: 'this is only the beginning!' They shall caw: 'Soon you shall be forgotten.' We shall answer: '*Non, non et non, Madame.*' "[7]

Vladimir Vasilievich concludes his short foreword to his essay "Pamiati Musorgskogo" [To the memory of Musorgsky] with the following words: "We are simply proud to say that we were the contemporaries of the greatest of all Russian men."[8] . . . Such was the faith with which Vladimir Vasilievich looked upon Musorgsky, and this faith was the reason why he protected him so vigilantly from adversity.

Vladimir Vasilievich never missed the staging of his favorite operas. The difficulties linked with the production of *Boris Godunov* and *Khovanshchina* were borne by the entire Stasov family as if they were their own. Vladimir Vasilievich's failures in his encounters with the powerful theatrical directors provoked sincere grief on the part of the whole family. In the end, the success of *Boris* was grandly celebrated by all of Musorgsky's friends.

iz Pis'ma k Andreiu Rimskomu-Korsakovu

FROM A Letter to Andrei Rimsky-Korsakov

M[odest] P[etrovich] was a person of great natural gifts, a *bogatyr* [epic hero] with the looks of *Chernomor;* incidentally, he did not mind playing the fool. The attraction he held for me, although I am not a musician, is an enigma I cannot fathom. I think that it was M[odest] P[etrovich] himself who sparked my sincere (albeit ignorant) enthusiasm for his talent, which at that time was far from recognized. . . . "Pull on, wheelhorse, pull on," he wrote.[9] Well, what sort of a *wheelhorse* am I? His genius profoundly impressed my instinctive nature, but I could only sense it; I was incapable of judging or comprehending it.

At the Stasovs', M[odest] P[etrovich] would improvise a lot when *under the spell* of inspiration, and he plunged us all into ecstasy.

While I was painting M[odest] P[etrovich]'s portrait in the Nikolaev Hospital, a *terrible event* took place: the death of Aleksandr II. During our breaks in the sittings we would reread many of the newspaper accounts which dealt with that frightful event.[10]

We were getting ready to celebrate Modest Petrovich's birthday.[11] He was on a strict program of no alcohol and was in a particularly healthy and sober frame of mind. . . . But, as always happens with alcoholics, he was constantly gnawed by Bacchus' worm; so he was already dreaming about a reward for his lengthy endurance. Despite stern orders given to the hospital attendants regarding the ban on brandy, "the heart is not made of stone," and one of the attendants, to celebrate M[odest] P[etrovich]'s birthday, got him a whole bottle of brandy (everybody loved him so). . . . The following day we were supposed to have our last sitting. But when I arrived at the appointed hour, he was no longer with us.[12]

I hear *Khovanshchina* (on the radio) quite often, and each sound, each individual note reminds me so much of him. . . .

After all, it had all been rehearsed at the Stasovs' in front of my very ears, and I, lucky man that I was, heard it performed by the author himself many times, so often that, in fact, I knew almost all of the melodies by heart. . . . Vladimir Vasilievich so greatly adored "his Musorianin" that when at times he could not sleep (from three to four in the morning), he would be immediately attacked by the artistic and historical possibilities arising from the wealth of the chronicles, whose *depths* he was then exploring with a historian's passion. Those manuscripts were kept in the basement of the Public Library, as well as in the section of which he was the head.

With all the sincerity and liveliness his titanic nature discharged, when V[ladimir] V[asilievich] would catch sight of me from afar, he would shout: "Look at what new materials I came across in our manuscript section!!" And thus it was that even before M[odest] P[etrovich] himself, I was often honored with a look at these extremely rare documents.

At my request, V[ladimir] V[asilievich] Stasov agreed to stand as my daughter Vera's *godfather* in 1872. V[ladimir] V[asilievich] arrived together with Musorgsky. Both the great musician and the great historian stayed with us common folk until late evening. M[odest] P[etrovich] greatly entertained us by playing the great Mozart, albeit, on a rather bad piano (there being no better one available). He improvised so many things that evening, and then he played "The Seminarian" and other pieces. He remembered several songs sung by choirs of beggars which he, obviously, had studied at the fairs. We laughed a lot. He performed all that by himself. . . .

Iu[liia] Platonova

iz Pis'ma k V.V. Stasovu

from a Letter to V. V. Stasov

Iuliia Platonova, née Garder (1841–1882), a soprano, was married to a military man named Tvanev. Platonova was her stage name. An opera singer, from 1863 to 1876 she was an artist with the Mariinskii Theater; later she became a voice teacher.

.   .   .

Musorgsky, with whom I became acquainted at my house, but had seen previously at Liudmila Ivanova's[1]—with Lukashevich, Kondratiev, Kommissarzhevskii, Leonova, and Petrov[2]—charmed everyone with his *extraordinarily sweet personality*. To meet him was to love him. Even the obdurate enemies of the new Russian school involuntarily succumbed to his charm, saying: "What a nice fellow, this Musorgsky is; too bad he has gone astray in his music!" These were the words of Napravnik[3] and of the artists who disapproved of the direction he had taken.

On Saturdays, the circle of admirers of this *new* music met at my home. Among the comrade-artists only Kommissarzhevskii came. He liked the opera *Boris* very much. Many others would be there too, but Musorgsky was the heart of the evening; he played and sang until the early hours of the morning. His declamation impressed more than just the connoisseurs of music. My husband and I recruited many more admirers for Musorgsky's talent, and we did so by inviting people from all over *to listen to Musorgsky*. As a result we soon had a circle of fervent champions of his talent.

At that time Lukashevich was a passionate admirer of mine, and my husband and I used our influence on him to recruit him into our circle. We succeeded because Musorgsky's fascinating talent had also affected Lukashevich. It was decided that *Boris* should be staged. But how? Following the proper channels, Musorgsky had formally presented his opera to the committee and the authorization had been denied.[4]

Having made up my mind to have *Boris* staged at whatever cost, I decided to make an outrageously audacious move. In the summer of 1873, when the Director Gedeonov[5] was in Paris, when it came time to renew my contract, I wrote to him laying down my conditions, the first of which was to have *Boris Godunov* staged for a benefit performance; if this were denied, I would not sign the contract and I would leave! I did not receive an answer, but I knew very well that I would obtain what I wanted since the management could not do without me.

Gedeonov arrived, and his first words to Lukashevich, who met him at the train station, were: "Platonova demands unconditionally to have *Boris* for a benefit performance. What can we do? She knows I don't have the right to stage an opera that had been rejected! Our only recourse . . . is to call another meeting, and let them study it a second time, for form's sake, and perhaps then they will agree to let *Boris* through."[6]

[The music committee rejected the opera again. Then Gedeonov, bypassing the committee's decision, ordered the staging of the opera] and this was the *first example* of a director exceeding his authority.

[The next day, Gedeonov called Platonova] and started to shout: "Here we are, Madam, look at the extremes to which you have driven me! Now, I risk being fired from my job, thanks to you and your *Boris*! And what good you found in it is beyond me. I am a long way from sympathizing with any of your innovators, and yet, because of them I have to suffer." "More credit to you, Your Excellency, that you, not personally in favor of this opera, are nonetheless so energetically defending its interests!" was my answer to him.

[After the Director's order to stage *Boris,* another obstacle arose.] Napravnik, hemming and hawing, inwardly furious, came to the Director and told him that *he did not have the time* for the rehearsals since he had many other things to do. It was then that we decided to hold private rehearsals at my house, under Musorgsky's direction. The Director ordered Pomazanskii to teach the choruses; Musorgsky eagerly began to work, lovingly studying along with us that music which enthralled us all; and in one month we were ready.

During the second performance, after the scene by the fountain, Grand Duke Konstantin Nikolaevich, a sincerely devoted friend of mine, but by the calumny of the Conservatory members, the sworn enemy of Musorgsky, approached me during the intermission with the following words: "And you like this music so much that you chose this opera for a benefit performance?" "I like it, Your Highness," I answered. "Then I am going to tell you that this is a shame to all Russia, and not an opera!" he screamed, almost foaming at the mouth, and then turning his back, he stomped away from me.[7]

Eduard Napravnik

"Boris Godunov" M. P. Musorgskogo
(opera postavlena 27 ianvaria 1874 g.)

Boris Godunov by M. P. Musorgsky
(Opera staged January 27, 1874)

Eduard Napravnik (1839–1916) was a composer and a conductor. From 1863 to 1916 he was the conductor with the Mariinskii Theater. This excerpt is from his notebooks.

. . .

Musorgsky—one of the members of the Russian circle ("The Mighty Handful") stood out from this group of comrades because of his originality. He had great natural gifts and was antagonistic toward any formal training; he was almost a musical illiterate. He had a realistic and revolutionary approach to music; nonetheless, at all times and places, he was true to his own genius. In his work as well as in Dargomyzhsky's, the text and the music constituted one, inseparable unity, a rare occurrence among operatic composers—especially in the recitatives in the folk scenes and in the scenes with the lead singers. Had he followed Rimsky-Korsakov's example and enthusiastically studied elementary theory, harmony, counterpoint, instrumentation, and so forth, one can only imagine what talented works he would have created in operatic literature! His irregular, careless life-style and his reluctance to work assiduously were the main factors which prevented him from achieving such success. His abnormal life-style shortened his brief span of years. He died at the age of forty-two, in 1881, in the Nikolaev Military Hospital, where in view of his lack of means, charitable souls found him shelter and a job as an orderly. The bass I[van] A[leksandrovich] Mel'nikov, who at that time was performing the part of Tsar Boris beautifully, and I visited him there more than once.

I was saddened and pained as I watched this talented jewel waste away. I used to meet him often at the house of the Petrovs—Osip Afanasievich was a famous bass of the Russian opera, and his wife, the contralto Anna Iakovlevna, was an artist with the same company. They were the first to perform Glinka's *A Life for the Tsar* in 1836 and *Ruslan and Ludmila* in 1842. At their place, Musorgsky played all his vocal compositions and sang masterfully in his hoarse voice. It was only thanks to his friend Rimsky-Korsakov that Musorgsky's operas were put in immaculate order, i.e., shaped up and orchestrated. It was in Rimsky-Korsakov's version that *Boris* was staged and was an unquestioned success. It has been revived, and lately F[yodor] I[vanovich] Shaliapin, with his masterful rendition of Boris, has pushed it into the foreground.[1]

Semyon Kruglikov

ɪᴢ *Musorgskii i ego "Boris Godunov"*

ꜰʀᴏᴍ *Musorgsky and His "Boris Godunov"*

Semyon Kruglikov (1857–1910) was a music critic and a professor. At one time he was the Director of the Moscow Philharmonic School. In Moscow he was a popularizer of the works of the composers of the "Mighty Handful."

·　　·　　·

Even before the raising of the curtain, the orchestra was playing the solemn ringing of the bells. I recall how the author played it on the piano and how perfect it was: the imitation of big and small bell ringing was masterfully captured.[1]

Arsenii Golenishchev-Kutuzov

Vospominaniia o M[odeste] P[etroviche] Musorgskom

Reminiscences of Musorgsky

Arsenii Golenishchev-Kutuzov (1848–1913) was a poet on whose texts Musorgsky based many of his compositions. See the Preface for more information about him.

.   .   .

On March 16 of this year, one of the most talented composers of the new Russian school of music passed away. Modest Petrovich Musorgsky died too early, as do the majority of gifted Russians. He did not win fame during his lifetime, and he did not achieve half of what he could have achieved under different circumstances, with the talents with which nature had endowed him.[1]

Why do our Russian gems die young? Does the reason lie hidden in themselves or is it in the milieu? God only knows. It is a difficult problem to solve. Whatever the reason might be, Musorgsky's voice was silenced too soon, and he sank into the grave mourned by a very small circle of friends and admirers who accompanied his mortal remains from the Nikolaev Hospital, where he died, to the cemetery of the Aleksandr Nevskii Monastery, where he was buried not far from Glinka, Dargomyzhsky, and Serov.[2]

Having enjoyed, during the last eight or nine years, very close, friendly relations with the deceased,[3] I wanted to jot down my reminiscences of him immediately after his death; these reminiscences would have rather fully covered Musorgsky's activities from the time of his finishing the opera *Boris Godunov* up to the time of his death. But having written a couple of pages, I decided that my work was going to be too influenced by the recent loss of a close and dear friend; that its character would be too personal and fleeting; that it would reflect the feelings understandable and forgivable in the friend of one who has just died, but of no use or interest to the majority of the readers who, fairly enough, ask of a biographer an impartial, sober, and realistic description of the personality who, for one reason or another, deserved his attention. I already feared being partial and I was afraid that I, although unwittingly, would err against the truth, and consequently would not pay a tribute worthy of Musorgsky through failing to recreate his moral and artistic image in its inviolable truth and faithfulness. It is for that reason that I had postponed my project for several years, restricting myself to writing down in a memorandum book separate reminiscences and bare facts as they came to mind. This memorandum book was to be used as the nucleus of the biography of Musorgsky, which I planned to write at a later date.

Meanwhile, first in newspapers, and then in "fat" journals, articles about Musorgsky began to appear with biographical information and critical judgments on his works. One of these articles, which had appeared in the last two issues of *Vestnik Evropy* [The European herald], signed by Mr. Stasov,[4] is one of the lengthiest, and it has unveiled even the most intimate details of Musorgsky's life and work. For the first time, Musorgsky appeared in the public eye not only as a composer but also as a human being. But he was arbitrarily depicted from one angle only, which, perhaps, least conforms with his artistic mission; this angle, in any case, fails to present all the traits of his distinctive and unique personality. In Mr. Stasov's article, Musorgsky was exclusively depicted as a member of a famous circle, a famous musical sect, to which he indeed belonged, but only for a short time. The theories of this circle were a heavy burden upon the natural inclination of his talent; but he was finally able to divorce himself completely from them when his talent had fully developed. Those who knew Musorgsky well could only blame the author of this article for his somewhat thoughtless and biased attitude toward the memory of the deceased composer; since having decided to write a biographical essay, he obviously had more than one objective, of which the elucidation of Musorgsky's personality was not even in the foreground. But the majority of the public who knew Musorgsky only through his compositions, would, as a result of reading this article, have a totally false notion about Musorgsky; and this notion began to find its expression in the press and in oral comments I often heard about Stasov's article. In view of the situation, I decided that I no longer had the right to remain silent, and, despite my previous resolution, I choose to publish my recollections immediately, even though they are in a very incomplete and fragmentary form.

I drew closer to Musorgsky during the summer of 1873. We had previously met each other occasionally in a private home where during musical evenings, excerpts from his *Boris Godunov* were at times performed.[5] During these evenings, a circle of young Russian composers gathered. It was an intimate, small, but at the same time very friendly circle; the members mutually supported each other, encouraged each other in their works, and loved one another, exaggerating with youthful enthusiasm the importance of each member in particular and that of the circle as whole. All this was very sincere and lively with, however, a touch of something very juvenile and immature. M[ilii] A[lekseevich] Balakirev was the only one who looked at the whole thing seriously and soberly; he had a stern attitude toward his young

comrades' compositions. Very soon, unfortunately, he completely divorced himself from the circle and had almost no influence on its subsequent development.

It was precisely at that time that fate brought Musorgsky and me together. We moved to the same house on Panteleimon Street—he had a furnished room with windows that looked out on the street, I had a small apartment which opened onto the courtyard.[6] I was writing poetry, passionately hoping to see it published one day; he had finished *Boris,* and for the time being was content that his opera was being satisfactorily performed by a circle of amateurs; he was dreaming about having the opera put on stage. Both of us were deeply convinced of our genius and determined that, without fail, each would say "a new word" in his chosen field. Musorgsky was older than I; what is more, he already belonged to a "circle"; he had his admirers and knowledgeable critics; and worst of all, he had his leaders. He believed that he had already "spoken his new word in music." What he still had to do was make that "word" universally accepted. As for me, I still shyly hid my writing from the majority of my acquaintances, and I continued "to create" secretly. Most likely, our similar predicaments helped us at first to understand each other; at any rate from the very beginning we both realized that we would become friends. Musorgsky's character—open, honest to the point of effeminacy, and delicate to the point of naiveté—accomplished the rest. Within a month, we were virtually inseparable; we confided our artistic projects to each other; we judged and criticized each other with a partiality that is only possible to inveterate flatterers or intimate friends. In short, we had become bosom friends.

Nine years later, as I reflect objectively on that period (although we thought we were happy then), I have become more and more convinced (and it is my unswerving conviction now) that neither before nor after would Musorgsky deviate so far from his true path as he did at that time. He had never been so false to himself; his talent had never been put to such a difficult and dangerous ordeal. Not before, not later. The sixties—an era of sudden change and regeneration throughout Russian life and society—provoked an unbelievable confusion in our ideas regarding the purpose of literature and art; of course, it also affected Russian music, and Musorgsky in particular. His responsive, sensitive nature, so easily influenced by external pressures, reflected perfectly the spirit of the time, with all its enthusiasms and mistakes, and if I may say, wild fanaticism. An artist-idealist, Musorgsky began to reject passionately art in general and music in particular. He convinced himself and others that sounds were only a means of conversing with people, of telling them the "bitter and naked truth"! Aristocrat to the marrow of his bones, reared and educated in a good, old family of landed gentry, and, as I have already said, delicate to the point of effeminacy and considerate to the point of naiveté, he tried very hard, and at times unfortunately succeeded, in cloaking himself with a rude, abrupt awkwardness that he had been convinced (of course, by others) was characteristic of true strength and genius. The results of such program were compositions like "Savishna" [Darling Savishna], "Sirotka" [The orphan], "Kozyol" [The he-goat], "Rayok" [Peepshow], "Klassik" [The classicist], "Seminarist" [The seminarian], and many separate numbers in the opera *Boris Godunov* in which the absence of music and beauty was utterly compensated for, in the eyes of his leaders, by the realism (or the comedy) of the content and by the "veracity in the sound." There was no end to their ecstasy when these compositions appeared. When I first knew him, he was always delighted to talk about the ecstasy his compositions occasioned and was always very willing to play and sing his latest works in the "new" taste. I remember as if it were yesterday what my reaction was on hearing the famous "Peepshow" for the first time: it was definitely beyond me; those present roared with laughter; everywhere one heard: "Marvelous," "Masterful!" and so forth. I was bewildered and I looked everywhere for an answer. Finally, I was given a detailed explanation of the meaning of the satire. I was told the names of those satirized, and eventually I was able to convince myself that "Peepshow" was indeed an astonishing work. Nevertheless, the same evening, on my way home with Musorgsky, I brought myself to ask him, somewhat shyly, if he himself thought his "Peepshow" was a work of art.

"It seems to me, Mr. Poet, that you deign to be displeased?" smiled Musorgsky good-naturedly.

"Oh, no, no," I was quick to reply. "That's not it at all! I only mean that 'Peepshow' is a joke—witty, wicked, talented, but it's still a joke, a prank. . . ."

"And how mad he got at me for that prank!" Musorgsky interrupted me. "At the concert, he met me, pushed me against the wall with such delicacy and shouted that he had recognized himself. He was laughing, but twitched with anger."

We arrived home.

"I don't feel sleepy at all," Musorgsky remarked. "Let's go to your apartment. I want to show you something."

We entered and turned on the lights, and then he sat down at the piano.

"I know what you need," he said and played "Kolybel'nia" [Lullaby] from *Voevoda* by Ostrovskii—a beautiful, musical work filled with unaffected feeling and simplicity, and I was sincerely and frankly taken by it.

"Well, that's totally different from 'Peepshow'!" I could not help exclaiming.

Musorgsky again smiled his crooked smile.

"That was dedicated to the memory of my late mother," he said.

"And to whom was 'Peepshow' dedicated?" I asked.

And we both burst out laughing.

Musorgsky stayed until dawn. All night he sang and played tirelessly, choosing with an amazing insight what, he knew, would particularly please

me. I remember that among other things he played "Saul"; "Noch'"
[Night], based on Pushkin's poem,[7] the last part of the scene by the fountain
from *Boris,* and then Marina's scene with the Jesuits and Boris's death scene.
It was only the morning light peering through the window that showed us
that it was time to go. [We shook hands heartily and parted], but we left each
other with the realization that we had much more in common than we had
assumed several hours earlier and that we would be seeing each other more
and more often.

And we did begin to meet often. We would have lunch somewhere and
then go straight to my apartment. I had a rather good piano. Musorgsky
would sit at it and improvise for two or three hours; he would come across a
felicitous musical phrase, repeat it several times, memorize it—and in a
couple of days it would appear with a text, as a passage of *Khovanshchina,*
the opera which Musorgsky intended to write even before the staging of
Boris. I must say that his *first improvised version,* in my opinion, was always
better, more beautiful, and even richer than the later one in its harmonized
and finished form. Musorgsky the artist improvised, but the Musorgsky who
put it on paper was a member of the circle; he was a musical innovator who
valued above all his mentors' opinion, whose tastes he knew and whose
approval he sought. To begin with, whenever it was possible, one had to
hide and muddle up the beauty and melodiousness of the theme in order to
avoid being criticized for being "sickly sweet and sugary," as was their cus-
tomary way of putting it. By the same token, the simplicity would then
disappear to be replaced by the "originality of the harmonies." The richness
of themes and organic succession of sounds that had flowed naturally at the
moment of genesis were forced to suffer a rearrangement, since that organic
sequence of sounds and richness of musical themes (it goes without saying)
represented in their fullness something true, which unfortunately reflected
the "classicism" of the "conservatory." It was necessary to remove this "retrograde flavor" whatever the cost. So the initial theme was cut off in the
middle, harmonies were shorn of their natural development, and the musical movements were left hanging in the air, to the great joy and rapture of
the leaders. Incidentally, I should add that some of the leaders, and the most
important ones at that, were indiscriminately enthusiastic since they had no
clear concept of the musical scholasticism with which they warred.[8] They
would have been incapable of determining what was really incorrect in a
given composition and wherein the "innovation" was to be found. They
only judged a piece by the spontaneous impression made on their ears,
although in all fairness it must be said that that impression never misled
them. Anything that was traditionally acknowledged outside the circle and
among mere mortals as soothing to one's ears was an offence to the leaders'
ears and vice versa. Their keenness in this respect went to such extremes that
whenever Musorgsky did not succeed in the difficult task of entangling and
camouflaging the initial beauty of a good musical theme, despite his best

efforts, and it sometimes forced its way out—they would say that the composition was "poor" and "mediocre." (Which is why I said above that it was at this time that Musorgsky diverged most from his true path.) The leaders' opinions prevailed even for the author himself, consequently he abandoned whatever failed to meet with their approval.

Here, I ought to confess frankly that at the time I too had fully adopted the views and taste of the circle, to whom I was introduced by Musorgsky. I could always tell which of his compositions (he usually showed them to me first) would please or displease the circle, and I sincerely convinced myself that it should be so. A really strange and inexplicable rule was at work: whatever was undeniably beautiful or unaffected, for some reason, always sounded unattractive to me; but what was misshapen and distorted satisfied my warped expectations. For instance, when Musorgsky was playing or singing, I avidly awaited something totally unusual or unexpected; I was looking for some sudden sound that could not even be imagined in advance, and when I heard that unexpected effect I was satisfied. If there was no such surprise it seemed that I had missed something.

I really cannot demonstrate this by musical examples—such a long time has elapsed and I am no expert in music. Therefore, I have decided to give an example of my poetic compositions which were strongly influenced at that time by my musical tastes.

I was then writing something similar to "Reminiscences"; these had a fragmentary nature, no beginning and no end. In short, they were rather peculiar and meaningless. Among other things, I had a description of Moscow which initially concluded with the following verses:

> Vot ploshchad' Krasnaia—Vasiliia sobor
> Krasoiu strannoiu moi privlekaet vzor.

> [Here is Red Square. The strange beauty of
> St. Basil's Cathedral attracts my eye.]

"Well, Sir, would you be so kind as to strike that one immediately and change it," Musorgsky told me when I read the poem. "It's so poor and weak—it has no power at all!"

Naturally, I agreed with him, and the next day I read him the verses in their new version:

> Vot ploshchad' Krasnaia—Vasiliia sobor
> Pestreet v storone, kak staryi mukhomor.

> [Here is Red Square. The many-colored St. Basil's Cathedral
> Stands aside like an old death cap.]

"That really is good! That's it!" exclaimed Musorgsky, and the same evening he read the poem to one of the leaders.[9]

I would never have dared to burden the reader with such a silly story, had it not summarized Musorgsky's characteristic frame of mind at that time, in that the "death caps" were, one can see, the quintessence of an entire program and an outlook on poetry and art in general. Later on all this would change. In his last years, Musorgsky almost totally renounced these earlier enthusiasms and delusions. Had he lived longer, without a doubt his talent would have emerged victorious from the struggle with the influence of the sixties and its oppressive surroundings and would have reached its height. But I will talk about that at a more appropriate moment. I would now like to talk about the staging of *Boris Godunov* and try to clarify the good and the bad influences its success had on Musorgsky's subsequent work.

It was January 1874. The rehearsals of *Boris Godunov* in the Mariinskii Theater were progressing quickly and successfully, Musorgsky was present at all of them and always came home happy and full of hope for its success. He could not praise the general attitude of the artists enough, and that was especially true about Napravnik, the conductor. According to Musorgsky, Napravnik gave a great deal of good advice; at his urgent request, many tedious passages were deleted, passages which added nothing to the opera, or passages which were not particularly well turned and which spoiled the general impression on the stage.[10] Thus he deleted the scene in Pimen's cell, the story about the parrot in the scene with Boris and the tsarevich, the scene of the striking clock, and several others. Musorgsky totally and sincerely agreed with Napravnik's opinions and passionately argued with those who accused him of compliance or lack of character.

"All this is absolutely impossible on the stage," he would often say to me after such arguments, "and these people refuse to listen to anyone. They don't need quality, they only want quantity. They say that I am weak willed, but they do not understand that the author, by himself, before the final staging of an opera, can never judge the impression a scene will make on the public. Meyerbeer had no pity and would strike out whole pages—and he knew what he was doing, and he was right!"

Afterwards, when (I don't know on whose initiative) the last act of *Boris* was to be deleted from the performances, Musorgsky not only approved of this change but was particularly satisfied with it.

He totally agreed that this last act was quite obviously unnecessary to the opera's course of action and that it gave the impression of something which had been added in a slapdash manner (in reality, that had been the case). Nevertheless, I was very sorry that it was completely deleted, because I thought it had many good musical points. So I told Musorgsky that I would have preferred to see *Boris* with this act, but that it should be placed earlier; that way the Pretender's entrance into the Kremlin would precede Boris's death. Musorgsky did not agree with me. He passionately defended the idea that the entire deletion was not only necessary to the drama and to the conditions of its staging, but that his author's conscience demanded it. I was surprised, and I asked him to say why.

"In this act," he answered, "for the first time in my life I lied about the Russian people. The people's jeering at the boyar isn't authentic; it is not the Russian way. When the people give sway to their angry passions, they condemn and kill their victims; they do not humiliate them."

I had to agree.

"That's the whole point, dear friend," he added sternly. "An artist shouldn't make a joke about such matters. In *Khovanshchina* I am not going to have what I had in *Boris,* although, it's likely that many people will be angry with me for that; except that now I am no longer afraid of their anger. And as for you, Mr. Poet, I advise you to take note of this rule: always be yourself, speak the truth only and . . . do not give a straw for anybody or anything, don't pay attention to anybody else's advice."

I emphasize these words of Musorgsky's particularly because they directly contradict the statements made in the biographical article I mentioned above. The article had said that the abridgment, or, as it was put, the castration of *Boris* by the Board of Directors, deeply outraged and distressed Musorgsky and that it even hastened his death. It was even more peculiar to read this, knowing as I did, that the author of the article had often heard Musorgsky himself say that he completely approved of the cuts in *Boris;* and although the author never agreed with Musorgsky on that point, in my opinion he still had no right to ascribe to the late composer feelings, that he, the author, wished him to have held. On the contrary, that deep respect and gratitude which Musorgsky constantly showed Napravnik (without whose consent the deletions in the opera naturally would not have occurred)— precisely because of his stern, artistic, and honest attitude toward the staging of the opera, the musical style of which Napravnik did not totally approve—should have been for Mr. Stasov sufficient proof that Musorgsky did not consider the deletion in *Boris* a castration.[11] Although the dead feel no shame, the living have no right to attribute to them these tendentious fables.

Let's go back to the staging of *Boris Godunov.* On the eve of the first performance Musorgsky paid me a visit. As usual he sat at the piano, and after playing a few chords, he stood up, closed the lid, and said with great resentment:

"No, I can't. It's all so stupid, but what can I do? I can't stop thinking about tomorrow. How will it all turn out?"

All evening we both tried to talk about totally extraneous matters. Musorgsky forced me to read excerpts from *Smuta* [Sedition],[12] a dramatic chronicle I was writing at the time. He pretended to listen with great attention, caviling at my wording, but I easily saw that his thoughts were aimed at one single question: what is going to happen tomorrow?

I must confess that the same question haunted me too. Musorgsky spent the night at my place, but he had a sleepless night, waking several times, and each time I saw him pace the room with his hands behind his back, deep in thought. In the morning he left, agreeing to meet at the Mariinskii Theater.

As is known, the performance ended in a triumph for Musorgsky; *Boris Godunov* was an absolute success. After the first act, which was received by the audience rather coldly, I began to worry seriously. This act, when performed by the author himself was magnificent, but on stage with an orchestra it did not turn out well at all. Nevertheless, the scene in the Inn, the scene at the Fountain in the Palace of the Kremlin, and particularly the scene of Boris's death made truly shattering impressions on the audience, impressions which did not fade away even during the totally unnecessary last act, which was dramatically much weaker than the preceding ones. At the end of the performance, Musorgsky was given many curtain calls, the audience cheering him most enthusiastically. Naturally, some protesting voices were heard, but they were drowned out by the roar of general delight. This success was neither accidental nor fleeting. During the winter, there were, I think, nine performances, and each time the theater was sold out, each time the public tumultuously called for Musorgsky.[13]

At the same time critical articles began to appear in the newspapers, and what was worth noticing was that all of them criticized rather than praised the opera. Even the famous musical critic, who at the time was writing in the *S[ankt] P[eterburgskie] Vedomosti* [St. Petersburg news], using the signature‡*, and who always wrote very warmly about the music of the circle to which Musorgsky belonged, dealt with the opera rather severely; he could not discover the good points in it and restricted himself to focusing on its serious shortcomings.[14]

Thus, the critics' opinion was divorced from the public's opinion, and Musorgsky's triumph was overshadowed by the realization that the voices of competent judges,[15] in defiance of the loud approbation of the public, were not on his side. In conclusion, who was right, the public or the critics? This was a question which naturally arose from such a contradiction. Unfortunately, Musorgsky did not ponder it long enough. Quite understandably his feelings as author on the one hand, and the protestations of myopic and fanatic leaders on the other, quickly convinced him that only the public that gave him its approval was right. He had no reason to pay any heed to the critics, moved as they were by anger and envy, and infected with ideas of conformity and retrogression. Such a hastily accepted conclusion on Musorgsky's part was a great and regretable mistake. Not only did it hamper the development of his talent and impede his inner striving for artistic self-perfection, but also it drew him away from his comrade composers, who, despite their sincere friendship for the author of *Boris Godunov*, could not praise this work for a perfection they did not see, as demanded by the leaders, since in many respects they genuinely and honestly agreed with the critics.

Therefore Musorgsky suddenly found himself outside the musical world, surrounded by people of every breed and color: artists, architects, university professors, civil servants, lawyers, all of them, needless to say, quite respectable people, but alas! not only were they not musicians, they knew absolutely nothing about music. [Yet] it was their opinion that Musorgsky accepted completely, and quite readily at that, since their judgments flattered his author's vanity. In listening to what they were saying, Musorgsky came to believe that the public hailed him precisely for all those "novelties" and the musical radicalism he had shown in *Boris:* for "Ai, likhon'ko" [Oh, it's dreadful], "Mitiukh, chego oryom?" [Mitiukh, why are we yelling?], "Turu, turu, petushok" [Tra la la, little rooster]; for all those unbelievable hostesses and Jesuits, for the tramps and Ivanushkys—the Holy Fools— with whom, at times, he would fill the stage, thus interrupting the course of his drama and violating its unity and continuity. In short, for supplementing the great and immortal work of Pushkin, which had no need of any such additions. That was precisely the reason why Musorgsky and I had many a heated argument and became estranged at that time. At that juncture I was a very staunch admirer of Pushkin, and I considered the distorting of his works an intolerable sacrilege. When N. N. Strakhov's article appeared in the newspaper *Grazhdanin* [The citizen], as I recall, quite sternly and seriously chastizing Musorgsky for his "corrections" of Pushkin's text of *Godunov,* despite my devotion to Musorgsky, I was in total agreement with him. But there was something very strange here: Musorgsky was particularly unable to bear any criticism of his text. He would quite readily talk about his music, without becoming upset, and very often agreed with the objections; but when the criticism bore on the text he had written, he was always irritated and never changed his mind. I should point out here that Pushkin was not particularly respected by the leaders, and, consequently, Musorgsky did not respect him much either. Even now I cannot quite fathom why he agreed to write an opera based on Pushkin's story. Perhaps, had he not had the prospect of a totally independent rewording of the story with the insertion of the various episodes, such as the nanny's fight with the parrot, or the tramps' jeering the boyar, or the hanging of the Jesuits; perhaps, without all this additional rubbish, in the frame of mind in which he then found himself, Musorgsky would never have begun to write *Boris*.[16] Incidentally, I am convinced that the great and solid success of his opera was only due to those scenes which were the most faithful to Pushkin's drama, in which few or no corrections were made, and in which Musorgsky's talent, relying on the great poet's text, was able to unfold the Pushkin story in all its might and breadth. This was what Musorgsky, his friends, and comrades refused to understand. They liked the opera precisely because of the very things which had made the least impression on the majority of its listeners and which were, often quite rightly, the issues targeted by the critics. In short, there was a serious misunderstanding between Musorgsky and his public. He utterly misconstrued the meaning of their approval and was more than ever persuaded that courage overcame all obstacles. "We shall hold high our banner 'Be daring' and shall not betray it," Musorgsky wrote on the printed libretto of *Boris Godunov* that he gave me.

Soon, with the composition of the musical illustrations for *Pictures from an Exhibition* by the architect Hartmann, he reached the acme of that musical radicalism, to whose "new shores" and to whose "unfathomed depths" the admirers of his "Peepshows" and "Savishnas" had pushed him so diligently. In the music for these illustrations, as Musorgsky called them, he represented kittens, children, Baba Iaga in her wooden house on chicken legs, catacombs, gates, and even rattling carts. All this was not done jokingly, but "seriously."[17]

There was no end to the enthusiasm shown by his devotees; but many of Musorgsky's friends, on the other hand, and especially the comrade composers, were seriously puzzled and, listening to the "novelty," shook their heads in bewilderment. Naturally, Musorgsky noticed their bewilderment and seemed to feel that he "had gone too far." He set the illustrations aside without even trying to publish them. Musorgsky devoted himself exclusively to *Khovanshchina*.

Could it be possible, people would ask me, that the success of *Boris* had nothing but harmful consequences for the development of Musorgsky's talent? No, would be my answer. Although for a short while this success firmly sent Musorgsky along that erroneous path to which he had been directed by the people and circumstances surrounding him, at the same time it provided him with self-confidence and independence, and allowed him to free himself from external influences. Musorgsky, having come to believe in *Boris,* also came to believe in himself; and he was, as I have already said, a great artist. Little by little his nature began to emerge and his creativity went on to that phase in its development which Mr. Stasov in his article called decadent, and which, in my opinion, was the beginning of a new and fruitful period of creativity.

In the meantime, the musical circle known as the "Moguchaia Kuchka" [The Mighty Handful], dispersed completely. The meetings which had taken place in the private house in which I had met Musorgsky, and which had served as a rallying point for the members of the circle, came to an end. Besides, the enthusiasm and the youthful eagerness had had time to cool down. The springtime floods had receded, and that yearning to create a revolution in music at whatever cost, to say the "new word," had given way to a more sober and serious outlook on art. M[ilii] A[lekseevich] Balakirev still remained totally aloof from the circle. The author of *Ratcliff* wrote *Andzhelo* [Angelo]. The author of *Antar* and *Sadko* was now composing formal quartets and symphonies and was reworking *The Maid of Pskov*, after having become a professor at the Conservatory. In short, I think I would not be mistaken were I to say that while Musorgsky, intoxicated with the success of his *Boris* and influenced by his worshippers, rushed on toward "new shores" and steadily lost the solid ground under his feet, his comrades, the composers, by contrast, turned themselves around and recognized that the study of the musical past was essential; sobered by this realization, they consciously embarked on the path which corresponded to their individual talents. If I am wrong, let those who are better informed correct me. In any case, I repeat, it was around that time that the "Mighty Handful" had disbanded. Its banner was held by Musorgsky alone; all the other members had left it and each pursued his own path; and I am deeply convinced, each of them made the right decision.

As for Musorgsky, from that time forward, he began to struggle inwardly with rather complex yearnings; this struggle, at various times and with differing vigor, often pushed him in totally opposite directions, depending on what was predominant at the given moment: the artist's nature or the obtrusive purposes foisted upon him. Moreover, as time went by, the discrepancy between what Musorgsky was doing and what he was saying or writing to his "admirers" became more obvious. For instance, in November of 1875, in reference to Saint-Saëns, he wrote to Mr. Stasov, in what was for him unnaturally rude, artificial, and unusual language, the following lines, which are almost incomprehensible coming from a composer:

> *It's not merely music,* words, palette and chisel that *we need*—no, the devil take you, you liars, hypocrites *e tutti quanti*—give us living thoughts, have live conversations with people, on whatever subject you've chosen! *You can't fool us with pretty, sweet sounds:* the lady luxuriously passes the box of bonbons to her dear friend, and that's all.[18]

Without even mentioning the imitative crudeness and artificiality of his style (which was also meant to be the expression of "originality and strength"), one must comment on the total absence of any clear, definite meaning in these lines, which were carefully copied *verbatim* from the biographical article by Mr. Stasov. Who is implied by the word "we," who does not need "music" [in music]? Who is sent to the devil, who are the liars and the hypocrites who arouse such an unnatural indignation in Musorgsky, and what was their falsehood and pretense? Finally, what does this "you can't fool us with pretty, sweet sounds" mean? And what about this "lady with a box of bonbons"? All this is very obscure and confusing. One thing is clear though: there is no need for "music" in music nor is there a need for "beautiful sounds"; and what is more important, those lines showed an affected eagerness for a fight foreign to the real Musorgsky. In that fight, he was unwittingly his own worst enemy. At the time he wrote this to Mr. Stasov, he was composing *Khovanshchina*. He began to create passages of "music" and "beautiful sounds" which intruded into his opera, regardless of the many inconveniences represented by a topic chosen for God only knows what reason, a topic fit neither for an opera nor for a drama. This intrusion is seen in the enormous number of songs sung by the principals whenever a convenient or an inconvenient occasion arises. These songs are a detriment to the notorious "realism," but on the other hand, they are, without a doubt, a great benefit to the music. It will suffice to enumerate the songs whose qualities I will not discuss here, since *Khovanshchina* is still unknown to the public,[19] to understand what an outstanding, if not totally predominant, role they play in the opera. The following is the enumeration of the songs in the order in which they are sung: "Podoidu pod Ivan gorod" [I shall go to Ivangorod]; the Streltsy song "Goi, vy liudi ratnye" [Hey, you, men of armor]; the peasants' song, "Zhila kuma" [There lived a godmother]; the song about the clerk, "Okh, ty, rodnaia Rus' " [O, thou, Russia, my dear homeland]; the song to the glory of Khovanskii, "Belomu lebediu put' prostoren" [Make a wide path for our white swan]; and finally the songs of the Old Believers: (a) "Bozhe vsesil'nyi, otzheni slovesa lukavye ot nas" [God Almighty, deliver us from the snares of the Evil One], (b) "Pobedikhom, posramikhom" [We have defeated, we have shamed]; Marfa's song "Iskhodila mladyoshen'ka" [The maiden wandered]; Shaklovityi's song, "Akh, ty, v sud'bine zlochastnoi, rodnaia Rus' " [Oh, how wretched is your lot, Russia, my dear homeland]; the Streltsys' song "Akh, ne bylo pechali" [Oh, we shan't have a care in the world then]; Kuz'ka's song about the gossip; the song of the peasant women at Khovanskii's, "Vozle rechki, na luzhaike pozdno vecherom sidela" [By the river in a meadow, I was sitting late at night]; "Plyvyot, plyvyot lebyodushka, ladu, ladu" [The swan glides on the water, tra la la]; and finally in the last scene the Old Believers' hymns before the mass self-immolation. The total come to twenty songs, some of which are repeated at different times during the opera. Moreover, in some parts of the opera, Musorgsky gave the words of his characters a pure song form which often did not correspond in the least with their content. All these songs and all these recitatives in song form, whatever their intrinsic merit, from an external and formal point of view were precisely the type of "music" that Musorgsky had rejected in his letter to Mr. Stasov, since the songs contained nothing but music, i.e., more or less "beautiful sounds." They cannot contain "living thoughts" or "live conversations with people," and therefore Musorgsky the composer, having filled his opera with "songs," found himself in total contradiction with Musorgsky the author of the letter to Mr. Stasov, where with all his intellectual might he rejected Saint-Saëns, "the music" and "the pretty, sweet sounds." The whole point is that an artist's spontaneity cannot be subordinate to intellect, especially when this intellect ... And those passages where Musorgsky yearned to express living thoughts or faithfulness to his topic remain dark blemishes.

Not wishing to go into details since, as I have already said, the public does not yet know *Khovanshchina*, I can only make a general observation which, I am sure, will be acceptable to almost all those familiar with the topic of this opera: all the power, beauty, and merit of the opera are to be found in its songs. It must be said also that, contrary to his initial intention of representing Marfa the Old Believer as a sort of Potiphar's wife (a very strange plan, not exactly consistent with the Russian folk theme), Musorgsky endowed Marfa with a profound lyricism, a delicate and feminine sensibility and a somewhat fantastic, magic, and even prophetic character, which of course was utterly foreign to the folk theme and particularly to the Old Believers. Nonetheless, characterizing her this way allowed him full play in musical creativity, and, moreover, due to the nature of musical creativity, he was able to embody it all in "beautiful sounds." Is there any other explanation for the "Scene of Marfa's witchcraft at the Golitsyn's house" other than the compulsion to create these sounds? The scene is not only totally superfluous to the course of the drama but also obviously impractical and artificial. Nevertheless, because of its music, it is a part of the most beautiful and inspired moments in the entire opera. The same yearning for a pure, and I would even dare to say, an ideal, beauty explains Musorgsky's effort to make Shaklovityi, contrary to historical fact, a man (even under the guise of a Jesuit or a Mephistofeles) who conceals the warm, passionate heart of a great patriot, grieving over the misfortunes of Russia. He is inspired in all his actions by a single desire: "Not to let Russia perish at the hands of evil mercenaries." As, I repeat, it is precisely in these digressions from the initial plan for *Khovanshchina* (the *narodnost'*, the "realism," and the "living thoughts") that all the beauty and merit of the opera are to be found. They are songs which are truly unnecessary to the development of the drama, but they have been inserted in every act.

We hope that the opera, orchestrated by the skillful and talented hand of one of our modern composers who knew Musorgsky intimately, sooner or later will be put on stage. Let the music critics then decide if I was right or wrong in my opinion about *Khovanshchina*. But let's leave judgments aside and go back to the facts.

In the fall of 1874, Musorgsky and I decided to share rooms. At that time, he lived on Shpalernaia Street. I had rented the two adjacent rooms. The doors between our lodgings could be opened so that we had a small apartment in which to settle down. Every morning until noon (when Musorgsky left for work) and every evening were spent together, mainly at home. During the winter, Musorgsky made some progress on *Khovanshchina*. And in addition to the opera he also wrote a song "Zabytyi" [Forgotten] based on my verses, and a collection of songs entitled *Bez solntsa* [Sunless],[20] based on verses which I had written one or two years earlier. I must emphasize that Musorgsky chose the poems himself, and his choice was not without a special significance. All five poems in the collection are purely lyrical; they have no images or pictures, their subjects are fleeting, emotional moods in Fet's vein. (When I say Fet's vein, let it be understood that I am not comparing myself to our great lyrical poet; if I dare to mention his name, it is only for the purpose of briefly and precisely identifying the character of the poems Musorgsky had chosen.) Musorgsky gave them a poetical, graceful musical form which pleased him a great deal.

"Many say," he told me once, "that my only qualities are fluid form and humor. Well, we shall see what they say when I show them your poems. The only element I have here is feeling, and the result isn't half bad."

The result was indeed good, but not to the taste of the "worshippers," who demanded a continuation and a repetition of "Peepshows," and "Seminarians," but Musorgsky was no longer capable of that style. His irritation with the critics of *Boris* provided me with an opportunity for suggesting that he resume work on a musical satire entitled "Rak" [The crab],[21] and he did. But after writing four or five measures, he abandoned it. Several months later, while in the country, I wrote him a letter asking him about the fate of "Crab." Among other things he wrote the following: "I had a good romp with "Peepshow," enough of that! I can find more serious work to do."[22]

Generally speaking, in 1875 Musorgsky was already becoming more and more independent. The formerly obedient steward of *someone else's orders* had begun to set his own themes and tasks more consistent with his nature and talent. *Khovanshchina* began to acquire a shape totally unlike the one that had been initially conceived. Musorgsky decided that many of the projected episodes should be deleted. For example, the appearance on Red Square of a Lottery Wheel (?!), amid a lot of noise and uproar in the "folk" scene composed earlier, was now struck out. "The comic and humoristic" scenes in the German Settlement, with their parody of German music in a retrograde Mozartian style, also disappeared.[23] They were replaced by the aforementioned elaboration of Marfa's and Shaklovityi's characters. Musorgsky wrote this latter role for Mel'nikov, and he wanted to provide the magnificent and full-scale voice of this artist with a wide musical range. In short, the period of "decline" had begun during which, according to Mr. Stasov's article, Musorgsky's talent started to weaken and, obviously, to ebb. Mr. Stasov's acknowledgment of the "apparent change," in my opinion, best corroborates what I previously said about the development of Musorgsky's independence and his new freedom from the yoke of other people's influence. The natural consequences of this emancipation was that the former "worshippers" and leaders were no longer able to sympathize with his altered direction, and they began to find his new works, "foggy, bizarre, disconnected, and even tasteless." It could not have been otherwise: the people who considered "Peepshow" a *chef-d'oeuvre* of talent, sparkling wit, and fluidity of form, and *Detskaia* [The nursery], or "Kozly" [He-goats], "Zhuki" [Beetles], "Raki" [Crabs], and so forth, as strings of pearls and diamonds, i.e., compositions worthy of "complete symphonies and operas," were not able to appreciate the new works. They were also incapable of understanding Shaklovityi's and Marfa's arias, or the album *Sunless*, or the nonprogrammatic piano pieces,[24] to which Musorgsky again addressed himself toward the end of his life. Nor could they accept the best passages of *The Fair at Sorochintsy,* which Musorgsky had begun,[25] which was also filled with clear, simple, and gentle poetry. This internal, spiritual world, a world of pure poetry to which Musorgsky was irrepressibly drawn by his artistic nature, must have indeed seemed to those accustomed to the clarity and form of "The He-Goat" and "The Beetle," as something particularly foggy, bizarre, and tasteless. At first, having noticed the change in Musorgsky, they were upset; but when their distress had no effect, and when Musorgsky not only failed to reform but proceeded ahead on this path, and even completely divorced himself from them, their distress turned into wrath; he was given up as being hopeless and he was looked on as "lost." He was indeed "lost," but certainly not in the sense understood by his friends from earlier times. Musorgsky's health, for a reason which had nothing to do with music, or work, or theatrical direction, was destroyed in the end. His weakened physique was simply unable to cope with the physical ailment which had stricken him. In 1879, when I came back to Petersburg, after spending more than two years in the country, I already found him physically weakened and ailing, and during those two years Musorgsky had lived . . .

While I was living in Petersburg, it was a rare day when Musorgsky did not come to see me; once there, he would play and sing all evening although he was composing less and . . .

As a result of this affliction, which finally took him to his grave, in the last two years of his life, he had almost ceased to compose. But what he did write clearly demonstrated that there was no decline in his talent. Quite the contrary, his works from this last period bore an imprint of maturity and profundity he had never achieved earlier. Among the works from this period one finds scenes from the last act of *Khovanshchina* and from the first act of *The Fair at Sorochintsy.* The very fact that Musorgsky, before finishing one opera had begun work on a second one, plainly demonstrated that his creative power was far from diminished; it was in search of a more apt and fertile subject than *Khovanshchina.* In *The Fair at Sorochintsy,* in addition to all its other merits, what had attracted Musorgsky was its touch of the fantastic contained in the stories about the red *svitka* [a Ukranian garment] and its sale. Musorgsky was more and more attracted by fantasy, to the point that several times he told me most seriously that once *Khovanshchina* and *The Fair at Sorochintsy* were finished, he intended to start a purely fantastic opera, but that he had not decided yet between two subjects: the legend of "Vii" or the legend of "Savva Grudtsyn,"[26] the Russian Faust, as he called him. One musical attempt in that vein had been "Poklonenie chyornomu kozlu" [Worship of the black he-goat] in "Mlada,"[27] an attempt made considerably earlier, in 1875. "Chetyre pesni smerti" [Four songs of death] and finally "Stsena koldovstva" [Witchcraft scene] in *Khovanshchina* came later. Musorgsky was extremely satisfied with all these ventures.

These endeavors were not destined to be fully realized, but their very manifestation is a clear indication of the direction Musorgsky was taking at the end of his life. Even on his deathbed, just a few days before the end, hoping for recovery, Musorgsky told me about his desire to start something important, something prominent.

"And you know," he added, "I would like to do something totally new, something that I have not touched before; I would like to take a rest from history, and generally from all this 'prosiness,' which won't let you catch a breath."

Holding back my tears with difficulty, I expressed my approval.

"And I am going to tell you something else," continued Musorgsky, "up till now, you and I have been busying ourselves with trifles. Let's work together on something big; you can write a fantastic drama, and I will put it to music in such a way that not a word will be changed, just as Dargomyzhsky did with *The Stone Guest*. But, shush, don't say anything to anybody. For the time being, let's keep it a secret."

Three days after this conversation, Musorgsky passed away.[28]

These fragmentary details that I have presented in my brief recollections do not contain one-tenth of all I could have written about Musorgsky. But, as I said at the beginning, biography and testimonies about remarkable men cannot and should not be hastily written immediately following their deaths. On one hand, the inadequacy of the sources, and on the other hand, the impossibility of making a totally objective classification and analysis of the information means that such endeavors can never be successful; they never achieve their goal, which is the total elucidation of the personality of which one writes. In the present article, I only wished to rectify some inaccuracies in the prejudiced views contained in the biographical essay by Mr. Stasov. I wanted to demonstrate that the period of Musorgsky's creativity, which, according to Mr. Stasov, was the most brilliant one, was in reality a transitional period, if I may say so, in which Musorgsky's talent was hampered by the dead weight of theories and tendencies foreign to his nature— burdens, which toward the end of his life, he was more and more able to cast aside. Furthermore, I wanted to make clear that Musorgsky's nature constantly drew him toward a pure, ideal poetry and beauty, toward a spiritual, perfect world, the only place an artist can find true gratification and peace of mind.

Musorgsky's great misfortune was that during the time when his talent was developing, he found neither in the time nor in the milieu in which chance had placed him, that guidance and support so necessary to a young talent. Glinka had found such support in the spirit of the forties, in a society in which musical circles such as that of the Counts Viel'gorskii could exist.[29] Had Musorgsky been born twenty years earlier, or perhaps, twenty years later, his name would be there, alongside the most illustrious names of European composers.

July 25, 1888. Village of Shubino

But fate placed Musorgsky in different circumstances, in which his enormous and original talent, unarmed by the power of knowledge, mistakenly directed, and condemned to a long and difficult struggle, had no time to develop in all its magnificence and force. It barely hinted to his contemporaries and posterity what Musorgsky should have been and what he could have achieved under different social circumstances.

N[ikolai] Cherepnin

Vospominaniia muzykanta

Memoirs of a Musician

Nikolai Cherepnin (1873–1945) was a composer.

·   ·   ·

My father entered the artistic milieu through his contact with his patients, among whom there were quite a number of leading musical and theatrical figures. In the welcoming ambience of the house of Dr. Golovin, his colleague, my father fell under the spell of the Musorgsky cult which reigned there. The creator of *Boris* willingly performed his "novelties" at Dr. Golovin's, playing with great inspiration.[1]

The summer when I was working on "Printsessa Greza" [Princess Dream] was a happy one and quite propitious for my musical work. At the time we lived near Oranienbaum. . . . In great agitation I would often walk past the little house where the famous singer Dar'ia Mikhailovna Leonova lived, [knowing that] Modest Petrovich Musorgsky was her great admirer, accompanist, and friend; he often crossed her threshold and created great musical works there.[2]

Malyi Iaroslavets, a Petersburg tavern, is closely linked with Musorgsky's name. The tavern . . . was the favorite place of the leading figures in Petersburg's world of the arts. Musorgsky was often there in the last few years of his life, usually in the company of his best friend, the writer I[van] F[yodorovich] Gorbunov, known for his public reading. Musorgsky called him the "national artist" and he dedicated his piano piece "V derevne" [In the country] (1880) to him.[3]

Dmitrii Stakheev

Gruppy i portrety
(Vospominaniia)

Groups and Portraits
(Memoirs)

Dmitrii Stakheev (1840–?) was a writer and journalist.

.   .   .

[1875]

Sometimes alone, sometimes in the company of several colleagues from my newspaper, I would head toward Malyi Iaroslavets, which was located in the same building then as it is now, close to the one that housed the editorial offices of *Russkii mir* [The Russian world].

We did not always have lunch by ourselves or have it in the same rooms. Sometimes when the tavern was very crowded, we ended up in rooms in which the usual *habitués* had their lunch, or more exactly, swilled their bottles of beer and wine. I am unable to name them all, as I was unacquainted with most of them. I remember that I used to meet Musorgsky there, presiding at a table loaded with bottles, and Sergei Vasilievich Maksimov,[1] talking in his hoarse voice about Siberian mountains, forests, and convicts; the actor Pavel Vasilievich Vasil'ev, who also assiduously drained his bottles of beer and wine; and the operatic bass Vladimir Ivanovich, who was also a Vasil'ev. Vladimir Ivanovich's principal difference with his boon companions was the fact that he drank nothing but pure vodka.

Vladimir Ivanovich was not seen often at Malyi Iaroslavets, especially not in the winter. His drinking companions said that he often declined their invitations to go to the tavern. "I can't," he would say, "it's not the right time now. These are hard times, my friends. Napravnik is a beast—and you must behave. Miss a rehearsal and he will peck you to death. He talks softly, makes small talk, and smiles, but it is obvious when you look him in the eye that he is ferocious and wicked. I can drink on Saturday. That's my day. It says: 'Remember the Sabbath day.' That's the day I can drink until dawn, and, if necessary, I can drink on Sunday too. Same thing during Lent, I can 'perform a good deed' to the glory of the all-Russian pure vodka. Lent, my friends, is a very nice thing: you can sing religious hymns and no Napravnik can stop you."

He would talk thus in his bass voice, while emptying a carafe of vodka and clinking glasses with Maksimov. I repeat, I did not see him often, but I did meet Maksimov, Gorbunov, and the other devotees of Bacchus many times in the Malyi Iaroslavets.

I remember a little vignette: Musorgsky sitting on a chair by a table loaded with bottles, holding a newspaper with both hands. One would not say that he was very stable on his seat, for although his back was rather firmly pressed against the back of the chair, he still swayed slightly to keep his balance. The open newspaper gave one the impression that Musorgsky intended to read it. But taking a close look at this face, swollen from excessive drink, and at his eyes wildly roving all over the sheet of paper, one could definitely conclude that Musorgsky was barely able to decipher one line even if he were to read it syllable by syllable. The room was silent. Gorbunov was telling something about A[leksandr] N[ikolaevich] Ostrovskii,[2] something about his trip with him to London; everyone was laughing, except for Musorgsky who puffed quietly under his breath. . . . Pavel Vasilievich got up from the bottle-covered table and tried to reach Musorgsky. Maksimov quickly stood up and grabbed him by the arm. "Don't touch him, don't touch him: he will fall!" he said hoarsely, shaking his beard.

Nikolai Bruni

Neskol'ko slov o Musorgskom

A Few Words about Musorgsky

Nikolai Bruni (1856–1935) was a painter. These memoirs were written at the behest of Andrei Rimsky-Korsakov but were never used.

. . .

[In 1877–1878 Musorgsky participated in the evenings at the Valuevs'.[1]]

The house was often filled with guests who formed the circle which Musorgsky frequented and which he considered his own; he obviously had a good time and could enjoy himself. . . . Theater, concerts, exhibits, home performances, and live tableaux were held. There were also modest but very lively balls. . . .

Usually rather pensive, extremely unassuming, almost shy, he would become amazingly animated when he sat down at the piano and played at our request. I especially remember one evening when, during the show which followed the live tableaux, surrounded by the young people, he sat down at the piano, lost in thought. We quieted down and waited; and suddenly wonderful sounds, full of inexpressible passion and force, unusually lively and enticing, began to flow from his hands. It was Glinka's *Kamarinskaia*.

[The young people who met at the Valuevs' home included the painter Mikhail Vrubel', who was later to become famous, and his sister.]

In order not to wake the adults, we would just gather up the leftovers from dinner and sit down and talk very softly. Musorgsky, who lived at the Valuevs',[2] would appear unexpectedly. Dressed in a robe and slippers, holding the flaps of his robe with one hand, he would give us a friendly smile as he approached the dresser, where he opened a well-known door. Then he would take out a carafe of brandy, pour himself a small glass, drink it, and after keeping us company for a bit, he would silently leave. . . . At that time, he looked very much like the portrait Repin painted of him. . . .

In my memory Musorgsky will always be a quiet, pensive, unassuming person, leading a different life—the one where creativity overpowers everything else. He somehow stood aside.

Anna Vrubel'

Vospominaniia

Memoirs

Anna Vrubel' (1855–1929), sister of the famous painter, was a school-teacher. Her memoirs were written at the request of A. Rimsky-Korsakov, but they were not used. She recalls her encounters with Musorgsky at the Valuevs'.

.   .   .

I always picture Musorgsky at the piano giving an unusually picturesque rendition of his works with truly shattering force. At the same time I see the astonishing modesty of the brilliant composer, a man who, for the sake of pleasing the young people, was willing to play the piano for hours on end just to accompany our dancing.

Once an outing to a beautifully hilly site was organized. A rather large group of people participated in this trip and admired the magnificent sunset for a long time. The heart of this group was Musorgsky. He was accompanied by his musical colleague—the singer Leonova.[1]

Aleksandr Molas

IZ *Moikh vospominanii o Moguchei Kuchke*

FROM *My Recollections of the Mighty Handful*

Aleksandr Molas (1856–1942) was a naval officer and the brother-in-law of Aleksandra Molas (née Purgold). Orphaned at an early age, he lived with his older brother's family.

.   .   .

From early youth my brother[1] was a close friend of the then young midshipman, Nikolai Andreevich Rimsky-Korsakov. Rimsky-Korsakov lived with his older brother, my cousin's husband, Voin Andreevich, the Director of the Naval School. Nikolai Andreevich and Modest Petrovich Musorgsky often performed in the big reception room, where they acquainted their relatives and friends with the operas *Pskovitianka* [The maid of Pskov] and *Boris Godunov* even before these works were staged.

Nikolai Andreevich Rimsky-Korsakov and my brother married two sisters; this brought them even closer together. Rimsky-Korsakov married the wonderful pianist Nadezhda Nikolaevna, and my brother the talented singer Aleksandra Nikolaevna. Musorgsky, on very friendly terms with both men, was particularly close to my brother: he was a *shafer* [he held the crown] at his wedding. He came to see us often, and not just to our musical gatherings on Tuesdays.

It goes without saying that Modest Petrovich Musorgsky was our permanent guest. He always came at dinner time and would stay the entire evening to accompany all the singers.

[Aleksandra Nikolaevna] really loved to sing in the intimate circle of the musicians and for her closest acquaintances. She could tirelessly sing all evening; however, performing at formal concerts was, in her own words, "sheer agony." Nevertheless, her official performances were always a great success. Her own unpretentious concerts, held in the small hall of the Singing Capella, had the atmosphere of a family affair. Here, she sang with pleasure and personally knew by name almost everyone in this audience, which wanted to listen to works by members of the Balakirev circle, performed according to the wishes of the authors themselves. After all, most of their works were usually performed in manuscript form, prior to their publication, by their authors, or by singers and pianists under the direction of the creators of these astonishing musical compositions. Nevertheless, Aleksandra Nikolaevna was also supposed to perform at formal concerts. I clearly remember one particular concert. When Balakirev had momentarily divorced himself from music, Nikolai Andreevich R[imsky]-Korsakov, Aleksandra Nikolaevna's brother-in-law, became the director of the Free School of Music of the Russian Musical Society.[2] The proceeds of those concerts supplemented the small budget of the School.

Rimsky-Korsakov asked Aleksandra Nikolaevna to participate in the forthcoming concert.[3] As she agreed with the purpose of the concert, she accepted the invitation to sing. Shortly before this, at one concert or another, she had heard one of the famous singers of Petersburg perform Musorgsky's "*Sirotka*" [The orphan][4] very poorly. The clumsy rendition of a highly dramatic song provoked smiles and even laughter in the audience, to the great consternation of Aleksandra Nikolaevna. She decided to demonstrate to the public, at whatever cost, how "The Orphan" should be performed.

Rimsky-Korsakov and Musorgsky were working on the program for the concert, and when Aleksandra Nikolaevna announced that she wanted to sing "The Orphan," Rimsky-Korsakov began to plead with her to change her mind, but to no avail. Then he pressed his case with Musorgsky: "Modest Petrovich, perhaps you can convince Sasha not to sing this song, which has just recently been such a failure!" "I can only be grateful to Aleksandra Nikolaevna for having given me the honor of choosing my song," declared Musorgsky. Consequently, Rimsky-Korsakov had no other recourse than to agree to the song: Aleksandra Nikolaevna would have categorically refused to participate in the concert.

In the first part of the concert Maria's aria was well received; there were either one or two curtain calls; it was a rather moderate success. At last Aleksandra Nikolaevna came on the stage for the second part of the program. My brother and I had the impression that she was pale: she was obviously nervous. Musorgsky calmly took his seat at the piano. Following the first introductory notes a faint moan was heard: "Barin moi milen'kii, barin moi dobren'kii" [Kind gentleman, good gentleman], and so forth. When Aleksandra Nikolaevna finished singing the words "S kholodu stynet krov', s golodu smert' strashna" [My blood grows colder, death by hunger frightens me], the audience seemed to have frozen up, and only the tears in the voice of the poor orphan could be heard.

After the song ended, there was silence for several seconds; Aleksandra Nikolaevna's face started to take on an expression of sadness. Then suddenly a deafening, unending applause with unanimous shouts of "bis, bis" from the entire audience was heard. Musorgsky wanted to follow the program and go on to the next number, but the audience stamped its feet and applauded, and repeated its request for "The Orphan." Aleksandra Nikolaevna, with a beaming smile, bowed to the public. Musorgsky jumped from his stool, kissed her hands and applauded her. They had to repeat "The Orphan" twice. . . .

Obviously, the singer had achieved her goal: Musorgsky's song had been appreciated by an audience at its true worth. The following remarkable incident corroborates this fact. In the 1920s, the elderly A[leksandra] N[ikolaevna] Molas came to live in the house belonging to the USSR Academy of Sciences in Leningrad. On hearing that, the president of the Academy, A. P. Karpinskii, paid her a visit to express his gratitude for that aesthetic delight she had given him half a century ago with her rendition of "The Orphan."

The day after A[leksandra] N[ikolaevna] Molas sang *Detskaia* [The nursery] at one of her concerts, dozens of copies of that work were sold in Bessel's music store.

When I was a little boy, Musorgsky, with his protruding eyes, in particular, impressed me as being a very gentle and kind person. It was impossible not to feel his unusual kindness, which sometimes bordered on the amusing. For example, when he paid us a visit at our *dacha,* he would brush mosquitoes away without hurting them, because he did not want to kill "a living being." He always readily accepted requests from singers to accompany them, free of charge, at concerts or in private homes. He considered it his responsibility to play every new composition of his for us, and he never declined to come to our place when his presence was required by Aleksandra Nikolaevna.

On one occasion, two or three of our close Muscovite acquaintances, great admirers of Al[eksandra] Nik[olaevna]'s singing, arrived in Petersburg and begged her to arrange a concert. Everything depended on whether Musorgsky was available on that particular evening. Unfortunately a concert of the Free School of Music of the Russian Music Society[5] had been scheduled several days before. Musorgsky was to accompany the bass Vasil'ev, the Second,[6] who was singing Pimen's aria from *Boris Godunov*. Therefore, Modest Petrovich was at a rehearsal at Vasil'ev's, an unusually hospitable person, who would never let you go without giving you supper. Our acquaintances could not postpone their departure to Moscow. During the day, Modest Petrovich came by, and during lunch it was decided that I, a student in the tenth grade of the Naval School, would go by around ten o'clock, when Vasil'ev would have finished his aria, to pick up Musorgsky, who would have warned Vasil'ev in advance, and then, perhaps, we would be able to leave the Petersburg area, where Vasil'ev lived in a small house. When I arrived at my destination and explained to the host the reason for my coming, I was very warmly invited to meet the composers and listen to the singing, which had not yet started. I informed him that I already knew the composers.

"So much the better," answered Vasil'ev and showed me in. The first one to meet me was R[imsky]-Korsakov. He was very surprised at seeing me, and he involuntarily exclaimed: "Shura! How did you get here?"

I had to explain the reason for my presence to him too. Cui and Borodin were also surprised to see me; however, there was no time for explanations: Vasil'ev had come in with the opera *Boris Godunov* in his hands, and Musorgsky was already sitting at the piano. It was with pleasure that I listened to the well-known, beloved aria sung twice; and when Musorgsky saw me he began to take his leave. Apologizing to Vasil'ev, he told him that he could not go back on his word to be at our place, where an entire audience was awaiting him. Thus, since it had been possible to bring Modest Petrovich, our concert was held, to everyone's delight. Aleksandra Nikolaevna was at her best, and she sang particularly well; and Modest Petrovich, delighted at the idea that he had been able to leave Vasil'ev without any trouble, was very sweet and obliging to our guests. He played and sang excerpts from *Sorochinskaia Iarmarka* [The fair at Sorochintsy], which he had begun to compose;[7] he also performed a Chopin Polonaise beautifully. In a nutshell, the evening was a brilliant success. Our guests could not find words enough to express their gratitude for the pleasure that had been bestowed on them. As for me, I was very proud that, thanks to my expedition, I had been able to bring Modest Petrovich to our house. He had a very pleasant baritone voice, and when he was in voice, he liked to perform his recently composed works. One day, he sang Shaklovityi's aria from *Khovanshchina*. When he finished, he said melancholically: "Unfortunately, there is almost no metal left. And what a clear, velvety voice it used to be."

Musorgsky's health was taking a turn for the worse. During the winter of 1880–1881 he had to be admitted to the hospital, where I[l'ia] E[fimovich] Repin, in four sittings, painted his wonderful portrait.[8] On March 16, 1881, Modest Petrovich died.

I was on a long voyage, and my brother sent a letter to me in Naples:

We have suffered a great loss: on March 18 we buried Musorgsky. His death has left us with a ineffaceable void. I am not only talking about the void in music, but in everything else. Now that he is no more, we clearly see how close we had been and what sincere relations we had had. Sasha is wasting away with grief.

Aleksandra Molas

IZ *Vospominanii*

FROM *Memoirs*

Aleksandra Molas, née Purgold (1844–1929), a singer, participated in the evenings at the home of Dargomyzhsky, Shestakova, and others. She was one of the best performers of Musorgsky's works.

.   .   .

My acquaintance [with Musorgsky] did not last very long, barely ten years, but it left an indelible imprint on my whole life; it had enormous influence on my singing and it provided me with many bright and wonderful moments. I met him as well as the other Russian composers, at the end of the sixties, at the home of Dargomyzhsky when he was composing *The Stone Guest.* The very next day Musorgsky brought me his songs and drafts from *Boris Godunov.*[1] Later, after I was married (Musorgsky was my *shafer* [he held the crown] at my wedding), he developed the habit of coming to our house often, and thus he became a very good friend of my husband's.[2] At first, M[odest] P[etrovich] was very much afraid that my marriage would interfere with my singing, and he was unhappy with the changes it brought into my life. But very shortly, he was convinced that not only had I not abandoned my singing but that I had begun to work at it much more than before and much more seriously. Soon, a nucleus of young, talented composers was formed. They would meet at our house two or three times a week; they would bring me everything new they had composed, and Musorgsky and I would perform those works while they were still in manuscript form. Our constant guests were V[ladimir] Stasov, Borodin, Cui, Rimsky-Korsakov, Shcherbachev, Lodyzhenskii, and later Glazunov[3] and many others.

I was on very friendly terms with Musorgsky; nonetheless he never talked to me about his youth. It was obvious that he was not satisfied with the way he had spent it. On the other hand he liked to talk about his childhood, how he grew up in the country, on his father's estate—it was one of his fondest memories. Later on, he was in the military; and it seems that for a time he fell under the influence of bad examples and damaged his health for the rest of his life. I met him when he had already resigned from the military and was living in extremely straitened circumstances. I know that he gave his elder brother his father's estate, saying: "My brother is married, he has children, as for me, I will never marry and I can make it on my own." Unfortunately, he did not live long enough to see the time when he would be fully understood and when his works would be rightfully valued.

M[odest] P[etrovich] was very ugly, but his eyes were amazing; they were so intelligent and so full of thought; only people with great talent have that kind of eyes. He was of medium height, nicely built, graceful, educated; he spoke foreign languages beautifully; he recited excellently, and he also sang, although he had almost no voice; still he sang with remarkable feeling. . . . He was invited everywhere, and he was the soul of the party. He liked children very much and tried to understand them, but he was afraid of the very young ones: he thought he could hurt them. Children understood that and also liked him a great deal.

When he compelled me to sing *The Nursery* for the first time, I was terribly afraid that I would not succeed with my rendition. But he told me afterwards: "That was exactly what I had in mind. You understood me beautifully; keep on singing it exactly like that, don't change the intonation or the expression, and I will be fully satisfied."[4] After that, I constantly sang it at our musical gatherings and in many concerts, always with great success. Generally speaking, whenever I sang his songs, they were successful, especially since Musorgsky was an exceptionally good accompanist and since he always accompanied me in public.

During the last years of his life, M[odest] P[etrovich] came to our house especially often: three or four times a week. He would come for lunch and would then stay all evening. My children shouted enthusiastically: "Musorianin is here, hurray!" After lunch, he would take a short nap in an armchair, and having rested, would sit down at the piano and let his imagination run free. Many portions of *Khovanshchina* and *The Fair at Sorochintsy* were composed in our house. M[odest] P[etrovich] always said that in our house he was able to rest his soul from a hard and distressing life. By nature Musorgsky was a remarkably delicate, gentle man; and in his works, despite seemingly rude, typically Russian expressions, there was never a feeling of impropriety. He did not think that everything Russian ought to be coarse, and he did not like it when performers underscored the rude expressions. Such an attitude is understandable when one considers that everything he composed was talented, realistic, and always apposite.

Musorgsky loved nature passionately. When he came to our *dacha,* in Pargolovo, where V[ladimir] V[asilievich] Stasov also lived, our big group would go on long outings, some of us on foot and some in carriages. I always rode a horse, since I loved horseback riding. . . . M[odest] P[etrovich] preferred to walk and look for mushrooms, which reminded him of his boyhood, and he always naively rejoiced when he came upon a good mushroom patch. He particularly liked sunsets, and we often watched them together. He had such an amazingly delicate and poetic soul! M[odest] P[etrovich] could not bear to see a fish caught on a hook. He said one should catch a fish with a net so that the fish would not suffer unduly; one should always avoid harming any living creature, and one should not cause suffering either moral or physical.

Intrigues and troubles were a terrible burden on Musorgsky. He was sick more and more often, and his nerves were utterly shattered. He became seriously ill in 1881; the illness lasted a short time. His weakened and exhausted constitution was unable to overcome the affliction, and he died in the hospital, surrounded by his close friends, on his birthday, March 16/28, 1881, at the age of 42. M[odest] P[etrovich] died during the night; the nurse's aid who was with him told us that he suddenly uttered in a loud cry: "Everything is over. Oh, poor me!"

Portrait of Musorgsky by S. Aleksandrovskii

Vasilii Bessel'

Moyo znakomstvo s Listom

My Acquaintance with Liszt

Vasilii Bessel' (1843–1907) founded a music publishing firm and a music trading company. In the 1870s he published the journal *Muzykal'nyi listok* [Musical leaflet] and in the 1880s, the journal *Muzykal'noe obozrenie* [Musical review]. V. Bessel's and Co. published many works by the composers of the Balakirev circle.

.　　.　　.

My acquaintance with Franz Liszt came about because of the policy of our firm. At first, I went to Weimar, on the advice of C[esar] A[ntonovich] Cui and of the late Musorgsky, to show Liszt the piano scores for the operas *The Stone Guest* by A[leksandr] S[ergeevich] Dargomyzhsky and *William Ratcliff* by C[esar] Cui, which had just come off the press. To allow Liszt to read the text of *The Stone Guest*, a German or a French translation had to be added (the opera *Ratcliff* had been published in both languages). Then Musorgsky, who knew German rather well, undertook to interline Bodenstedt's translation of *The Stone Guest*, which seemed quite close to the original, and gave me that copy for Liszt.[1]

Nikolai Lavrov

iz *Vospominanii*

FROM *Recollections*

Nikolai Lavrov (1853–1927), a pianist, was a professor at the Petrograd Conservatory. His recollections were recorded in 1918–1919 by Victor Beliaev, then a professor at the Petrograd Conservatory, who wrote the following account.

·   ·   ·

In St. Petersburg a circle of musical amateurs devoted to dramatic performance was formed in 1879. This circle appeared to be a branch of a similarly named circle formed a year earlier, under the direction of K. K. Zike, to stage opera performances. This circle of amateurs met in the Hotel Demut.

The members of the new circle met several times a week to study music. Toward the beginning of the 1879–1880 season, at A[natolii] K[onstantinovich] Liadov's invitation, Musorgsky joined this circle. He became a member at the same time as D[ar'ia] M[ikhailovna] Leonova, who had already retired from her operatic career and was directing a music school with Musorgsky. Musorgsky was often the accompanist at the circle's weekly musical evenings, and from the first evening he impressed Lavrov with the unusual expressiveness of his talented and passionate manner of playing the piano, a manner which always profoundly impressed his audience. Lavrov had particularly vivid recollections of the evenings in which Musorgsky played the accompaniment for a series of songs by Balakirev, Rimsky-Korsakov, and others. However, his most vivid memory of that period was Musorgsky's and Leonova's renditions of "Pesnia o blokhe" [Song of a flea] and the fantasy "Buria" [Storm].

The "Song of a Flea" had provoked quite a sensation in the circle; the audience had burst into applause. Musorgsky's ability for picturesque accompaniment was most strikingly illustrated there: at times one could actually hear a flea jumping. The arpeggios in the middle of the song were exquisite and were definitely in the style of Rubinstein. Lavrov had never before had the opportunity to hear such a rendition of an arpeggio, nor was he ever to have the opportunity again. The thundering *fortissimo* of the grand piano did not drown out Leonova's voice for one second; each word of the song could be heard clearly.

After one of the evenings in which Musorgsky and Leonova had participated, the audience became so enthusiastic that everyone gathered by the stage and asked Musorgsky to play from his own works. Leonova prompted the audience to ask him to play "Storm." At that time Lavrov was still unaware of the fact that Musorgsky could play as a soloist, and so he was surprised to see Musorgsky sit down at the piano and start playing "Storm." In this performance Musorgsky greatly perplexed not only Lavrov (who was more or less unacquainted with the new music and unaccustomed to it) but also Liadov. Lavrov was utterly bewildered, since he was not able to find any music in "Storm." But there was one thing he could not deny: the unbelievable perfection of the imitation of the sounds. In the rolling passages where Musorgsky reached the highest notes of the instrument, one had the perfect illusion of waves crashing on the rocks.

Lavrov and Liadov never heard this piece again, and they did not know whether it ever existed on paper or even in rough draft. Although they were amazed by it, they did not know what to make of it. Lavrov, at least, always talked about "Storm" with a puzzled look on his face.

The circle was very kind to Musorgsky, but unfortunately, even at that time he was already an absolutely confirmed drunkard, a total alcoholic. When he finished a number, he would immediately start sipping cognac. He would get drunk very quickly, and since his central nervous system was already affected, he had the manners of a person who even when sober gave the impression of being drunk. But when he was indeed intoxicated, the impression he made was distressing, even if at times comic: he would strike a theatrical pose and make strange gestures. This happened to him quite often on stage while he was playing, especially during a rest.

In the last years of his life, there was about his figure a kind of slackness; a red face, a bluish nose, all of which, from the first glance, indicated the typical alcoholic. His face was always slightly puffy, and this puffiness was somehow asymmetric. In his manners he had certain pretensions to good breeding—after all, he had previously been an officer of the Guards—but his manners were old-fashioned.

In his last years his constant residence was the restaurant Malyi Iaroslavets, where he was respected and loved by everyone from the waiters to the *maître d'hôtel*. He almost never had any money, but he was trusted and was allowed to run a tab. After Modest Petrovich's death, Stasov, having sold some of Musorgsky's compositions to Bessel',[1] paid the debts Musorgsky had accumulated in the restaurant, which were around one thousand rubles.

When Musorgsky was very drunk, and this would usually occur quite late at night, just before the restaurant closed, he would confide in the senior barman and often told him: "I will die, but one day you will remember my name with pride."

He would say this with such sincerity and conviction that the barman always believed him.

Balakirev's closest friend, T[ertii] I[vanovich] Filippov, a Government Comptroller and a great connoisseur of Russian folk songs, saved Musorgsky from starvation by giving him a Post in the Government Control. As he was Musorgsky's superior, he was lenient to the point of injustice and self-compromise, and forgave him everything. Musorgsky did nothing at work and would arrive drunk after a sleepless night. Tertii Ivanovich never reprimanded him for such behavior, and permitted Musorgsky such indulgence by saying: "I am a servant to the artists."[2]

Musorgsky was hired in the Government Control the day after Balakirev asked Filippov—a very close friend—to provide the composer with a job. Musorgsky's obligation was to collect his salary on the 20th of each month.

A. Leont'ev

Rasskaz o Musorgskom

Rasskaz o Musorgskom

A Vignette about Musorgsky

A. Leont'ev was a general.

. . .

Was it a dream or did it really happen? In either case, it was an unforgettable experience for me. It took place in Petersburg in 1878, perhaps in 1879, the date does not make any difference. It was late at night, in a private house and in a small, intimate company of no more than six or seven people, after a hearty supper. Among those present that night were the former *diva* of the Russian opera Leonova, the famous actor Gorbunov, and Musorgsky. Not yet forty years old, he had an unhealthy look and was already growing quite decrepit. He sought consolation and oblivion more and more frequently in alcohol, where he also looked for his strength and inspiration; he was quickly going to ruin—such was the picture of poor Musorgsky.

The grand piano was open; lighted candles stood on it. Suddenly the laughter provoked by Gorbunov's story was interrupted: Musorgsky was taking his seat at the piano. He softly played the first chords of a melody we had never heard before; Leonova had already taken her position next to the pianist. The song, tender and heartrending, "Plyvyot, plyvyot leby-odushka," etc. [The swan glides on the water],[1] was heard.

This song was followed by other excerpts taken from his last and greatest work—*Khovanshchina*—which was in process of composition. Suddenly, Leonova fell silent: she could no longer follow Musorgsky, who was playing and improvising as he went.

We were all witnesses to the exhilarating process of inspiration that the genius, falling more and more into ecstasy, was going through. With titanic strength he was fighting to master the ever-developing theme that he alone could hear. It seemed that in playing, the composer fought for ascendency over the artist performer. Finally, the last powerful chords resounded. It is impossible to describe his eyes; their expression had changed, and they were cast down. Suddenly he looked up as if searching for a way out or for the answer to a conundrum. . . . When he finished he closed his eyes and dropped his hands in a gesture of helplessness. All of us were trembling violently. . . . What was the reason? Tension? Fear? For whom? For Musorgsky? For Russia? For us personally? Or it was because we had caught sight of a divine manifestation in a frail and ailing human being? No one dared interrupt the silence. Leonova, who up to that point stood motionless by the piano, quickly turned away and soundlessly went to the back of the room. Tears were streaming down her face. Gorbunov sat perfectly still, all shrunk down, his massive head on his knees. Everyone was frozen to his chair. "Modest Petrovich," the host finally dared to whisper to Musorgsky, who remained sitting at the piano, utterly exhausted, "why don't you spend the night here?" Musorgsky glanced at him, his eyes still afire with inspiration and his excited face momentarily lit by a gentle, grateful smile. But he raised his hand in such a decisive farewell that our host did not have the audacity to repeat his invitation. And Musorgsky was the first to leave. Even after his departure no one ventured to be the first to utter a word. . . . I never saw Musorgsky again. It had been said that his death was the result of his excessive passion for alcohol. What nonsense! What blasphemy! Even if there is some physiological truth in that statement, he mainly fell victim to the burden of fulfillments that exceed the human potential to which he was condemned by his genius, and . . . to poverty.

Ivan Lapshin

IZ *Khudozhestvennogo tvorchestva*

FROM *Artistic Creations*

Ivan Lapshin (1870–1952) was a professor of philosophy at Petersburg University and, after 1923, at Prague University.

.   .   .

Musorgsky was an outstanding pianist. C[esar] A[ntonovich] Cui told me that, in his opinion, Musorgsky was so gifted that if he had cultivated this talent, he would have rivaled even Anton Rubinstein.

As is known, in 1879 Musorgsky and the singer Leonova made a concert tour of southern Russia. He appeared on stage as an accompanist and a soloist. His talent as accompanist was highly appreciated by the public everywhere, and he was given curtain calls of his own, separate from the singer, because of his amazing renditions of the piano part of, for example, "Lesnoi Tsar' " [The forest king] by Schubert.

Musorgsky acquired his fateful taste for alcohol in his youth, and it grew stronger in the seventies. Professor S. V. Rozhdestvenskii[1] told me the following:

> In 1880 my parents and I were living in Leonova's *dacha* in Oranienbaum. I was eleven years old. I saw M[odest] P[etrovich] Musorgsky in the garden and in the park every day. He looked remarkably like his famous portrait painted by Repin. His suit always looked somewhat shabby; later Mr. Druri[2] told me that he had often acquired second-hand clothes for the unfortunate composer. . . . Once a week at Leonova's there was a reception followed by a dinner. Usually "Musin'ka" was in charge of the dinner. From the room in the rear one could hear the clatter of dishes and the uncorking of bottles. Each time Musorgsky came out, he was more and more "in his cups." After dinner the concert would begin. Musorgsky played the piano (by now quite "ready") as accompanist and soloist. He performed his own works with amazing perfection, producing a "shattering effect" on the listeners. This is confirmed by A. A. Vrubel', who often heard Musorgsky at F. M. Valuev's, where he performed "Blokha" [The flea] with diabolical force, and according to her, "he performed even better than Shaliapin."[3] At that time Musorgsky was suffering from the frightening

hallucinations often observed in alcoholics; this was also noted by D[ar'ia] M[ikhailovna] Leonova in her recollections (see *Istoricheskii vestnik* [Historical herald], 1891). Cui told me that he gave Musorgsky the robe he wears in Repin's portrait.

Musorgsky loved what the British call "practical jokes,"* even when he was the victim. In his youth, according to Professor S. Ia. Tereshin (a close friend of one of the composer's most intimate friends, Nikolai Konstantinovich Larin⁴), one winter morning Larin, Musorgsky, and two other friends were returning home in a carriage from a musical evening. It was already four in the morning. On the way Musorgsky and Larin had been having quite a row. Suddenly Larin stopped the carriage, walked over to the Semyonov Parade Ground, which they were passing, and, raising his arm in a solemn gesture, proclaimed before the empty square: "I publicly announce that Musorgsky is a scoundrel!" This unexpected "joke" cheered Musorgsky up so much that his anger instantly vanished.

Ia[kov] P[etrovich] Polonskii,⁵ who knew Musorgsky well and who, along with his wife, had gone to visit the great composer when he was ill, told me that he had heard Musorgsky's rendition of a piano piece which reproduces the emotional state of a dying political prisoner in the Peter and Paul Fortress, while in the background, out of tune, chimes the hymn "Kol' slaven"⁶ [How glorious is our Lord in Zion].

The famous archeologist V[asilii] G[rigorievich] Druzhinin kindly informed me that a few days after Dostoevsky's death (January 28, 1881) at a literary gathering devoted to his memory,** when they brought in the portrait of Dostoevsky framed in black crepe, Musorgsky sat down at the piano and improvised a funeral knell, similar to that heard in the last scene of *Boris*.† This was the next to the last public appearance by Musorgsky, and his musical improvisation was his farewell, not only to the deceased poet of "the humiliated and the insulted," but also to all the living.⁷

---

*In English in the original text.—Trans.

**On this evening Grigorievich read "Mal'chik u Khrista na yolke" [A boy at Christ's for Christmas]. The program for the evening was announced on February 4. On February 9 Musorgsky again performed as an accompanist.

†Musorgsky had the ability to compose "in the presence of other people." Thus, he composed Marina's monologue while visiting the Stasovs and the Rimsky-Korsakovs. All evening long he repeatedly went over to the piano and played passages and, in the presence of his friends, gradually composed the entire monologue. N[adezhda] N[ikolaevna] obligingly provided me with this information.

Vasilii Bertenson

Vasilii Bertenson (1853–1933) was a physician and an amateur musician.

. . .

Modest Petrovich Musorgsky, who, alas, achieved fame only after he was dead, when this purely national talent became not only Russia's property but the property of all Europe, had a great magnetic attraction for me when I was merely a student. Practically speaking, no charity concert was held without Musorgsky. Musical evenings in the seventies, organized by the students of all the institutions of higher education for the benefit of their needy comrades, were unthinkable without his participation.

Modest Petrovich was an outstanding accompanist. Although poor as Job himself, when it came to philanthropic concerts, he accepted no money for his work.

It so happened that one winter I was responsible for organizing a concert for the benefit of the medical students. Even three weeks before the concert, I was already rushing about all day from artist to artist.

Anyone who has had the responsibility of organizing a charity concert, which, in those days, as far as the artist was concerned, was invariably without monetary reward, knows that this honorable responsibility was not, by any means, a sinecure.

Although I boldly announced to all the participants that Musorgsky was going to be the accompanist—which immediately influenced their favorable decision—I must confess that, at the moment, I was unwillingly deceiving them.

The fact was that the author of *Boris Godunov,* still in the prestigious Preobrazhenskii Regiment, was rumored to be drinking hard; therefore, asking him three weeks in advance to participate in a concert meant that there was no way of knowing if on the designated day one could rely on him. Although I would doubtlessly have obtained his promise to participate, naturally, I would not have had a guarantee that, on the given day, he would not be too drunk to play or even too drunk to recognize his own father.

As a special attraction, I was fortunate enough to obtain, in addition to artists from the Russian opera, the splendid tenor Ravelli, from the Italian opera. At the time he was singing in the Bolshoi Theater.

In anticipation of an "encore" I asked the singer to study the famous song by Kushelyova, "Skazhite ei" [Tell her], which the famous Tamberlik had performed so many times. It was not yet completely forgotten.

The day before the concert Ravelli told me he wanted to meet his accompanist, and, with this purpose in mind, he asked Musorgsky to come to his house the following day, as early as possible, for a rehearsal.

The day before, I had received Musorgsky's agreement to participate; happy at having found him sober, I again went to him to fulfil Ravelli's request.

But to my horror I found Musorgsky more intoxicated than wine itself. Babbling on, he assured me, in French for some reason, that there was no need to go see the Italian, that he would manage, etc.

No exhortation or request had any effect on him: with a drunkard's stubbornness, he kept repeating: "Non, monsieur, non: maintenant c'est impossible. Ce soir je serai exacte [sic]." [No, sir, no: it's impossible right now. I will be on time tonight.]

Musorgsky was then living in a small unkempt room. There was a bottle of vodka on a dirty table and some kind of poor food. . . .

When I took my leave, he stood up with great difficulty, but nevertheless saw me to the door. Making a low bow, perhaps not totally worthy of Louis XIV but utterly amazing for someone who was completely "soused," he added: "Donc, à ce soir!" [So, see you tonight!]

Having received nothing for my pains, I returned to my tenor and told him that I had not found Musorgsky at home. I was finally able, although with great difficulty, to convince Ravelli to participate in the concert, despite my having been unable to contact Musorgsky. Besides, I said, my accompanist was a marvelous and extremely capable one.

I immediately dispatched a friend to get Musorgsky. My friend had volunteered to watch for him and had promised to bring him, in any case, long before the beginning of the concert.

Indeed, promptly at seven o'clock Musorgsky was in Kononov Hall, where the concert was to take place.[1]

Unfortunately, in the greenroom, Musorgsky continually helped himself to the various drinks, which were right at hand, and he got more and more intoxicated. Suddenly, my Italian tenor, trying a roulade, discovered that his voice had lowered, and therefore he decided to sing all his repertoire half a tone or, if necessary, a whole tone lower.

That was the last straw!

I ran to Musorgsky and asked him if he could solve the problem Ravelli presented to us. Standing up with a certain gallantry, Musorgsky reassured me with: "Of course, why not?" also in French (the fact was that Musorgsky spoke only French to educated people even if he was just slightly tipsy). To reassure the tenor, he suggested that he sing his entire repertoire in *mezza voce*.

Musorgsky, who undoubtedly was hearing the Italian songs sung by Ravelli for the first time, so charmed the Italian with his talented rendition and his ability to play in any key, that the latter started to hug him saying: "Che artista" [What an artist].

Both Ravelli and Musorgsky had an immense success, especially the singer, despite the fact that, in the encore "Skazhite ei" [Tell her], he sang some false notes; but with the support of Musorgsky's masterful playing, he was able to pass the test honorably.

Poor Musorgsky, because of the daring realism in his music, tinted, as it was, with surprisingly vivid national colors, stood alone among the Russian composers. He died in the Nikolaev Military Hospital. It was thanks to my brother's intercession that Musorgsky—terminally ill and literally without shelter—found a refuge in the hospital as my brother's orderly. In everyone's opinion Musorgsky lived too soon and died too young.

Had he lived in our time, had he acquired a more serious musical education, this naturally talented man would have molded his creative powers into a different shape, and his creativity would have evolved in a completely different manner.

Perhaps A[nton] G[rigorievich] Rubinstein was right in saying that Russians have a strong inclination for music and are gifted for it, but because of a general lack of enlightenment and a Slavic carelessness, they are invariably dilettantes.

Dar'ia Leonova

iz *Vospominanii*

FROM *Memoirs*

Dar'ia Leonova (1829–1896), a contralto, was also a voice teacher. From 1852 to 1873 she was an artist with the Russian opera. After leaving the stage, she gave many concerts and made a concert tour around the world.

. . .

Two scenes from the opera *Boris Godunov*, composed by Musorgsky, were performed at my recital. Musorgsky, who was living at my *dacha,* was working on two of his operas—*Khovanshchina* and *The Fair at Sorochintsy*—and he finished them while he was there.[1]

Shortly before my benefit performance for Kommissarzhevskii, I had played the part of the hostess of the Inn in two acts from Musorgsky's opera *Boris Godunov*. I thought that nothing would work better than to have these two acts for my benefit performance, since the public had liked them so much. But as soon as I voiced my wish to do so, I was told that I had to obtain the rights to perform these two acts; I would have to pay the composer his royalties. I retorted that quite probably Musorgsky would not wish me to pay anything since we were close acquaintances. And, naturally, when I mentioned this to Musorgsky he answered that he would consider himself only too happy to see the two acts in my benefit performance.[2]

I would like now to turn to how I began the voice classes. I met the composer Musorgsky before the opera *Boris Godunov* was staged. He would visit me occasionally. Having noticed his many oddities as well as extremely positive characteristics, both as a man and an artist, I wanted to get to know him better. On my return from a trip[3] I found many opportunities to meet Musorgsky at the house of mutual close acquaintances, where he was then living,[4] and little by little we became good friends. He overcame his reluctance and confessed that, having heard and believed various rumors, he had been afraid of me, but that now he was convinced that the rumors were completely false. Musorgsky was unique among men. He loved people so much that it was impossible for him to find anything wrong in another person. He judged everybody else by himself.

Anyone who knew Musorgsky well was able to see that he was not an ordinary man; he never got involved in intrigues; he could not believe that an educated, intelligent man would wish to harm or play dirty tricks on anyone. In short, he was angelic. When he was composing *Khovanshchina* he often visited me; after composing a passage, he would immediately come to my place in Oranienbaum to show me how he wanted it sung. I would then sing it, and he was always delighted with my execution. That was how he composed *Khovanshchina*.

Soon he was convinced that I was not in the least the wicked woman my enemies had described to him, and when I decided to go on an artistic tour of Russia, he readily joined me, and we traveled together.[5] It was, incidentally, in the Ukraine that he collected many regional motifs. During the summer preceding his death, he lived in my *dacha,* where he finished *Khovanshchina* and *The Fair at Sorochintsy.* It was there that we decided to start my school. He had great hopes for this enterprise, as it would allow him to earn a living, since his means were very, very limited.

However, during the first year, we had very few students. He was saddened by this, but both of us eagerly devoted ourselves to our endeavor, hoping that through our concerted efforts we would attract students. In our classes we introduced totally new methods of teaching. For example, when there were two, three, or four voices, Musorgsky wrote duets, tercets, and quartets so that the students could practice their solfeggio.[6] This technique worked very well in our instruction. Musorgsky was astonished at how successful I was at training voices.

It looked as if our enterprise was going to be a success, but before the season ended Musorgsky died. Most likely, his death was brought on by his artistic temperament and his material hardships. He lived in dire poverty. For example, one day when he came to me, he was extremely nervous and irritable; and he told me that he had no place to go, that his only recourse was to live in the street. He had nothing left at all and saw no solution to his predicament. What was I to do? I began to comfort him, saying that although I was far from wealthy, I would share everything I had with him. My words calmed him down somewhat. That evening we were going to the house of General Sokhanskii, whose daughter, our pupil, was to sing for the first time before a large gathering at their house.[7] She sang very well, which probably soothed Musorgsky. I saw how nervous he was as he accompanied her. But everyone agreed that she sang very well, considering that she had been taking lessons for such a short time. Everybody was pleased, and the parents thanked us profusely. After the singing, dancing began, and I was invited to play cards. Suddenly Sokhanskii's son rushed to me and asked if Musorgsky was subject to nervous attacks. I assured him that as long as I had known him I had never heard of anything of the sort. Apparently, he had just suffered a seizure. A physician who was present attended him, and when the time came to go, Musorgsky was completely recovered and on his feet. We left together. When we got to the apartment he implored me to allow him to stay, alleging a nervous, fearful condition. I gladly acquiesced, knowing that if something were to happen to him in his lonely apartment, there would be no one to help him. I put him in a small room and requested that the servants keep an eye on him all night and ordered them to wake me immediately if he were ill. He slept the whole night in a sitting position. In the morning when I went to the dining room for tea, he came in in a very good mood. I asked him how he felt. He thanked me and answered that he felt fine. With these words he turned to the right and suddenly fell full length on the floor. My fears had not been groundless: had he been alone he would most certainly have suffocated; but we immediately turned him over, helped him to bed, and sent for the doctor. Before evening he had two more seizures. That evening I called his friends who took an interest in him, most significantly Vladimir Vasilievich Stasov, Tertii Ivanovich Filippov, and the others who loved him. All those present agreed that in view of the complex treatment, and in view of the necessity for constant care, they should persuade him to enter a hospital. They explained how important it was and how good it would be for him. They promised to get him a beautiful private room. For a long time he refused to agree; he only wanted to stay at my place. Finally, they persuaded him. The next day he was taken to the hospital in a carriage.[8] At first, he began to improve, but then he became worse and worse and shortly after he died.

Pis'mo v redaktsiiu gazety *Novoe Vremia*

Letter to the Editor of the Newspaper *New Time*.

(Published March 21, 1881)

In M[odest] P[etrovich] Musorgsky's obituary published in no. **1814** of *New Time* it was said among other things that "this year he was working as an accompanist in a voice school," which I had opened the previous fall. Both an inaccuracy and some misinformation have slipped in here. Allow me to ask you to correct both.

Firstly, it has long been known that the late Musorgsky was an incomparable accompanist. We never had such a brilliant accompanist, and there is no one to fill the vacuum. He brought "accompanying" to a degree of perfection and virtuosity heretofore undreamed of by a concert musician. With his accompaniment he had, indeed, said a "new word" and demonstrated its importance to the artistic integrity of a performance. To follow in his footsteps has become a difficult and challenging task. It was for that reason that the majority of artists always wanted to sing at concerts where M[odest] P[etrovich] was to be the accompanist; and therefore, no concert of any importance was held without his participation.

Secondly, in my classes, M[odest] P[etrovich] Musorgsky was not simply the accompanist; he was also my closest collaborator, my adviser, and my assistant. We conjointly elaborated our program of courses, and it was jointly that we carried it out. And I might add that it was at his urgent request that I had started these courses.

His talent as a musical declamator, an innate and typically Russian talent, his sound knowledge of technique, of singing instruction, and of stage conditions, made his advice and directions particularly priceless for anyone preparing for a dramatic and operatic career. My lengthy experience as a singer entitles me to express the belief that with Musorgsky's death both my students and Russian musical art suffered an irreparable loss.

The lives of prominent personalities such as the late Musorgsky would not be completely ruined if it were not for an evil fate that blights the destinies of our best national men of talent. The chair of musical declamation, created in the Conservatory of the Russian Musical Society, which has in its custody the fate of our national art—a chair, which up to now the Society has been trying unsuccessfully to fill—should have been given to Musorgsky. In doing so the Society would doubtlessly have benefited from the immense contribution he would have made in this field. And the resulting social status, combined with the character of his talent, would probably have saved and substantially extended the life of the creator of *Boris* and *Khovanshchina*, a man who died such an untimely death.

Rest in peace, honest Russian talent, you who invariably and consistently strove toward "new shores."

Aleksandra Demidova

Vospominaniia

Memoirs

Aleksandra Demidova (1860–1949) was a schoolteacher. A soprano, she was Leonova and Musorgsky's student.

.   .   .

I went to the address where the courses were offered. I found the apartment near Sennaia, near the Kokushkin Bridge, on the Kriukov Canal. I went up a rather modest staircase to the third floor and entered a small anteroom. I was greeted by a stout Russian beauty, who affably informed me that it was indeed here that a music school had been instituted. . . . She loudly called "Modest Petrovich," and from the adjoining room a middle-aged man entered. He was of medium height and rather uncomely looks, with wavy hair. He was dressed in a frayed frock coat. He rather sternly invited me to approach the piano.

I was asked where and with whom I had studied, and when I answered, he showed his annoyance: "I am absolutely uninterested in all this Italian stuff!" He picked a music book, and opening it at random, began to play Schubert's introduction to "Zhaloba Devushki" [The maiden's complaint]. I was astonished. . . . I had never dreamed that an accompaniment could so clearly recreate scenes from nature. I suddenly felt that I could really see the rocks, the forest, and the weeping maiden. . . .

After the Schubert I sang some other songs, and when I finished, Musorgsky jumped up, and in a totally different voice said, "But this is Bosio!" (a famous Italian singer). "That's what we need! Dar'ia Mikhailovna!" Modest Petrovich called. "Come here! This is exactly what we need."

Leonova came in, and the three of us began talking about my studies. Modest Petrovich brightened up and became almost an entirely different person; he was excited and declared immediately that we could now begin studying real Russian music, and that with this new asset we would be able to form a student quartet. . . . It was suggested that we study *A Life for the Tsar, Ruslan and Ludmila,* and *Rusalka*; but all of this was to be in the future; for now, we were to study the songs of Glinka and Dargomyzhsky.

Musorgsky was frequently taken ill. . . . During the lessons, in the adjoining dining room his refreshment was usually at hand: a plate of mushrooms and a small glass. Dar'ia Mikhailovna bemoaned the fact that he resorted to it all too often and that he was obviously getting worse. . . .

The then famous Government Comptroller Tertii Ivanovich Filippov worried a great deal about Modest Petrovich; he tried to help him as much as he could, but he was unable to change anything at this late date.

[During that season] Dar'ia Mikhailovna's Saturdays guests often listened to us students, since they were interested in our progress. Thus, for instance, Rimsky-Korsakov praised me for my high "do" in the trio "ne tomi, rodimyi!" [Don't torment me, darling!]. . . . Leonova sang the aria from *Khovanshchina* straight from the manuscript. Donskoi, a talented student, sang Vladimir's "Medlenno den' ugasal" [The day was slowly dying away], from *Prince Igor*.

Often good things were said about us, the students of Leonova and Musorgsky, and we were invited to private concerts.

At Leonova's evenings Musorgsky was her faithful accompanist. From his works Leonova performed the ballad "Zabytyi" [Forgotten]. Carried away by his own accompaniment, Musorgsky often digressed and improvised such modulations and chords that we students were astonished and ravished; and Leonova performed the melodies which streamed from his hands with amazing subtleness.

Modest Petrovich had time to translate Agatha's aria for me, from "Volshebnyi strelok" [The magic archer] by Weber.[1] He was irritated by the existing poor Russian translation, and he reworked it in his own way.

[The students were not allowed to visit Musorgsky in the hospital so they received news of his condition from Leonova.]

[March 18] A sullen day in March. . . . A wet snow was falling. His students and an enormous crowd of fellow artists carried our friend and teacher to his eternal place. . . .[2] There was a huge wreath from all of us students. Orphaned now, we returned to Dar'ia Mikhailovna's. She was grieving deeply; we tried to console her to the best of our abilities, expressing the hope that everything we had learned from Modest Petrovich would not be lost to Russian music but that we would sacredly preserve it.

Lev Bertenson

K biografii M[odesta] P[etrovicha] Musorgskogo

Material for a Biography of M. P. Musorgsky

Lev Bertenson (1850–1929) was a surgeon and an amateur musician.

· · ·

Not only has the last word about Musorgsky not been said, but at the present time there is not even an essay in which this brilliantly shining, brightly dazzling semi-precious gem of Russian musical talent has been duly studied and appraised at his true worth. Therefore, every grain of information about him, even the smallest one, ought to be taken into consideration when one gathers the materials for an exhaustive monograph on the great musician.

Motivated by this thought and influenced by the fortuitous reading of a French article about Musorgsky, I have decided to tell what I know about him, even though I am not a professional writer. I feel entitled to take up this endeavor, since I was Musorgsky's physician right before he died. I was in close contact with him and served him lovingly and loyally during his last illness. Moreover, long before his death, I knew him and admired his works, well before the public knew them. I had heard them at the homes of mutual friends as well as at my own, where Modest Petrovich was always a welcome and dear guest to me and to my wife—the singer O. A. Skal'kovskaia. Because of the favorable circumstances in St. Petersburg and my particular and innate attraction to artistic talent, which I have had since early youth, I was very close to quite a few musical figures of my time (the brothers Anton and Nikolai Rubinstein, G. Veniavskii, K. Davydov, Napravnik, Tchaikovsky, Henselt, Laroche, and others); I was especially close to the talented and progressive group composed of Balakirev, Vladimir Stasov, Cui, Rimsky-Korsakov, and Borodin. This circle was well known in its time as the "Mighty Handful," and it even had its own forum, i.e., the musical satires by C[esar] A[ntonovich] Cui in the newspaper *S. Peterburgskie vedomosti* [St. Petersburg news] (when V. Korsh was its editor). This circle selected Musorgsky as a member and, so to speak, brought him up.

Although the idea of doing my part in collecting the materials on

Musorgsky was provoked by the fortuitous reading of a short article by a French music critic dealing with the opera *Boris Godunov* (I will talk about that later), I had often felt this desire to write about our great musician previously—ever since an article by the noted music critic M[ikhail] M[ikhailovich] Ivanov was published in the newspaper *New Time* (April 20, 1909). In that article M[ikhail] M[ikhailovich] Ivanov described the circumstances in which Musorgsky died in Nikolaev Military Hospital (where in a time of great need he had been admitted through my efforts). At the time, his article stirred the emotions and created indignation among Musorgsky's friends and greatly distressed me.

I shall start with Ivanov's article, which, even now, has the power to disturb me deeply, as soon as I tell how Musorgsky came to be a patient in the Nikolaev Military Hospital.

When Musorgsky, then retired, having no regular income and living in the most terrible and wretched conditions, fell seriously ill, his closest friends—V[ladimir] V[asilievich] Stasov, C[esar] A[ntonovich] Cui, N[ikolai] A[ndreevich] Rimsky-Korsakov, and A[leksandr] P[orfirievich] Borodin—approached me individually and as a body as "a physician who loved and respected musicians and men of letters," with the request to place Musorgsky in a good hospital. This request disturbed and distressed me very much, for I could not foresee any possibility of carrying it out properly. At that time I worked in two hospitals: the Rozhdestvenskii City Hospital for common laborers, with general wards only, and the Nikolaev Military Hospital for soldiers and officers. In both institutions I was only a junior staff physician, i.e., rather an unimportant member with no administrative power. I could have only acted as a modest intercessor for the request of such important people as Rimsky-Korsakov, Stasov, and the others. In the City Hospital nothing could be done, not even by the Lord Mayor himself; and Nikolaev Military Hospital, as its name indicates, was open only to lower military ranks and officers. Since Musorgsky, according to his passport, was then registered as a retired civil servant from Government Control, there was no hope of placing him in that hospital. Nevertheless, I promised his friends, not without some embarrassment, to do my best for the great man. I rushed off to the head physician. The first onslaught on my superior was not only a failure, but I was reprimanded for asking for the impossible. But as I began to take my leave, saddened and dispirited, my stern superior came up with an extraordinary solution to the hopeless situation. He stopped me and offered to accept Musorgsky in the hospital as the "hired civilian orderly of intern Bertenson" if, naturally, the ailing man and his friends could agree to such a lofty rank. . . . Needless to say, I was very happy with this unexpected and successful outcome to my intercession, and having secured the consent of the above-mentioned friends (the patient was not asked because he was unconscious with a high fever). I immediately placed Musorgsky in the hospital. Thanks to the kind disposition of the head physician, it was possible to make more than simply "good" arrangements for the patient: he was placed in the quietest and the most isolated part of the hospital, in a spacious, sunny room with a high ceiling, furnished with the necessary (although not stylish) furniture. The care could not have been better: two nurses from the Krestovozdvizhenskii Commune, hospital attendants, and a doctor's assistant had been assigned to him. The diet was more than satisfactory, for, in addition to an officer's ration, Musorgsky received many different dishes in generous amounts from close friends and acquaintances, who constantly showed him their loving care.

Now, to return to M[ikhail] M[ikhailovich] Ivanov: in the above-mentioned article, which was devoted, properly speaking, to the personality of N[ikolai] A[ndreevich] Rimsky-Korsakov and to the analysis of this great musician's work, based on his posthumous notes and personal points of view, the music critic of *New Time,* in passing, also speaks about the highly talented Musorgsky. He mentions his life, his works, his successes, his "progressive decline," and the fact that, at one time, he "had been abandoned by both his friends and his boon companions." Ivanov concludes his article by saying that he had seen the conditions at Nikolaev Hospital, where Musorgsky had been placed as an orderly, because of the efforts of the "compassionate L. B. Bertenson."[1] "These were wretched conditions, the sight of which wrung one's heart," exclaims Ivanov. . . . This remark, which did not reflect the true conditions, was categorically refuted, not only by my afore-cited remarks, published in *Golos* [Voice] (No. 79, 1881) but also by the grateful attitude Borodin, Cui, and Rimsky-Korsakov showed for the administration of Nikolaev Military Hospital, the nurses, and myself. Furthermore, it was refuted again in Stasov's article, also published in *Voice,* with the title "Portrait of Musorgsky."[2]

Mikhail Ippolitov-Ivanov

IZ *50 let russkoi muzyki v moikh vospominaniiakh*

FROM *Recollections from Fifty Years of Russian Music*

Mikhail Ippolitov-Ivanov (1859–1935) was a composer and a conductor. After 1893 he was a professor at the Moscow Conservatory, and after 1905, Director. He did not know Musorgsky very well. His notes are more of a "second-hand, third-hand" nature.

. . . .

V[ladimir] V[asilievich] Stasov was the center as the trustee of Glinka's behests and the source of Balakirev's inspiration. He was art's brightly burning luminary, not only in music but also in painting and sculpture. Great artists accepted him as a true voice of art. Stasov has given a very accurate characterization of the "Mighty Handful"; he said Balakirev was the most inspired; Cui, the most graceful; Rimsky-Korsakov, the most learned; Borodin, the most profound; and Musorgsky the most talented.

During my last year at the conservatory the "Mighty Handful" totally dispersed. The young eaglets had grown up and left the nest for a glorious flight. Rimsky-Korsakov, who had already composed *Sadko, Antar,* "Serbskaia Fantaziia" [Serbian fantasy], and the operas *The Maid of Pskov* and *May Night,* was working on *Snegurochka* [Snow maiden]. Musorgsky had written *Boris* and was in the process of writing *Khovanshchina.* Borodin had finished the musical picture *V srednei Azii* [On the steppes of Central Asia], two symphonies, and was working on *Prince Igor.* Cui had written three operas: *The Prisoner of the Caucasus, Ratcliff,* and *Angelo.* A star of first magnitude, A[leksandr] K[onstantinovich] Glazunov,[1] had just appeared on the horizon. The musical gatherings at Balakirev's had moved on to the Rimskys' and to the Borodins', and occasionally to the Stasovs'. Musorgsky came to these evenings once in a while, but only for a short time. He was frequently ill and rarely seen anywhere but at the restaurant Malyi Iaroslavets. The constant visitors at these gatherings were Liadov, Glazunov, F[eliks] Blumenfeld, Borodin, Stasov, the Molas and Il'inskii families, and V. M. Zarudnaia, a student from the Everardi Conservatory, a soprano with a beguiling timbre of voice. She had been the first one asked to sing the roles of *The Snow*

Maiden, of Iaroslavna, and even Hanna in *May Night.* The male roles always went to V[ladimir] N[ikanorovich] Il'inskii. He was an extremely musical young physician who had a pleasant, although not strong, baritone voice. He had been the first to perform the principal men's roles of the operas by Korsakov, Borodin, Musorgsky, and Cui, as well as all the many other new songs to be sung at these gatherings. Il'inskii was a fanatically dedicated popularizer of Musorgsky's works. He unfailingly performed them at the Solianyi Gorodok concerts, which were given for the benefit of the students. Musorgsky himself was always the accompanist. M[odest] P[etrovich] Musorgsky was an excellent pianist and an ideal accompanist. At that time he was the faithful traveling companion of the then-famous singer D[ar'ia] M[ikhailovna] Leonova in her concert tours. Everywhere they went he liked to force the audience to listen to excerpts from songs by Schumann and others to spite Leonova, who always wanted to leave the stage as quickly as possible. At all our gatherings, wherever they were held, before they were over, Zarudnaia and Il'inskii would sing Maria and William's duet from the opera *Ratcliff.* This duet particularly enchanted us all.

I returned to Petersburg at the end of the summer of 1881. I had settled down for the winter, but I had to move out of my sister's and find a room, somewhere near the Conservatory since it was difficult to make the walk from Ekaterinhoff to Teatral'naia Street twice a day. My sister agreed to my moving to the Il'inskiis', at 109 Nevskii Prospect, where they took me in as if I were one of the family. Since at the time I was accompanying V[ladimir] N[ikanorovich] Il'inskii in all his performances at the Korsakovs', the Borodins', and the Stasovs', we soon became close friends. We studied for our finals together. He was graduating from the Medical Academy, and I was graduating from the Conservatory, so we would both often study until dawn. Sometimes, seeing our light, on his way back from a meeting, Borodin would stop by and have a cup of tea and talk about *Prince Igor.*

Musorgsky also visited the Il'inskiis often.[2] He never stood on ceremony; if they were not home, he would sit down at the piano and improvise until they returned. The maid often complained to the master of the house: "He bangs away on it so! One day he'll break it, and then I'll be held responsible. And I'll be told that I was not careful enough." After his trip with Leonova to the Crimea, Musorgsky particularly liked to play "Buria na Chyornom more" [Storm on the Black Sea], a rather confusing work with a lot of thundering. V[ladimir] V[asilievich] Stasov jokingly tried to convince him to write a musical picture "Earthquake in Japan." He said that one day, during D[ar'ia] M[ikhailovna] Leonova's stay in Japan, the rickshaws were bringing her down a mountain, and since she was a hefty woman and they could not support her weight, they dropped her. As she fell down the mountain, she demolished an entire village and killed several hundred Japanese; the disaster later was attributed to an earthquake. Stasov found this an excellent joke, but Musorgsky disliked the sarcasm and kept a morose silence.

I met Modest Petrovich Musorgsky at the end of 1878, when it was not yet apparent that he was an alcoholic. His clothes, although not very smart, were clean, and he walked with his head held proudly; his distinctive haircut gave him a jaunty look. Later, when he began to degenerate rapidly, he still always appeared properly dressed in public. He would usually talk about himself and attack us—the younger generation. "You young people," he said to me during a walk, "sitting in your conservatory only want to learn your *cantus firmus* and nothing else; do you think that the Zaremba formula, 'the minor key is our original sin, but the major key is our redemption,' or that 'rest, movement, and rest again' exhausts everything? No, my dear ones, I believe that if you want to sin, then go ahead and sin; if there is movement then there is no return to rest; one must go forward, destroying everything on his path." While saying this he proudly shook his head. The last time I saw him before his illness was in the restaurant Malyi Iaroslavets, where Laroche, Glazunov,[3] and I stopped by to see him. We found him totally erratic. He immediately lashed out at Rubinstein, Balakirev, and Rimsky-Korsakov for their erudition; and after repeating "one must create, one must create," several times, he fell silent. . . . Then, looking up at me with sleepy eyes, he suddenly asked: "And how do you remove stains from a morning coat?" "I try not to make any stains, Modest Petrovich," I answered. "Well, I use green soap," he said, "it works wonders." That was the end of our conversation. In the spring he fell ill with *delirium tremens;* Stasov and Borodin were able to get him a bed, as a retired military man, in the Nikolaev Military Hospital. He was very weak, but he talked in a perfectly rational way, recalling his performances with Il'inskii. At times he would have violent fits of delirium which left him totally exhausted. On the eve of his death he felt very well, and I[l'ia] E[fimovich] Repin had time to color the sketch of his famous portrait. But that was the last spark of a mind that was dying out; during the night of March 16 he died of a heart rupture. All the lovers of Russian art gathered at his funeral. F[eliks] M[ikhailovich] Blumenfeld and I carried the wreath sent by the Conservatory; how ironic that it was from an institution which never acknowledged him.

At the end of 1881 the Theatrical Directors resumed *Boris Godunov*.[4] M[ilii] A[lekseevich] Balakirev got tickets and invited the Rimskys, Borodin, the Il'inskiis, the Stasovs and me. It was with inexpressible sadness that we gathered in the box. During the performance I noticed several times that A[leksandr] P[orfirievich] Borodin brushed away a tear; overwhelmed with emotion and unable to listen to the scene of Boris's death, he left the box. Everyone was deeply distressed and felt the drama in the life of this great Russian musician.

Mikhail Ivanov

iz *Nekrologa Musorgskogo*

FROM *Musorgsky's Obituary*

Mikhail Ivanov (1849–1927) was a composer and a music critic. He was on the staff of the newspaper *Novoe vremia* [New time].

. . .

Everyone was as unprepared for Musorgsky's death as they had been for N[ikolai] Rubinstein's.[1] His constitution was so strong that no one ever thought that he was in any serious danger. [But] Musorgsky's foe was that unfortunate propensity which has destroyed so many talented Russians. He was driven to his grave by that fatal passion, which held him in a vice, as well as by the irregular life of an artist, which affects the nervous system. It was only about a month ago, in mid-February, that Musorgsky became ill. His illness was quite complex. He had a liver disorder, an adipose heart, and an inflammation of the spinal cord. He was in need of intensive care, and we could never have let him stay at home. The distressing situation of the composer at the beginning of his illness is difficult to imagine. He had always had a Bohemian life-style, but in the last two or three years he forsook almost everyone and was leading the life of a vagabond. Just before falling ill he had rented a room in *chambres garnies* somewhere on Ofitserskaia. But it was inconceivable that we leave him alone and sick in a furnished room. So his friends determined to find him a place where he could be properly cared for. He was entrusted to the care of Dr. L[ev] Bertenson, who, to assure his isolation and the best conditions for his treatment, had him taken to the Nikolaev Military Hospital. Dr. Bertenson looked after him with the utmost care. Musorgsky was given a private room; Dr. Bertenson came to see him twice a day; and the composer's friends did not leave him alone either. He had constant visitors. The treatment was successful. He quickly began to improve, and in such a marked manner that he was positively unrecognizable: everyone hoped that he would be totally cured, and that he would find a return to his previous life-style unthinkable. Money had already been gathered to finance a trip to the Crimea or abroad, where he could rest and fully recover. In short, everything had been done to pull him out of the impossible conditions in which he had been living in Petersburg. These conditions were truly appalling. In the last few years he had been forced to leave the Government Control, where he had been working. From a financial point of view, his retirement did not cause him any privation, since, I repeat, his friends came to his rescue: he had been paid in advance for his music (some of which had already been written). Consequently, he was not in dire need of money; but he was deprived of this last restraint, which employment—to a certain extent—represented for him, and he totally ceased to control his fateful weakness. Alcohol, sleepless nights, erysipelas on one leg, and strenuous mental activity (during these last years he had worked assiduously) quickly exhausted his strength. Nevertheless, by nature, his constitution was so strong that, provided with reasonable conditions and with sensible treatment, he promptly began to improve. The hopes of his friends, however, were not to be fulfilled. On account of his own gross imprudence, a sudden change for the worse occurred.[2] It became clear that recovery was no longer a possibility. His arms and legs were paralyzed. Under different conditions this might not have been too grave, but taken into account with all his other ailments, these symptoms foretold the end. Properly speaking, Musorgsky's last two days were one long agony. Paralysis was gradually taking hold of his respiratory organs: he was able to breathe only with difficulty and constantly complained about the lack of breath. However, up until the last minute he was mentally alert. Saturday, his condition was hopeless. But he himself did not want to believe that the end was near. When the question arose of officially giving Mr. T[ertii] Filippov (a person close to the composer) the copyright for Musorgsky's works, because of the composer's susceptibility, his friends were at a loss as to how to proceed with the deal without aggravating the sick man's condition.[3] They were also afraid of his seeing any of the newspapers which informed their readers of the hopelessness of his condition and described his agony. But even during the last two days Musorgsky demanded to have the newspapers read to him or requested to have them held in front of him so that he could read himself. On Sunday, his condition improved. The respite was temporary, the result of the various medicines prescribed for him, but he rejoiced and hope once more awoke in his heart. He was already dreaming about traveling to the Crimea or to Constantinople. Gaily, he told various anecdotes and recalled several events from the past. He unceasingly asked to be helped to sit up in an armchair. "I have to be polite," he said, "ladies are visiting me; what are they going to think of me?" This activity helped to hearten his friends, but it was the last gasp of a dying man; he spent Sunday night as usual—not any better, not any worse; at five o'clock in the morning he died. At his side he had only two doctor's assistants. They say that twice he uttered a loud cry, and that fifteen minutes later everything was over. The previous evening Mr. Bertenson, who was in charge of him, told me of his dangerous condition. At ten o'clock in the morning I went to see him in the Nikolaev Hospital. I was shown his ward. In the doorway, I ran into Count Golenishchev-Kutuzov. "You wish to see Musorgsky? He is dead."

It was his birthday. I entered the ward. My heart was involuntarily wrung by what I saw. The conditions in which Musorgsky died: his total solitude and the barren hospital surroundings in which a prominent talent had to die produced in me great melancholy. The big room with its plastered walls looked inhospitable, despite its tidiness. Except for the bare necessities it was empty. I could see that in this room an impoverished soul had died. Half of the room was partitioned off by a grey screen, behind which there were several other beds. Just across from the entrance there were a wardrobe, a writing desk, two chairs, and two small tables with newspapers and five or six books, one of which was Berlioz' treatise "On Instrumentation." Like a soldier, he had died with his weapon in his hand. To the right of the door there was a small bed, and on it was Musorgsky's body, covered with a grey hospital blanket. How he had changed! His face and hands, white as wax, made a strange impression on me—as if a total stranger were lying here. The expression of his face was, incidentally, peaceful; one could even have thought that he was sleeping, were it not for the deathly pallor. An involuntarily bitter feeling stirred my heart: I thought about the strange fate of our Russians. To have such talent as Musorgsky had had (his talent was recognized by everyone, even though they did not share his aspirations), to have all the qualities, to be superior, to live—and then to die in a hospital, among strangers, without a friendly or a loving hand to, at least, close his eyes. What is this fate that hounds our gifted ones. . . .

Soon, several of Musorgsky's close friends gathered: Vladimir Vasilievich Stasov, his brother D[mitrii] V[asilievich] Stasov, N[ikolai] A[ndreevich] Rimsky-Korsakov, Mr. Kel'chevskii the uhlan officer, a former roommate of Musorgsky's, and some others, including two ladies (one of whom, I believe, was Mr. Rimsky-Korsakov's wife).[4]

I[l'ia] E[fimovich] Repin, who had recently arrived from Moscow and who was an old friend of Musorgsky, was fortunate enough to have painted his portrait shortly before he died. The portrait had very successfully caught the expression of the composer's face. Soon this portrait will be part of a traveling exhibit.[5]

M[odest] P[etrovich] Musorgsky passed on in the prime of life. [Short biographical details follow.]

He was a highly likeable and good-natured person. It is extremely rare to find in the artistic world such a forgiving man, with so much tolerance for others' opinions. He had been, at times, the target of very wicked pranks, but his behavior, even toward unfriendly people, was invariably even-tempered and affable. Even though he sometimes scoffed at their banter, he did so in an extremely mild manner; in such instances his sense of humor, as well as his awareness of his own talent, prevailed. His humor, as is known, is seen in many of his works. I hope to speak about his work shortly; at the moment, I want to point out that he left two operas: *Khovanshchina*, which is completely finished although not orchestrated, and *The Fair at Sorochintsy*, which, on the contrary, has great gaps and is far from complete. Lately, he had been thinking about another opera—"Biron," but its music had not been written; he just played some excerpts for his friends and obstinately refused to put them in writing, saying that he "had it all very well memorized in [his] head."[6]

There were no limits to his generosity. A very great number of Petersburg concerts—especially charity concerts—were dependent upon his participation: on every stage he could be seen at the piano, diligently accompanying the artists. . . . With the same generosity he accompanied and willingly played excerpts from his operas in private circles and homes. It seems that his last visit to the editorial office of *New Time,* where he was a frequent visitor, took place on the eve of his illness.[7]

Yes, we have lost a great talent, and we have so few of them.

[Objecting to some details in the description of Musorgsky's last years as given by Rimsky-Korsakov in *My Musical Life,* in 1909 Ivanov brought forth the following thoughts, based on personal recollections.]

To say that Musorgsky's decline resulted from his opera's being taken out of the repertoire is unworthy of comment. Many others had seen their works taken off the stage and did not succumb as Musorgsky did. Nevertheless in the above-mentioned lines there is a good deal of truth. I knew Musorgsky during the last three or four years of his life, but at the time I was a very young man and did not pay enough heed to much in life. Still, even then, it seemed to me that Musorgsky had been abandoned by both friends and boon companions. He was always lonely, and this loneliness was felt very sharply by such a soft and tender nature. During that period he was deeply touched by any kindness shown to him, any kind word spoken to him. But it was only in passing that kindness and sweet words came his way. Nobody gave him a serious thought, and in the big city he undoubtedly felt lonely. I do not know what the author of *My Musical Life* means when he uses the term "professional composer" or for what reason, in the case stated, he uses it half ironically. Musorgsky, incidentally, was not, even in his last years, a true "professional composer"; he was only a "professional accompanist." Accompanists can now receive good money for their work, and some even cleverly manage various special deals; but that was not the case earlier, when the accompanist could not bring in a single farthing. Everyone appeared on stage "as an honor." Musorgsky was no exception. Contrary to the belief established by Musorgsky's friends, that he played the piano masterfully, I boldly state that the opposite is true. He was no pianist at all, and only people who themselves played badly could have thought that he played well. But he did follow the singer very well and was sometimes capable of a finely turned "phrase," as Korsakov said. When Musorgsky retired, he was left without means: he was unable to give concerts either as a soloist or as a composer. His only recourse was to become an accompanist in D[ar'ia] M[ikhailovna] Leonova's school, where he conscientiously pounded the scales for the students' solfeggio. Obviously, such a life could not have been gratifying for him, and he took to drinking brandy.[8] Furthermore, if his friends began to regard his compositions critically, as Korsakov himself indicated, there was no reason for other people not to do likewise. This was perfectly normal, and Musorgsky hardly would have suffered from their opinion. But because of Stasov's excessive efforts, a cold atmosphere had grown up around him. Stasov so violently attacked all those who refused to believe everything he shouted about Musorgsky, that many people turned completely away from the author of *Boris*. During Musorgsky's last years a particular atmosphere of general indifference was created, and it is this atmosphere which killed the tender nature of the composer. Stasov overdid it, as did the bear of the fable.[9]

Musorgsky fell ill at the home of Leonova. The latter was so frightened she requested that the ailing man—a man who had served her faithfully—be taken away as quickly as possible from the apartment of a woman already aged and all alone. Musorgsky had toured the provinces with her as her accompanist, and probably earned little if anything, since one can guess that Leonova, at the ebb of her career, did not make good box-office returns. Musorgsky's living conditions in his last years were simply appalling. The poet A[pollon] N[ikolaevich] Maikov told me how startled he was when he paid a visit to Musorgsky. It was two o'clock in the afternoon. Musorgsky lived in a small room on Ofitserskaia. Maikov found him sleeping in the armchair in evening dress. On the table were several bottles; there was nothing else in the room. I believe it. I also saw the conditions in which Musorgsky lay when he was at the Nikolaev Hospital, where he had been placed as an "orderly," thanks to the efforts of the compassionate L[ev] B[ernardovich] Bertenson. These wretched surroundings wrung one's heart. On the day of the composer's death I described his last days in a newspaper article, and in telling the truth I incurred Stasov's wrath[10] and the indignant displeasure of Leonova and her friends.

If one were to ponder carefully the history of Musorgsky's collapse, even in the form in which it is told in *My Musical Life,* one would be deeply touched. How far removed can truth be from what we think! The arrogant Musorgsky, as he was portrayed by so many people, was the same unfortunate artist who, like an abandoned child, was grateful for the smallest kindness or attention paid him.

Il'ia Tiumenev

IZ *Vospominanii o Rimskom-Korsakove*

FROM *My Recollections of Rimsky-Korsakov*

Il'ia Tiumenev (1855–1927), a student of Rimsky-Korsakov, was a novelist, painter, composer, writer of operatic libretti, and translator of the texts of Wagner's dramas. He kept a detailed diary, which he transformed into memoirs. He gives a precise account of the facts, although once in a while they show the bias of the "Rimsky-Korsakov camp."

.   .   .

On January 16, 1879, I was present at the first concert of the season at the Free Music School, arranged by Nikolai Andreevich [Rimsky-Korsakov].[1] At this concert we heard for the first time: "Kel'ia v Chudovom monastyre" [A cell in the Chudovo Monastery] from *Boris Godunov*,[2] Konchak's aria from *Prince Igor*,[3] and three complete numbers from *May Night*.[4]

To be honest, it was strange to listen to Vladimir Ivanovich Vasil'ev the First,[5] clean-shaven, in evening dress, with white gloves, half-sing, half-recite the immortal monologue of Pushkin's eternally famous monk-chronicler, who sat in his isolated cell at night in front of his manuscript. Near the tall figure of Vasil'ev the First stood the short figure of Vasilii Mikhailovich Vasil'ev the Second,[6] also clean-shaven and in evening dress—in the role of Grigory Otrepiev. In any case, one has to be thankful even for this evening-dress recital of the "Cell," since in the Mariinskii Theater, this scene, one of the principal scenes in Pushkin's *Boris Godunov*, was unceremoniously deleted.

From the following winter season, 1879–1880, I recall the first concert of the Free Music School, held on Tuesday, November 13. At this concert for the first time ever Nikolai Andreevich's new version of the scene at the Pecherskii Monastery, from *The Maid of Pskov*, was performed. It included the song of pilgrims about Alexei the Man of God; the scene of the tsar's hunt; the storm, with its song, which has become the now-familiar song of the young girls: "Akh ty, dubrava, dubravushka" [O, you leafy forest, dear leafy forest]. But our musical pleasure was not limited to those pieces. In the same concert, Nikolai Andreevich presented us with three new excerpts from *Prince Igor*. . . .[7]

All our musical generals were present. Cui, Borodin, Musorgsky, Stasov, the singers Leonova, Skal'kovskaia, and others. Furthermore, I was very pleased to learn from Nikolai Andreevich that the little old lady present at his concerts and always sitting with the guests of honor in a special soft armchair was none other than Liudmila Ivanovna Shestakova, née Glinka, the composer's sister. . . . "All of us like her very much," added Nikolai Andreevich, "from time to time, we pay her visits, we show her our works, and we enjoy her kindnesses toward us."

During the School's second concert, Nikolai Andreevich introduced us to excerpts from *Khovanshchina*: the Streltsy chorus, Marfa's song, and the Persian Dance. This was a new delight for us, and we particularly liked the chorus and the dance.[8]

IZ *Dnevnika*

FROM *The Diary*

February 16 [1881] (Monday). Yesterday, I heard the sad news that Musorgsky suffered a third seizure. On Saturday the 14th, Kostia[9] saw Tertii Ivanovich Filippov, who told him about his two earlier seizures. Filippov said that Modest Petrovich could not even sleep, or more exactly could not lie down, and that he would only sit on a sofa and doze for a few hours.

Kostia incidently added that Filippov told him that Musorgsky's condition had not caused any concern and that the seizures had not had dangerous consequences. Let's hope that Modest Petrovich's strong constitution will cope with this ailment, which will make us all happy, and that he will still bless us with more of his talented compositions.

March 16 (Monday). Berman[10] came in the evening with sad news: today in the Nikolaev Military Hospital, M[odest] P[etrovich] Musorgsky passed on. The scythe of the accursed grim reaper has been swinging through our Russian men of talent. He goes on mowing and mowing: Dostoevsky, Pisemskii, N[ikolai] Rubinstein, Azanchevskii,[11] and now Modest Petrovich! Will we ever see the end of this merciless harvest?

Modest Petrovich lived and died almost completely alone (it is said that he has a brother in Moscow[12] and nobody else it seems); besides, his material situation was far from enviable.

At the end he was placed in the care of Sergei Petrovich Botkin[13] (either because he knew him or because of Borodin's influence), but, in all likelihood, his situation was already quite hopeless, although it seemed that he started to recover from his two seizures. Stasov and Korsakov are taking care of the funeral. Korsakov asked Berman to make arrangements for an office for the dead tomorrow at eight in the evening with the Dumskii Circle, which will be done. Berman asked me to order a wreath on behalf of the Circle; I will go tomorrow.

Yes, our music has suffered a great loss! He was, perhaps, the most gifted one and in his mass of bizarre and confused work, so often, nuggets of pure gold sparkle in its depths! As regards the spontaneous national character of M[odest] P[etrovich]'s work, he was without any doubt the most "national" of all. . . .

March **17** (Tuesday). The entire morning I was busy with the wreath. At about eight o'clock in the evening we gathered in the church of the Nikolaev Military Hospital (near the Smol'nyi Institute). The church—a huge building with high ceilings and numerous windows—was lit only by four candles burning at the corners of the coffin. Although the wall lamps were also lit, they were burning so dimly that the church was in semi-darkness. The face of the deceased (already lying in the casket) was covered with muslin. A wreath from the Conservatory had been placed at the head of the coffin, and on its sides there were several tubs with decorative plants.

About two hundred people, mostly women, had gathered. Later, I learned that they were students from the Conservatory and the Free Music School. In the crowd I saw Stasov, Rimsky-Korsakov with his wife, Dr. Bertenson, and a General with a Stanislav ribbon, who turned out to be A[leksandr] P[orfirievich] Borodin. The people from our circle stood together. The service for the dead began; now the church was less dark, because of all the lighted candles. The face of the deceased was uncovered. It was deathly pale, the eyes were sunken, the face had sagged, but its expression was peaceful.

"So sviatymi upokoi" [With the saints give rest], beautifully executed by our people, made a very strong impression on me. There was no loud weeping, no sobs, as M[odest] P[etrovich] had no close relative left. (He did have a brother in Moscow, who, according to the rumors, visited him in the hospital, but whether he was present at the mass or not, I do not know: nobody said anything about him, nor did anybody point him out.)

After the service Berman, Solovyov, and I went to take a look at the wreath, shaped like a lyre, which I had ordered in the morning. For the sake of greater "verisimilitude" Kostia had advised us to add three green sticks for strings, and that was done. The result pleased us. From the flower shop, we went on to Mikhail Andreevich's for tea. On the way he talked to us about Musorgsky's last years.

When Modest Petrovich left his work at the Government Control (where he had been placed by T[ertii] I[vanovich] Filippov, although he was totally incapable of doing any work), he found himself without any income; Leonova's singing school, where he worked as an accompanist, most likely was not very profitable. Tertii Filippov—on very friendly terms with Musorgsky—had bought all of his compositions (except, probably, those already published)—past, present, and future. And together with Ostrovskii

(Mikhail Ivanovich, the writer's brother) and somebody else, Tertii Filippov gave Musorgsky 100 rubles a month (the purchase of his compositions was very likely a pretext for this subsidy). . . . [14]

As we arrived at Mikhail Andreevich's, we were still talking about Musorgsky. Mikhail Andreevich told us how one day, Modest Petrovich, while a guest at Tertii Filippov's, because of his extremely good nature and kindness, not only accompanied all who sang that evening, but also fulfilled the duties of a dance pianist; i.e., at the request of his hosts, he played waltzes, polkas, quadrilles (mainly of his own improvisations); and how at another occasion he sat somewhere in a corner and dozed. An earlier story by Berman about an evening at Filippov's was immediately recalled. Musorgsky was playing his *Khovanshchina* in front of the Aeropagus of the "Mighty Handful" (Korsakov at that time was absent). What a pity it was to see how those present (especially Cui) constantly pestered him by suggesting various deletions, changes, curtailings, and so forth (and strange as it might seem, the least critical one was Balakirev, who despite his benevolent attitude, was a despot). Such a pulling about and cutting to pieces of a new work, in which the ink was barely dry, done publicly, in front of everyone, and not privately, was not only the height of tactlessness but the epitome of downright hard-heartedness. The poor, unpretentious composer silently agreed, and deleted. . . . It left such a pitiful impression, at least in Berman's eyes.

As for me, Musorgsky did not give me the impression of being such an exceptionally unpretentious person, were I to judge him on his behavior in the dressing room of the Mariinskii Theater or at one of Leonova's concerts (in Kononov Hall). During that concert, he was listening to an orchestral performance of Schubert's "Lesnoi tsar" [The forest king]. Musorgsky apparently was in the greenroom, but since the door was open I could see him. He was standing, his head lowered, as if oblivious to everything else around him, but he reacted to almost every word with a peculiar gesture, with a peculiar movement of his body. For someone who did not know him, one would have said that he was simply striking a pose. But I saw in his behavior another reason: the slight agitation was due not only to the music but also to another cause, namely, his serious illness, which was already undermining his health.

Yesterday Berman met Ivan Fyodorovich Gorbunov: "A copper coffee pot can also burn out on alcohol," remarked Ivan Fyodorovich, "and a man is far more fragile than a coffee-pot."

Today Gavriushko[15] said that lately the author of *Boris* did not even have his piano, but with great pleasure was using the old cymbals belonging to Gavriushko, with whom he lived in furnished rooms. . . .

March 18 (Wednesday). As I left the house I met Kostia . . . we arrived at the hospital on time. Our wreath had already been brought (it cost 41 rubles). There were fewer people in the church than yesterday, but these people were most important: Balakirev, Korsakov, Nadezhda Nikolaevna,[16] Borodin and his wife, Cui and his wife (Berman saw Davydov,[17] who showed up for a few minutes), Napravnik, Mel'nikov, Kamenskaia and her husband Prianishnikov,[18] both Morozov brothers (the stage manager of the Russian opera and the cellist of the Mariinskii Theater), D[ar'ia] M[ikhailovna] Leonova, all three Stasov brothers,[19] N[ikolai] F[eofemptovich] Solovyov,[20] Ivanov from *New Time,* and others. It is said that, right there in church, Stasov gave Ivanov a dressing-down for the article on Monday . . . (for having included intimate details on the personal life of the deceased). After this, Ivanov moved around the church deeply offended, and at the cemetery he complained to one of his acquaintances for this public reproof.

The funeral procession was to begin at nine thirty in the morning, but Borovskii (the deacon from Smol'nyi) was late, and then something else delayed it. Anyhow, the procession began at ten o'clock (prior to that the blessing was sung by the choir). There were about fifteen wreaths: one from the friends of the composer (it was the biggest one); another from the Conservatory; ours, from the Free Music School; one with the inscription "To the Author of *Boris Godunov*," from Leonova's students; one from "Russian Hearts"—it was not very big but it was elegant—and then there were many others without inscriptions.

When we came out of the church there were no more than a hundred people, who for the most part were busy with their wreaths. Neither the Conservatory nor the Free Music School came (each had sent five or six representatives). The casket was put on the hearse and the procession set out. It was obvious that those in charge of the funeral were not very experienced: they were not even sure which road to follow, and our whole procession looked very much as if the deceased were being seen off by all his relatives.

Having gone for a couple of miles toward Slonovaia,[21] Korsakov, who was in front with the wreath "From Friends," ran back to us, asking: "Are we taking the right road?" "Yes, yes," we assured him. I explained to him that this was the best way, and that after Slonovaia we would turn left toward the Nevskii [Prospect]. He calmed down, asked again about which turn to make, and went to catch up with his wreath. Balakirev, accompanied by an unknown gentleman, apparently a close acquaintance, had taken a cab and driven to the Monastery: he was concerned about whether the cross was ready for the grave.

Our procession was moving along without any singing, since there was no one to sing: everybody was busy carrying a wreath. We had all hoped that the choirs from the Conservatory and the Free Music School would sing "Sviatyi Bozhe" [Holy God], at least on the street during the procession, but, as we said above, nobody came.

We were moving rather quickly (faster than at Dostoevsky's funeral), and before we realized it we had reached the Monastery. At the gates we sang

"Holy God" impromptu, the best we could, and the result was rather good. Almost everyone sang: even some women's voices were heard. Those who were carrying the wreaths were called back to the casket; they assumed that there the blessing would be sung, but it was not, due to a lack of planning. We kept on moving forward and once again sang "Holy God." On entering the second gate we sang it a third time, and still singing it, we brought the casket into Dukhovskaia Church. There everything was already in place. The Hours had been read, and the Nevskii choristers were there: the entire choir.

T[ertii] Filippov and Chumachevskii,[22] with the help of Mikhail Andreevich, had supervised the funeral. Filippov and Pobedonostsev obtained a free grave in the Tikhvin Cemetery; and Chumachevskii paid a visit to an archimandrite he knew, the ecclesiastic censor Iosif (he looked like a very nice, modest little man), who promised to officiate free of charge. The main precentor of the Nevskii Choir—L'vovskii (a former student of Zaremba)—announced that for such a distinguished composer he would bring his entire choir (*gratis*), and he did.

As soon as the casket was placed on the catafalque, the mass began. The wreaths had been put on and around the casket. Now Stasov approached the casket with a young lady (probably a niece or a relative). She was carrying two ribbons, one white and one red, and she fixed them to the wreaths alongside the casket. On the red ribbon, embroidered in long steel beads, was "Toward new shores!!!" and on the white one—in red Church Slavonic letters, "Oi, i slava zhe tebe za Borisa, slava!" [O! Glory to thee for Boris, glory!]. Probably there were similar ribbons with inscriptions on the other side, but it would have been improper of me to go around the casket and have a look. I am under the impression that these ribbons had belonged to the garlands presented for the first production of *Boris* and had been kept either by the composer or by some friends of his (maybe Stasov himself).[23]

Although Filippov had caught a cold at the tsar's funeral[24] and had not yet totally recovered, he was nevertheless present with his entire family. During the mass Balakirev stood at a distance leaning against a column (in the right corner of the church). Several times I turned back to look at his expressive face and his deep intelligent eyes. He was wearing a long, thick cloth overcoat, and under the collar one could see a blue tartan scarf; his cloth hat was very shabby.

I forgot to mention that while we were on the way another wreath had been added, with the inscription: "To the Artist from the Students of St. Petersburg College of Mines." During the mass other wreaths arrived. There should also have been a wreath from our students, but for some reason it was missing.[25] The day before, during the service for the dead, Cherkasov had said that someone was organizing a collection at the Academy since, apart from any artistic preferences, the students ought to express their gratitude for the constant and considerate participation by Musorgsky at their benefit concerts.[26] New people arrived: Stravinskii, Velinskaia, Schreder,[27] I

Medal struck in France in honor of Musorgsky

think (judging by the portrait), the artist Maksimov,[28] and others. Many people were already waiting for us at the church, and during the mass the large church nearly filled up. A wreath from the Bestuzhev School[29] had also been brought in.

Following "Gospodi vozzvakh" [Verses] (the host had been consecrated earlier), Berman, Kostia, and I went out "for a smoke." Since Berman had not eaten or drunk anything since morning, we went with him to have some tea at the tavern on the corner across from the Monastery, and from there we went on to the Tikhvin Cemetery, the final resting place of Glinka (right at the entrance and to the left) and (much further on and to the right) of Dargomyzhsky and Serov, and not far from them a place had been reserved for Modest Petrovich.

. . . Modest Petrovich's grave had been lined inside with bricks covered with lime: obviously the work had been done by expert hands.

In the church, when we returned, the priest was preaching about the power of music and its beneficial influence on the soul, on the progress of the entire society as far as goodness and love were concerned. . . . In conclusion, turning to Musorgsky's death, the preacher reminded his listeners of the saying that "the chain is no stronger than its weakest link," pointing out the embryonic state of our musical art, where talented people are more indispensable and valuable than in any other branch of the arts. Although the preacher was far from an accomplished orator, his sermon was rather good.

The funeral service was conducted by the archimandrite, and it was quite solemn. Those in charge of the funeral did not think to pass out candles, so the people, on their own, rushed out to buy them. At the candle table Stasov was kept very busy giving out the free candles, which had arrived too late; however, as there were not enough of them, the people bought what they needed.

The funeral service came to an end. After the farewell to the deceased, once more the wreaths were moved—there were already twenty of them—they were lined up and then taken from the church. The casket was carried by the friends of the deceased. There was a huge crowd at the grave. Berman and I planted our wreath in the snow without reaching the grave, and we climbed on a nearby bench. After the blessing the casket was lowered into the grave. Following this, Mel'nikov, with his pleasant, deep voice, read a poem sent by Lishin[30] (for some reason he was unable to attend). It was a rather good poem, with several nice thoughts. After the poem, people expected speeches, but there were none; even Stasov kept silent. The only thing that was said came from Nikolai Andreevich, who had been uncommunicative and even secretive on the subject of alleged musical works. Going through the crowd, in an intentionally loud voice (probably it had been prearranged), he said to Stasov that he intended to go over everything the deceased had left behind and edit it, and that everything was going to be finished and published, starting with *Khovanshchina*. For the musicians such a statement was dearer than a number of speeches. The public, which stood at a distance, began to disperse little by little. But by the grave, where the grave diggers had begun to close up the vault, it was as crowded as before. Finally the vault was closed, and the grave was filled up. As soon as the white wooden cross, with a proper inscription, was put up (the one that Balakirev had taken charge of), they began to tidy up the grave, which was all covered over with our wreaths. When the grave diggers began to close up the vault, some of those in charge of the funeral began to wonder whether the wreaths should also be placed in the vault. But Balakirev and Borodin were against the idea. This small episode pointed up the purely family character of the funeral. All the while it was drizzling, and when the casket was lowered into the grave, it began snowing; and it became terribly muddy and slushy around the grave. I put our wreath right in front of the cross and then tore a couple of leaves from the branch representing the curve of the lyre, in memory of the never-to-be-forgotten composer.[31]

Peace, thrice peace to your remains, kind, responsive man, with your gentle and forgiving heart. A man who, with his talent, had so fervently served his beloved great homeland!

N. Kompaneiskii

1. In the fall of 1852 Musorgsky entered the Cadet School of the Imperial Guards, which had been founded in 1823 and reorganized in 1838. His elder brother, Filaret, had entered the school the year before. From 1849 to 1851, Musorgsky had studied in a German school (Petrischule), and from 1851 to 1852 he was at a preparatory boarding school run by A. Komarov.

2. We ought to make some corrections to the description of the school as given by Kompaneiskii. According to the memoirs by the famous traveler-geographer P. Semyonov-Tashanskii, who had graduated from the School in 1845, General Sutgof was far from being the uncouth "martinet" described by Kompaneiskii. He was an educated man, fluent in German and French, and an expert in French history. He valued education and saw to it that the School had the best teachers and that the pupils made progress. The Cadet School of the Imperial Guards was one of the best educational institutes in Petersburg. The teaching program was well organized according to the standards of the time; and the highly qualified teachers knew how to stimulate the pupils' inquisitiveness and their yearning for knowledge. The curriculum was extensive, ranging from humanities and foreign languages to special military disciplines. In the year before Musorgsky entered the School, the literature instructor, A. Komarov, resigned from the School of Guards. (He was a friend of Gogol's and Belinskii's, and it was in his preparatory school that Musorgsky had studied.) Among the instructors were the famous professors Sukhomlinov and Perevlevskii (who replaced Komarov and whom Musorgsky would later remember with gratitude). All these positive sides of the educational life were combined with the life Kompaneiskii described (see P. Semyonov-Tashanskii, *Memuary* [Memoirs], vol. 1, Petrograd, 1917).

3. See below, note 1 of F. Musorgsky's recollections.

4. From Musorgsky's early works, only *Porte-enseigne Polka,* for piano, has been preserved. It was composed in 1852 and dedicated to his comrades at the School (see note 1 of F. Musorgsky).

5. Musorgsky recalls the priest Kirill Krupskii as follows: "While in the School I often visited Father Krupskii, our religion instructor . . . thanks to him I was able to get to the core of ancient religious music—Greek, Catholic, Lutheran." (Autobiographical note in *M. Musorgskii Literaturnoe nasledie. Pis'ma i avtobiograficheskie materialy* [Literary heritage. Letters and autobiographical material] Moscow, 1971, p. 267.)

6. Musorgsky finished the School of Guards in the summer of 1856 and enlisted in the reserve of the Preobrazhenskii Regiment. In October of the same year, when the reserve regiment was dismissed, he was transferred to the Preobrazhenskii Regiment.

7. Musorgsky retired in the summer of 1858 because he had decided to dedicate himself wholly to music (see below, V. Stasov's recollections).

8. Stasov sheds light on the time Musorgsky spent in the Regiment by providing information on the musical interests of the Regiment.

9. The chorus of *Porazhenie Sennakheriba* [The destruction of Sennacherib], based on Byron's verses, was composed in 1867. It was performed for the first time on March 6 of that year at a concert of the Free Music School under Balakirev's direction.

10. Kompaneiskii repeats the generally accepted legends about Musorgsky's illiteracy and his inability to work systematically. The first was rejected a long time ago by history, and the second one is refuted by the composer's letters and his Autobiographical Note.

11. Anton Rubinstein's opera *Demon,* based on Lermontov's poem, had its première in the Mariinskii Theater on January 13, 1875.

12. A musical prank composed in 1870 for voice and piano with a text by Musorgsky. It ridiculed Petersburg music critics Rostislav (Feofil Tolstoi's penname), A. Serov, and A. Famintsyn.

13. Final chorus of Glinka's opera *Zhizn' za tsaria* [A life for the Tsar]. It was performed by Musorgsky on a piano built by the Petersburg master piano builder Virt.

14. "Molitva devy" [The virgin's prayer], a popular piano piece by T. Bondarzhevskaia-Baranovskaia, was performed in the salons of that time.

15. Between 1862 and 1866 Musorgsky was composing the opera *Salammbô,* based on Flaubert's novel. The following passages have been preserved: Act 1, Scene 1—"The song of the Balearic Islander"; Act 2, Scene 2—in the Temple of Tanita in Carthage; Act 3, Scene 1—in front of the temple of Molokh (the glorification of Molokh); Act 4, Scene 1—in the dungeon of the Acropolis, the prison in the cliff, Mato in chains; Act 4, Scene 2—"The women's chorus." Later on Musorgsky used parts of the *Salammbô* music for *Boris Godunov.*

16. A. Serov's opera *Iudif'* [Judith] was staged at the Mariinskii Theater in May 1863.

17. Musorgsky did not take voice lessons *per se*. According to the recollections of his contemporaries, he had a very pleasant, but not strong, baritone voice.

18. Aleksandr Serov (1820–1871) was a critic and a composer. In his youth, he was a friend of Stasov's; he was close to Balakirev. Later he became an implacable enemy of the composers belonging to the Balakirev circle. Serov disapproved of Musorgsky's chorus so severely that his review of the concert in which it was performed for the first time did not even mention its title.

19. There is absolutely no information about Musorgsky's comrades who were "burning out their lives in endless carousing." The only aristocrat who was a friend to Musorgsky was A. Golenishchev-Kutuzov, who was much younger than the composer (see his recollections below and the notes pertaining to them). Besides, it is known that Golenishchev-Kutuzov was not a debaucher. Kompaneiskii himself speaks in the following paragraphs about Musorgsky's tragedy. The subsequent story about the staging of *Boris Godunov* is also based on rumors and is told inaccurately.

20. There is no information about the soirées with the "renowned composer." Most likely this also lies in the realm of gossip and legend. Corroboration for this assumption can also be found in the distorted information about Musorgsky's participation in the concerts. The singers valued Musorgsky very highly; furthermore, he never refused to participate in charity concerts for the students, and he performed willingly. There is no connection whatsoever between his performances as a popular accompanist and his alcoholism.

21. Apparently Kompaneiskii is talking about Pyotr Stepanovich Chaikovskii. The episode he describes never happened.

22. Kompaneiskii apparently visited Musorgsky at the end of February.

23. O. Petrov died February 28, 1878.

V. Stasov

Stasov's recollections of Musorgsky were taken from several works by Stasov:

The biographical essay "Modest Petrovich Musorgskii," first published in the journal *Vestnik Evropy* [The European herald], May 1881, pp. 285–316, and June 1881, pp. 506–545. It has often been reprinted, most recently in V. Stasov, *Stat'i o muzyke* [Articles on music], 3d ed. (Moscow, 1977).

"M. P. Musorgsky's Obituary," published in the newspaper *Golos* [Voice], no. 76, March 17, 1881; reprinted in *Articles on Music*.

"Perov i Musorgskii" [Perov and Musorgsky], originally published in the journal *Russkaia Starina* [Russian olden times], May 1883, pp. 433–458; reprinted in *Articles on Music*.

The pamphlet "Pamiati Musorgskogo" [In honor of the memory of Musorgsky], written for the unveiling of the monument on the composer's grave on November 27, 1885. After some minor changes it was published in the journal *Istoricheskii vestnik* [The historical herald], March 1886, pp. 644–656; reprinted in *Articles on Music*.

"Dvadtsat' pisem Turgeneva i moyo znakomstvo s nim" [Twenty letters of Turgenev and our acquaintanceship], first published in *Severnyi vestnik* [Northern herald] 10 [1888]:148; reprinted in A. Orlova, *Musorgsky's Days and Works*, p. 140.

The letter to N. Findeizen appeared in translation in A. Orlova, p. 191.

1. Stasov's memory fails him: Musorgsky retired in 1858. On May 1, he requested that he be relieved "because of family circumstances," and on June 11, his resignation was accepted by an order of the Preobrazhenskii Regiment. (A. Orlova, *M. P. Musorgsky's Days and Works: A Biography in Documents* [Ann Arbor: UMI Research Press, 1983], pp. 65–66.)

2. Lermontov was at the School of the Imperial Guards before its reorganization. He left the School in 1834.

3. Dargomyzhsky's opera *Kamennyi gost'* [The stone guest]. It was based on the unaltered text of a "small tragedy" by Pushkin. When he started to compose the opera Dargomyzhsky wrote: "I am trying to do something unbelievable: to write music based on *The Stone Guest*—as it is, without changing a single word" (letter to L. Karmalina, dated July 17, 1866, in *A. S. Dargomyzhskii, Avtobiografia. Pis'ma, Vospominaniia sovremennikov.* [Autobiography. Letters. Memoirs of his contemporaries], Petersburg, 1921, p. 119). Musorgsky admired the author of *The Stone Guest* and he dedicated the first number of his *Detskaia* [The nursery] ("Ditia s nianei") [With Nursey] to Dargomyzhsky with the words "To the great teacher of Musical Truth."

4. The Balakirev circle was also known as "Novaia Russkaia Shkola" [New Russian school] or "Moguchaia Kuchka" [The Mighty Handful]. The latter name came from an article by V. Stasov, "Slavianskii kontsert g. Balakireva" [Mr. Balakirev's Slavic concert], about a concert held during the ethnographic exhibition in 1867. Stasov expressed the wish that the Slavic guests would "forever remember the poetry, the feeling, the talent, and the skill of the small but already mighty handful of Russian composers." At first, enemies of the movement used this expression ironically, but later it became common usage.

5. This song is based on verses by Polezhaev.

6. Cui's opera *William Ratcliff*, based on Heine's work, was composed between 1868 and 1871 and performed in the Mariinskii Theater in 1869. This opera, as well as most of Cui's other works, is forgotten. The only song by Cui which is still

remembered is "Sozhzhyonnoe pis'mo" [The burnt letter], based on Pushkin's poem.

7. Rimsky-Korsakov was a Cadet in the Naval Academy from 1856 to 1862. He was introduced to the Balakirev circle in the fall of 1861 by a friend of Balakirev, the famous piano teacher F. Kanille, with whom Rimsky-Korsakov was studying. Rimsky-Korsakov had his first lesson in composition with Balakirev. Later he wrote: "Not only had Balakirev never had a systematic course in harmony and counterpoint . . . he, apparently, did not even recognize any need for these studies. . . . He was an excellent pianist, an outstanding reader of music, a fine improvisor, gifted by nature with a sense of correct harmony and voice-leading; he possessed a composing technique which was partly a natural gift and partly due to practicing his own attempts at composition. He had all the qualities required of a composer. He owed this to his enormous musical erudition, which was reinforced by his unusual, keen, and durable memory. . . . As a critic, *a critic of technique*, he was astonishing. He immediately grasped an imperfection of form . . . and he would, at once, sit at the piano and, improvising, show how to correct or change the composition. Due to his despotic character, he demanded that a given composition be redone exactly as he had indicated; and often, entire passages of works written by someone else belonged to him and not to the real author. He was unquestioningly obeyed since he had an extremely forceful personality. . . . However, despite his intelligence and brilliant abilities there was one thing he did not understand: what was good for him in the matter of musical education was far from good for the others. . . . Furthermore, he tyrannically demanded that his pupils' taste correspond exactly to his own." (N. Rimskii-Korsakov, *Letopis' moei zhizni* [My musical life] [Moscow 1955], pp. 17–18.)

8. Rimsky-Korsakov's Symphony in E-flat minor was performed for the first time on December 19, 1865, at a concert of the Free Music School. It was conducted by Balakirev and was extremely successful. Chronologically this work was the first Russian classical symphony, although it was not a landmark in the history of music. As a rule, the Russian composers of symphonies are Tchaikovsky (the first two movements of his First Symphony were played in 1867; in 1868 it was performed in its entirety) and Borodin (his First Symphony was heard in 1869).

9. Stasov enumerates Rimsky-Korsakov's songs based on poems by L. Mei, A. Kol'tsov, N. Shcherbin, and L. Afanas'ev. The symphonic picture *Sadko* was created in 1867 and performed for the first time that year. The theme for *Sadko* had been given by Stasov to Balakirev; Balakirev gave the same topic to Musorgsky, who, in turn, suggested it to Rimsky-Korsakov. The programmatic symphony *Antar* (Symphony No. 2) was at first to be a symphonic poem; it was based on a fairy tale by the famous Russian orientalist Osip Senkovskii. It was composed in 1868 and had its first performance in 1869.

10. About Borodin's First Symphony see note 8. His songs "Falshivaia nota" [The false note] and "Spiashchaia Krasavitsa" [The sleeping beauty] were based on his own texts. The first one was dedicated to Musorgsky.

11. During these years Musorgsky composed the following songs and romances: "Zhelanie" [Desire], to words by Heine, "Svetik Savishna" [Darling Savishna], "Seminarist" [The seminarian], "Ozornik" [The mischievous one], "Kozyol" [The he-goat], "Klassik" [The classicist], "Sirotka" [The orphan], to his own text, and "Evreiskaia Pesnia" [Hebrew song], based on words by L. Mei.

12. "Svetik Savishna" [Darling Savishna] was written in September 1866.

13. Anton Rubinstein (1829–1894) was a pianist of genius, a talented conductor and composer, and a prominent figure in the social and musical world. He played an exceptional role in Russian musical life as the founder of the Russian Musical Society and of the Petersburg Conservatory. Tchaikovsky was one of his students.

14. See the introductions to their memoirs in the present volume.

15. Musorgsky nicknamed the elder sister "Donna Anna Laura" and the younger one "our dear orchestra."

16. Osip Petrov (1807–1878) was an outstanding Russian bass. See the memoirs of N. Kompaneiskii and L. Shestakova in this volume.

17. Musorgsky began to compose the opera *The Marriage,* based on the unaltered text of Gogol's prose comedy, during the summer of 1868. While working on the first act (he did not compose anything further) Musorgsky wrote: "In *The Marriage* I am crossing the Rubicon. This is lifelike prose in music; it is not a disregard of simple human speech by the musician-poets; it is not speech cloaked by a heroic robe; it is respectful of human speech, a reproduction of that speech." (Letter to L. Shestakova dated July 30, 1868; this passage and all his letters are quoted from *M. P. Musorgskii, Literaturnoe nasledie, Pis'ma i avtobiograficheskie materialy* [M. P. Musorgsky. Literary heritage. Letters and autobiographical materials] [Moscow, 1971].) The work with this experimental opera was limited to the composition of one act; the Rubicon had been crossed, the mastering of a supple recitative had been achieved, and in the fall of 1868 Musorgsky undertook another work: the opera *Boris Godunov.*

18. On the manuscript of the piano score Musorgsky wrote this dedication: "I bequeath my student efforts to the eternal possession of dear Vladimir Vasil'evich Stasov, on his birthday. January 2, 1873. Modest Musorgsky alias Musorianin." (All the dedications are reprinted in A. Orlova, *M. P. Musorgsky's Days and Works.*)

19. The first version of the opera *Boris Godunov* was first presented to the Board of Directors of the Imperial Theaters in the early spring of 1870. The decision of the committee on operas was made in February 1871. They denied permission to stage the opera. The official reason for the denial is unknown.

20. Victor Hartmann (1834–1873) was an architect and an artist. Musorgsky's *Pictures from an Exhibition* was based on Hartmann's drawings.

21. Collection of texts of Russian songs by the folklorist Pavel Shein (1826–1900).

22. When composing the opera *Boris Godunov* Musorgsky used volumes X, XI, and XII of N. Karamzin's *Istoriia Gosudarstva Rossiiskogo* [History of the Russian state]. (A detailed study appears in A. Orlova and M. Shneerson, "After Pushkin and Karamzin," in *Musorgsky. In Memoriam 1881–1981,* Russian Music Studies #3, edited by Malcolm Hamrick Brown [Ann Arbor: UMI Research Press, 1982]. The Russian version of this article was published in the journal *Grani,* No. 119, 1981, with the title "Vopreki 'ustanovkam i skhemam' [In defiance of "Directions and schemes"].) Khrushchyov was not a *voevode* in Kromy, but Boris's envoy to Kromy.

23. Daniil Mordovtsev (1830–1905) wrote historical novels and historical essays.

24. *Drevnie russkie stikhotvoreniia* [Ancient Russian poems], that is, *Sbornik velikoruskikh narodnykh istoricheskikh pesen* [Collection of great Russian popular historical songs], by I. Khudiakov (Moscow, 1860). Stasov forgot that he had met Musorgsky at the concert of the Russian Musical Society in November 1868.

25. The singer of tales T. Riabinin came to Petersburg in November or December 1871. Musorgsky recorded from his singing performance the tunes of the *bylina* "Pro Dobryniu i Vasiliia Kazimirova" [Dobrynia and Vasilii Kazimirov] and "Pro Volgu i Mikulu" [Volga and Mikula] (published in *Onezhskie byliny, zapisannye Aleksandrom Fyodorovichem Gil'ferdingom* [Byliny of Onezh, recorded by Aleksandr Fyodorovich Gilferding] [Petersburg, 1873], pp. 435–438).

26. Vladimir Nikol'skii (1836–1883), philologist, Pushkin scholar, and Musorgsky's friend, was one of the regular guests at L. Shestakova's. Not only did he advise Musorgsky to transpose the scenes of the finale in *Boris Godunov,* but it was precisely on his advice that Musorgsky chose Pushkin's tragedy as the subject of this opera.

27. Dargomyzhsky died on January 5, 1869. By that time the "Prologue" and the "Scene at the Inn" from *Boris Godunov* had been composed.

28. Vladimir Purgold (1818–1895) was a prominent civil servant, an amateur singer, and the uncle of Aleksandra and Nadezhda Purgold. The sisters lived in his home after their father's death. Alina Khvostova (1846–1904), mezzo-soprano, was a singing instructor at the Petersburg Conservatory.

29. Rimsky-Korsakov's *Pskovitianka* was being composed almost simultaneously with Musorgsky's *Boris Godunov*. Its first performance was held in the Mariinskii Theater, January 1, 1873. The first performance of three scenes from *Boris Godunov* was held on February 5 of the same year.

30. For information concerning Fyodor Komissarzhevskii and Iu. Platonova see *Vospominaniia* [Recollections] by Iu. Platonova, below.

31. Nikolai Lukashevich (1821–1894) was the master costumer in charge of the repertoire of the Imperial Theaters. He was close to Iu. Platonova.

32. P. Stasova sent the garland for Musorgsky not to the theater but to his house. Coming back from the theater he stumbled in the dark on something prickly and got scared. Later he wrote to P. Stasova: "I am still the same Musorianin, although I have become inured to the success after you had wreathed it." (Letter dated July 23, 1873.)

33. Musorgsky gave one photograph to V. Stasov and another to P. Stasova. On the first was written: "Here I am straight from the first rehearsal of my *Boris,* my dear *généralissime.*" On the second he wrote: "To Poliksena Stepanovna Stasova. That is how I looked after my first rehearsal of *Boris*; well, take me but not as No. 6280 [the number of the photograph] but as Musorianin. January 10, 1874. And because of the garland you sent me I feel pressured. I must do what I must. Thank you, dear. The same Musorianin."

34. Stasov has in mind the following critics: N. Solovyov, from the newspaper *Birzhevye vedomosti* [Stock news]; G. Laroche, from the newspaper *Golos* [Voice]; V. Baskin (the pen name of Foma Pichikato), from the newspaper *Peterburgskii listok* [Petersburg leaflet]); A. Famintsyn, from the journal *Muzykal'nyi listok* [Musical leaflet]; and finally C. Cui, from the newspaper *St. Peterburgskie vedomosti* [St. Petersburg news]. The last article was unexpected, and it was as knife in the back. Cui reproached the author of *Boris Godunov* for having composed the opera with haste and immaturity as well as for being complacent. After reading Cui's article Musorgsky wrote to Stasov: "It seems that *Boris* had to appear for people to show their true colors. The tone of Cui's article is odious." (Letter dated February 6, 1874.)

35. During Musorgsky's lifetime *Boris Godunov* had 21 performances.

36. For the second version of *Boris Godunov* Musorgsky wrote the Polish Act (two scenes) and the scene at Kromy; he developed the role of the hostess of the inn (the song "Poimala ia siza seleznia" [I caught a dove-gray drake]); he reworked the scenes in the cell and in the tsar's chambers; he wrote a new version of Boris's monologue; and he added the genre scenes. He also deleted the scene at St. Basil's Cathedral.

37. From the words "I shall never forget" to the end of the paragraph, this is an excerpt from a letter from V. Stasov to A. Kerzin, dated April 20, 1905 (*Muzykal'nyi sovremennik* [Musical contemporary], no. 2, 1916, letter XIV.) Rimsky-Korsakov writes in detail about his life with Musorgsky (see *My Musical Life*).

38. Stasov gives the wrong title to Musorgsky's vocal cycle; it should read "Pesni i pliaski smerti" [Songs and dances of death].

39. Vania is a trouser role in the opera *Zhizn' za tsaria* [A life for the tsar]; Ratmir, another trouser role, is from the opera *Ruslan i Liudmila* [Ruslan and Ludmila] by Glinka.

40. "Sirotka" [The Orphan] ("Barin moi milen'kii") [King gentleman, good gen-

tleman]) is a song by Musorgsky based on his own text and composed in 1868. As for its shattering rendition by A. Petrova, see also Shestakova's "My Evenings," below. The author himself corroborates this in the autograph of the manuscript he offered to the singer: "Concocted by Musorgsky without any *marks* (one cannot infringe on genius) for the brilliant Anna Iakovlevna Vorobyova-Petrova. Even he did not dream *what* Anna Iakovlevna Vorobyova-Petrova could create out of this humble 'Orphan.' May, 1874. Musorgsky." (From *Sovetskaia muzyka* [Soviet music], no. 10. 1967, pp. 70–71.)

41. A list of the subjects recorded by Golenishchev-Kutuzov has been preserved: "1. The Rich Man. 2. The Proletarian. 3. The Grand Gentleman. 4. The Dignitary. 5. The Tsar. 6. The Young Girl. 7. The Peasant. 8. The Child. 9. The Merchant. 10. The Priest. 11. The Poet." The facsimile exists only in the Russian text.

42. Between 1872 and 1880 the following passages of *Khovanshchina* were composed: In 1873 Marfa's song "Iskhodila mladyoshenka" [The maiden wandered] and the scene of Marfa with Susanna; in 1874 the Introduction "Rassvet na Moskve-reke" [Dawn on the Moscow River]; in 1875 the first scenes of the first and third acts, and the beginning of the second act; in 1876 Shaklovityi's aria from the third act, the Persian Dance, and the end of the second act; in 1878 Marfa's divination scene from the second act; in 1879 Marfa's song "The Maiden Wandered" was orchestrated; in 1880 the beginning of the last scene and the conclusion of the third act, and the first scene of the fourth act (Khovanskii's chambers). "Our *Khovanshchina* is completed, except for a short passage in the final scene of the mass self-immolation by fire: we will need to chat about it together, for this 'rascal' is totally dependent on stage technique." (Letter to V. Stasov, dated August 22, 1880.)

43. During his last years, starting with 1876, in addition to his work on *Khovanshchina*, Musorgsky wrote "Polkovodets" [The field marshal], the fourth and concluding number of *Pesni i pliaski smerti* [Songs and dances of death]); a series of pieces for *Sorochinskaia Iarmarka* [The fair at Sorochintsy]; songs based on words by Aleksei Tolstoi; some works for piano; and the song "Blokha" [The flea].

44. This passage refers to the final wording of the *Khovanshchina* libretto. During the summer of 1880, to satisfy his clients (they were to give him a subsidy when *Khovanshchina* was completed), Musorgsky feverishly deleted entire passages of what had already been composed. The manuscripts have been preserved, and nothing in them indicates that the composer planned to make any deletions. One can assume that the shortened version of the libretto was not the author's final intention but a sort of "document" testifying to the completion of the opera (which in reality was not entirely finished). Unfortunately, it is exactly this, the incomplete libretto, that M. Pekelis—the editor of the volume in which the literary texts of the composer are included—used as the basic text of *Khovanshchina* despite the musical version. Besides, Pekelis did not take into account the composer's unfortunate condition in the summer of 1880, the last year of his life. (The libretto is published in *M. P. Musorgskii Literaturnoe nasledie. Literaturnye proizvedeniia* [M. P. Musorgsky literary heritage. Literary works.] [Moscow, 1972], pp. 124–148.)

45. Musorgsky himself wrote to V. Stasov on August 27–28, 1880: "Khovanshchina is already on *the eve* of completion: but the instrumentation—Ye, gods!" Meanwhile, as early as August 2, 1876, Musorgsky had written to Shestakova: "Almost everything is composed; now one has to write and rewrite. If only I did not have to go to work as well, that's what stands in the way."

46. Several "conclusions" to *Sorochinskaia Iarmarka* [The fair at Sorochintsy] exist. V. Shebalin's version is considered the best.

47. The vocal cycle *Bez solntsa* [Sunless], based on A. Golenishchev-Kutuzov's verses, belongs to the dawn of Musorgsky's creativity. It was composed simulta-

neously with the ballad "Zabytyi" [Forgotten] and *Kartinki s vystavki* [Pictures from an exhibition] in 1874. The songs "Spes' " [Pride passes by, puffed up], "Oi, chest' li to molodtsu" [Ah, is it an honor for a young man to weave flax?], "Gornimi tikho letela dusha nebesami" [The soul calmly flew through the heavenly empyrean], "Ne bozhiim gromom gore udarilo" [Grief does not crash like God's thunder], and "Rassvetaetsia, rasstupaetsia" [Grief disperses and gives way] are based on verses by A. Tolstoi.

48. The two capriccios for piano—"Na iuzhnom beregu Kryma (Gurzuf u Aiu-Daga. Iz putevykh zametok)" [On the southern shore of Crimea. (Gurzuf at Aia-Dag. From travel notes)] and "Bliz iuzhnogo berega Kryma (Baidary)" [Near the southern shore of Crimea (Baidarki)]—were composed in 1879. "Buria na Chyornom more" [Storm on the Black Sea] has not been preserved. The project "Bol'shaia siuita" [Big suite], for orchestra with harps and piano on themes from the Transcaspian region, was apparently never written.

49. Beginning with 1872 not only are Musorgsky's letters to Stasov filled with simple complaints about his "unhappiness at work" but these letters show the composer's depressed state of mind, due to the fact that he had to go to work (see above, Preface).

50. Musorgsky worked from December 21, 1868 to September 30, 1878 in the Department of Forestry of the Ministry of State Properties. Tertii Filippov (1826–1899), an important civil servant and a State Comptroller, was an amateur musician and expert on folk art. (Rimsky-Korsakov recorded folk songs right from Filippov's lips; the collection of songs was published under the names of Filippov and Rimsky-Korsakov.) Filippov was a great admirer of Musorgsky's talent. He literally saved the composer from starvation and poverty at a time when the composer was under threat of dismissal from the Forestry Department. (Musorgsky was unable to fulfil his duties, his bouts of hard drinking having become habitual.) Filippov hired Musorgsky as a member of the temporary commission of the Government Control on October 1, 1878. But the composer's condition was worsening; he was incapable of working, and on January 1, 1880, he was dismissed, despite all of Filippov's efforts. Then Filippov, Stasov, and several other admirers of Musorgsky joined together and provided him with 100 rubles a month for the completion of *Khovanshchina*. Simultaneously another group (Ukrainophiles) collected 75 rubles for the completion of *Sorochinskaia Iarmarka* [The fair at Sorochintsy]. Unfortunately all this help came too late; it was impossible to save Musorgsky.

51. The opera *Boris Godunov* was not taken out of the repertoire but it was performed very rarely. Its last performance during Musorgsky's life, the 21st, was held on February 9, 1879. *Boris's* "castration" (i.e., the deletion of the scene at Kromy) began with the thirteenth performance, on October 20, 1876. At the time the scene in the cell had never been performed.

52. Musorgsky and Leonova's concert tour in southern Russia and later in the principal cities of Russia ended in Tver'. That this tour was an enormous success is evident, not only from the newspapers, but also from Musorgsky's letters. The following spring (1880) Musorgsky and Leonova returned to Tver' with two concerts, which were also very successful. For their stay in Yalta, see S. Fortunato's recollections below.

53. See K. Wolfurt, *Mussorgskii* (Stuttgart, 1927) and M. Ivanov's "Obituary" in the present work.

54. Musorgsky's birthday was not on March 16 but March 9. For details see A. Orlova, *Musorgsky's Days and Works . . .* , pp. 47–48. See also Nikolai Novikov, "Ego rodoslovnaia" [His genealogy] *Sovetskaia muzyka* [Soviet music], No. 3, 1989,

pp. 32–38; and *U istokov velikoi zhizni* [The sources for a great life] (Lenizdat, 1989), pp. 65–66.

55. In Musorgsky's letters to Stasov there is no reference to this theme, but it seems that they had conversations about it.

56. In Turgenev's *Dym* [Smoke] (1867), chap. 14, one of the characters—Potugin—has a scoffing monologue about Russian art in general and Glinka in particular.

57. "Rogdana" was an unfinished fantastic opera by Dargomyzhsky.

58. The music for Shakespeare's tragedy *King Lear* was composed by Balakirev between 1858 and 1861.

59. The first version of the chorus of *Porazhenie Sennakheriba* [The destruction of Sennakherib] (1867) was dedicated to Balakirev and its second version (1873) to Stasov.

60. From 1867 to 1869, while Balakirev was the conductor of the Russian Musical Society, he popularized the works of the Russian composers. Because his activity provoked the displeasure of the "pro-Germans," he was relieved of his duties. This event in turn caused the indignation of all the Russian musicians, whatever inclinations they had. Tchaikovsky responded with an irate article in *Golos iz moskovskogo muzykal'nogo mira* [Voice from the Muscovite musical world], in which, among other things, he wrote: "It would be very sad if the expulsion from a higher musical institution of a man who was its adornment did not provoke the protest of the Russian musicians. . . . Mr. Balakirev can now say what the father of Russian philology uttered when he learned of his expulsion from the Academy of Sciences: 'One can dismiss the Academy from Lomonosov,' said the genius 'but Lomonosov cannot be dismissed from the Academy'" (in the newspaper *Sovremennaia letopis'* [Contemporary chronicle], no. 16, 1869; reprinted in P. Chaikovskii, *Muzykal'nye kriticheskie stat'i* [P. Tchaikovsky, Articles of musical criticism] [Moscow, 1953], pp. 28–30).

61. The family of the artists, the Makovskiis, tried their best to show *Kamennyi gost'* [The stone guest] to Turgenev. It was then that K. Makovskii drew his caricature of the Balakirev circle (which has been attributed to his wife, Elena Makovskaia). For details, see below, Shestakova, "My Evenings."

62. Apparently Musorgsky did not tell Stasov about his meeting with Turgenev on March 22, 1874, when the writer visited the Petrovs and had the opportunity of getting to know Musorgsky's works as performed by O. and A. Petrov and by the composer himself. Turgenev wrote to Pauline Viardot about this encounter and the strong impression it had made on him. (Letter dated May 22, 1874 in Ivan Tourguénev, *Nouvelle correspondance inédite*, vol. 1 [Paris, 1971].)

63. Turgenev regarded Tchaikovsky especially highly. Regarding the opera *Evgenii Onegin* [Eugene Onegin], he wrote to Tolstoi: "undoubtedly remarkable music; the lyrical, melodious passages are especially good." (Letter dated November 27, 1878. Quoted from A. Orlova, *Dni i gody P. I. Chaikovskogo, Letopis' zhizni i tvorchestva* [Days and years of P. I. Tchaikovsky. Chronicle of his life and works] [Moscow, 1940], p. 192.)

64. Nadezhda Opochinina (1818–1874) was eighteen years older than Musorgsky. From his youth he was her enthusiastic admirer, but it is difficult to say whether Opochinina shared his feelings. There is no proof of intimacy. However, the works he dedicated to her betray these deeply hidden feelings for her. He dedicated the following works to her: "Strastnyi eksprompt" [Passionate impromptu] for piano, with the inscription: "Memories of Bel'tov and Liuba" (from Herzen's novel *Kto vinovat?* [Whose fault?]); a song based on Kurochkin's verses "Rasstalis' gordo my" [Proudly we parted]; "Noch' " [Night], which is based on Pushkin's poem; "Zhelanie" [Desire] ("Khotel by v edinoe slovo" [In one single word I would like]), based

on Heine's verses, with an undeciphered inscription: "Dedicated to Nad. Petr. Opochinina (in memory of her criticism of me)." In addition, the musical lampoon "Klassik"[The classicist] was also dedicated to Opochinina. The vocal prank "Strekotuniia beloboka" [The white-flanked magpie] was dedicated to her and her brother. Nadezhda Opochinina—an outstanding and strong-willed person—might have been Marfa's prototype in *Khovanshchina*. And Musorgsky might have had her in mind when he wrote to Stasov: "If a strong, passionate and beloved woman powerfully embraces the man she loves, then, although he realizes that there is violence, he does not want to escape from this embrace, for the violence is a 'boundless bliss,' for because of this violence 'the young blood blazes with flame.' I am not ashamed of the comparison: however you twist and flirt with the truth, one who has experienced love in all its freedom and might *has lived,* and he remembers *how beautiful life was,* and he will not throw a shadow on a past bliss." (Letter dated October 18, 1872.) The unfinished song "Zlaia smert'. Nadgrobnoe pis'mo" [Wicked death. Funeral letter] (based on Musorgsky's own text) is also dedicated to the memory of Opochinina.

65. Mariia Shilovskaia (1830–1879; née Verderevskaia; by her second marriage, Begicheva) was an amateur singer and a student of Glinka and of Dargomyzhsky. Apparently Musorgsky talks about his youthful passion for Shilovskaia in one of his letters to Balakirev (from Moscow, where he was then a guest at the Shilovskies'): "There was a time when I nearly went under, not musically, but morally—I crawled out; however, you will find out later what really happened—if our conversation should touch this matter—there was a woman involved." (Letter dated January 19, 1861.) There is no name mentioned, and apparently they never talked about it. About Musorgsky's love for the singer Aleksandra Latysheva (née Lileeva, 1830–1872) nothing is known.

F. Musorgsky

1. In 1849 Musorgsky began to take lessons with Anton Herke, a famous piano professor in St. Petersburg, immediately after the latter's arrival in Petersburg. (Herke later became professor at the Conservatory; Tchaikovsky was also one of his students.) The composer writes in his Autobiographical Note: "My father, who adored art, decided to develop his son's aptitudes; and his subsequent musical studies [after lessons with his mother] were with Anton Herke in Petersburg. The professor was so pleased with Musorgsky that he assigned him, a twelve-year-old boy, to play the concert rondo by Herz during a concert held in the house of the lady-in-waiting Riumina." (*M. P. Musorgskii, Literaturnoe nasledie.* [M. P. Musorgsky, Literary heritage], p. 267.) After his father's death, when the family's financial situation deteriorated, Musorgsky's lessons with Herke were less frequent at first; later they were stopped completely.

2. Johann Kaspar Lavater (1741–1801) was a famous Swiss philosopher physiognomist.

3. Musorgsky met Aleksandr Dargomyzhsky (1813–1869) through his friend F. Vanliarskii. They were at school and in the regiment together. Vanliarskii was very fond of music.

4. Regarding Musorgsky's service, see above, note 50 in V. Stasov's memoirs.

5. From the summer of 1856 to the spring of 1862 Musorgsky lived on Grebetskaia Street, near Raz″ezzhaia Street, in Tuliakov's house. Following Filaret's wedding and their mother's departure for the country, the brothers established their residence in house number 22/27, at the corner of Znamenskaia and Basseinaia streets. (This address was established recently and appeared in the newspaper

Vechernii Leningrad [Evening Leningrad] of June 15, 1989.) The former apartment of the Musorgsky brothers has been used as a post office for a long time. Filaret Musorgsky's wife was Tat'iana Balakshina (1837–1897). The friendly relationship between the composer and his sister-in-law is evident from the dedication he wrote on the photograph album he offered his *belle-soeur*: "To my dear sister Temira Musorgskaia in memory of her having come with my brother Filaret Musorgsky to the first performance of the opera *Boris Godunov*." (The album was preserved in the Musorgsky family and has been donated by Filaret Musorgsky's granddaughter to the composer's museum in Russia.)

6. Filaret is thinking of the so-called commune where the composer lived with his friends. At the time, young people shared quarters in communes, having been influenced by the novel *Chto delat'?* [What is to be done?] by N[ikolai] Chernyshevskii (1828–1889). Musorgsky's commune was located in house number 70 on Ekaterinskii Canal. Musorgsky dedicated his piano piece "Detskoie skertso" [Children's scherzo] to Nikolai Levashev, one of the members of the commune.

A. Borodin

1. Musorgsky resigned in 1858.
2. Mendelssohn's Third ("Scottish") Symphony.
3. Musorgsky had written the Scherzo in B-flat major in 1858.
4. Sergei Botkin (1832–1889) was a famous physician-therapist, one of the founders of Russian clinical medicine, a professor at the Surgico-Medical Academy, Borodin's comrade, and an amateur musician.
5. Rimsky-Korsakov's First Symphony in E-flat minor (second version in E minor). Rimsky-Korsakov was at sea from October 1862 to May 1865.

M. Balakirev

1. Musorgsky began to take lessons with Balakirev at the end of 1857.
2. In his Autobiographical Note, the composer himself tells about his studies with Balakirev: "The nineteen-year-old composer covered the entire history of the development of musical art—with examples, with exacting and systematic analysis of all the foremost musical works in chronological order. This study was always accompanied with the execution of the musical works on two pianos." (*M. P. Musorgskii, Literaturnoe nasledie.* [M. P. Musorgsky, Literary heritage], p. 268.)
3. This is absolutely false. Musorgsky ceased to consult Balakirev at the beginning of the summer of 1867, as a result of the master's rejection of "Witches" in *Night on Bald Mountain*.
4. The fact that Balakirev divorced himself from the circle was a result of the sharp change which took place in Balakirev himself. Material hardships played a great role: his father's death, the necessity of having to care for his sisters, the failure of his concerts in Nizhnii-Novgorod, and his break with the Russian Musical Society. Balakirev began consulting a fortune-teller, and he turned into a bigot. His despotic character played a great part in his break with the circle. Balakirev was unable to understand that his disciples had matured, that they had grown independent in their creativity and individuality. Borodin wrote that Balakirev had lost his mind. Borodin was not very far from the truth: a psychological breakdown must have taken place. Later on, Balakirev again began to meet his old comrades, but the previous relationships were not reestablished. In his *Letopis' moei muzykal'noi zhizni* [My musical life], Rimsky-Korsakov wrote about this extensively and in detail (although quite tendentiously). See also the correspondence of Balakirev and Stasov as well as Borodin's *Letters*.

A. Unkovskaia

1. Unkovskaia's father, Vasilii Zakhar'in, an amateur singer, was close to the Balakirev circle during its earlier period of activity.
2. Unkovskaia's mother, Avdot'ia, née Arsen'eva, was an amateur pianist. She was the sister of the Sanskrit scholar Aleksandr Arsen'ev, who was also close to the Balakirev circle (he had been nicknamed "Mustafa" by the circle). Unkovskaia also mentions her mother's other brother, Konstantin, who was also an amateur singer.
3. Nikolai Borozdin, a lawyer and amateur musician, was nicknamed "Pyotr" (Peter) and "Petra" by the Balakirev circle.

V. U.

1. The family of the opera singer Pyotr Gumbin (a baritone).
2. "Lieber Augustin" was a popular Austrian and German song; the waltz is from Gounod's opera *Faust; Kamarinskaia* is a fantasy for orchestra by Glinka.
3. Andzholina Bosio (1824–1859), an Italian soprano, performed in Petersburg between 1856 and 1859, and it was there that she died.
4. Osip Petrov was the first to perform the part of Ivan Susanin in Glinka's opera *Zhizn' za tsaria* [A life for the tsar]. He performed this part for half a century.
5. A card game.

N. Rimskaia-Korsakova

1. The first encounter of the Balakirev circle and the Purgold sisters took place on March 5, 1868.
2. A black or brown mineral, the chief source of metallic tin.
3. Ivan the Terrible has a role in the opera *Pskovitianka* [The maid of Pskov] by Rimsky-Korsakov; and Tsar Boris is the main character in the opera *Boris Godunov* by Musorgsky.
4. Nadezhda Rimskaia-Korsakova's diary from before her marriage gives interesting additional details on Musorgsky's character. It deals with the first years of their acquaintance: "He has a way—probably because of excessive vanity—of never starting a conversation, of never making the first move, of never forcing someone else to speak, as if he were afraid of showing that it gives him pleasure to talk with that person. He wants those who consider it a particular pleasure to talk to him to make the first move. The same thing also happens in other cases: because of vanity, he is never the first one to volunteer to bring his songs. Although he knows what pleasure they give, he waits to be asked. Again for the same reason he never asks Sasha to sing, although I know perfectly well how highly he thinks of her singing. Particularly when he is by himself. . . . In such a case, he usually comes with the idea of performing some work of his own, to show something new, and he wants exclusive attention, he wants to fill the entire evening with himself. In short, the result is (at least I have come to this conclusion) that the most important trait in his character is this vanity. . . . I disagree with those who think that he is not intelligent. He has a peculiar, original, and very spirited mind. But sometimes he abuses this spirited turn of mind out of a desire to strike a pose, to show that he is quite unique or because it is ingrained in his nature. The first is probably true. He has too much pepper in him, if one can express oneself this way. The nickname that my sister and I gave him (we also nicknamed all the others) is Humor. I find it quite appropriate since humor is indeed his most important trait. But he lacks warmth, and gentleness. Dear "Iskrennost' " [Candor; Rimsky-Korsakov's nickname] has so much of it. Perhaps he does not have the ability to be easily carried away and to love. I am not yet sure of that.

But, I repeat, he does not possess gentleness and indulgence toward the others." (Entry of August 29, 1870.) Later she added: "All this is incorrect; or at least many things are incorrect; generally speaking, this description of him is not good." "It is incorrect only as far as gentleness and warmth are concerned; he has both of them, as I had the opportunity to discover myself." (A. Rimskaia-Korsakova, *N. A. Rimskii-Korsakov, Zhizn' i tvorchestvo*, [N. Rimsky-Korsakov, life and works] [Moscow, 1935], Part 2, pp. 85–86.

5. In the scene at Khovansky's in the opera *Khovanshchina*.

6. The first performance was in a concert of the Free Music School under Rimsky-Korsakov's direction on November 27, 1879. (See below, memoirs by Rimsky-Korsakov and by Tiumenev.)

7. This statement is an example of the biased attitude of Musorgsky's friends. It is difficult to believe that, with his keen ear and his startling memory, he "did not notice" the changes made by Rimsky-Korsakov in the "Persian Dance." More likely, it was the result of his illness. But again, possibly, it was due to his usual tactfulness. Finally, the composer was not planning on dying soon—and he might have accepted with gratitude the assistance of Rimsky-Korsakov, who had come to his aid for the concert. And who knows whether Musorgsky would have kept the changes made by Rimsky-Korsakov, were he to work on the orchestration. Perhaps he would have created his own version.

S. Fortunato

1. V. V. Stasov, Fortunato's natural father.

2. Dmitrii Stasov (1828–1918) was a lawyer and a well-known figure in the musical world and in society.

3. The dates of Leonova and Musorgsky's concerts in Yalta have not been established absolutely. More than likely, the two concerts were held on September 7 and 8. In any case, in his letters to Shestakova and V. Stasov (September 9 and 10), Musorgsky says that in several cities, as well as in Yalta, works by Glinka and by the composers of the Balakirev circle had been performed. Therefore, by September 9, the concerts in Yalta had already taken place.

4. Musorgsky wrote about his stay in Yalta: "And what wonderful places we have seen, what lovely scenery, what a vivifying air. . . . Crimea's southern shore is magic: either formidable and inaccessible, frowning with the clouds hanging above the cliffs, or tender and hospitable with the most luxurious, charming gardens, which seem to be built of air, dressed from head to foot with rare, twining vegetation; through this intricate garb one can see the light, fretted cornices with lacy galleries and balconies. And in addition to all this a bright blue sky and a sea green as an emerald." (Letter to P. Shcmaev, September 19, 1879.)

5. Borodin's opera *Kniaz' Igor'* [Prince Igor] and Cui's opera *William Ratcliff*.

V. Komarova-Stasova

1. V. Komarova-Stasova was born in 1862; therefore, she is talking about the year 1869.

2. The second series of *Detskaia* [The nursery]: "Na dache. Iz detskoi zhizni" [At the *dacha*. From childhood] has two songs: "Kot Matros" [The sailor cat] and "V Iukki verkhom na palochke" [In Iukk' riding on a stick]; the songs "Son" [Dream] and a fourth one (without title) were not preserved, and possibly were not written down.

3. From *William Ratcliff*, an opera by Cui.

4. Konchak's aria from the opera *Kniaz' Igor'* [Prince Igor], by Borodin.

5. The three scenes were performed on February 5, 1873. The première of the entire opera was held on January 27, 1874.

6. The cast of *Boris Godunov* was as follows: O. Palechek—Rangoni, O. Petrov—Varlaam, I. Mel'nikov—Boris, F. Kommissarzhevskii—The Pretender. A. Krutikova took the part of the hostess much later; at the première it was sung by A. Abarinova. Komarova-Stasova's memory fails her: when only the three scenes were performed, it was Leonova who sang the part of the hostess.

7. The benefit was for the manager of the opera company, G. Kondrat'ev.

8. The first performance of the opera *Kniaz' Igor'* [Prince Igor] took place in 1890 after Borodin's death (the opera was finished by Rimsky-Korsakov and Glazunov). M. Kariakin sang the role of Konchak.

9. Komarova-Stasova is giving the titles of the scenes in the tsar's chambers from the opera *Boris Godunov*.

10. "Sirotka" [The orphan] was composed in 1868, "Zabytyi" [Forgotten] in 1874, and "Trepak" in 1875.

11. Tararui is the historical nickname of Ivan Khovanskii. From the episodes enumerated here, only one scene has been preserved: that of the destruction of the clerk's booth. It was deleted by Rimsky-Korsakov in his version of *Khovanshchina*.

12. The drama *Smuta ili Vasilii Shuiskii* [Sedition] was also by Golenishchev-Kutuzov. See his reminiscences below.

13. Ol'ga Andreevna Gulevich.

L. Shestakova

1. Shestakova's and Dmitrii Stasov's daughter Olia (Glinka's godchild) died at the age of ten in 1863.

2. Shestakova was present at the celebration of V. Stasov's birthday on January 2, 1866.

3. Dargomyzhsky died January 5, 1869.

4. Dargomyzhsky died without finishing *Kamennyi gost'* [The stone guest]; Cui completed it, and Rimsky-Korsakov orchestrated it. Prior to Dargomyzhsky's death, Balakirev wrote the Overture on a theme from the three Czech scenes; he planned and began to write the fantasy "Islamei" for piano and the symphonic overture "Tamara." Other songs written by Musorgsky during that period were: "Po griby" [Gathering mushrooms], "Pirushka" [The feast], "Strekotun'ia-beloboka" [The white-flanked magpie], "Ozornik" [The mischievous one], "Kozyol" [The he-goat], "Klassik" [The classicist], "Po-nad Donom sad tsvetyot" [On the Don a garden blooms], "Kolybel'naia Eryomushke" [Yeremushka's cradle song], the first song from the cycle *Detskaia* [The nursery] ("Ditia s nianei" [The infant with Nursey]; the children's song "Vo sadu, akh vo sadochke" [In the garden]; and "Ia tsvetok polevoi" [I am a flower of the fields] ("Evreiskaia pesnia" [Hebrew song]). The opera *Boris Godunov* was planned during the fall of 1868; prior to it, Musorgsky wrote the first act of the opera *Zhenit'ba* [The marriage].

5. Musorgsky presented *Boris Godunov* to the Board of Theatrical Directors in the spring of 1870. In the first version the hostess did not have the song "Poimala ia siza seleznia" [I caught a dove-grey drake].

6. For information about Platonova see her recollections below.

7. On Eduard Napravnik see the head note to his memoir, below. Gennadii Kondrat'ev (1834–1905), a baritone, was the principal manager of the Russian opera from 1872 to 1900.

8. The committee on opera rejected *Boris Godunov* in February 1871. Musorgsky's reaction to this decision came as a great surprise to his friends. Rimsky-Korsakov wrote to A. Purgold on February 14: "The insensible Tigra [Musorgsky's nickname

in the circle] . . . knows everything about *Boris*'s fate and he has reacted to it absolutely unlike one might have expected, and consequently his reaction has been quite different from what everyone expected." (A. Orlova. *M. P. Musorgsky's Days and Works*, p. 229.)

9. Shestakova erred: the entire episode happened in 1871. See also V. V. Stasov's recollections.

10. The caricature of the Balakirev circle (which is kept in the museum of the theater named for A. Bakhrushin in Moscow) was drawn not by Elena Makovskaia but by her husband, Konstantin Makovskii. In the lower left-hand corner one sees the initials K. M. It seems that it was his wife's idea, but it was he who drew it. It is quite possible that Shestakova forgot the details, hence her mistake. V. Komarova-Stasova reports that this picture had been offered to Shestakova by E. Makovskaia, and that for a long time it was hidden in a back room. Later Shestakova gave it to V. Stasov; and from him it passed into the hands of his brother Dmitrii. After Dmitrii's death V. Komarova-Stasova gave the picture to the Bakhrushin Museum "because it is a document of paramount interest and value, which, in an extremely talented manner portrays all the representatives of the Mighty Handful." (Vladimir Karenin, *Vladimir Stasov* [Leningrad, 1926], Part 1, p. 375.)

11. Stasov holds the trumpet of glory; riding on the trumpet is the architect and artist Victor Hartmann depicted as a monkey; and on Stasov's shoulder sits the sculptor Mark Antokol'skii, depicted as Mephistopheles.

12. The scene in the Inn was written for the first version of the opera. The song of the hostess is a later addition (see above, note 36 of Stasov's recollections).

13. The première of *Pskovitianka* [The maid of Pskov] was held on January 1, 1873; the three scenes from *Boris* were given on February 5.

14. The prototype for the seminarian in the song *Seminarist* [The Seminarian] was Vasilii Molchanov from the Velikie Luki Seminary. He had been "assigned" to the village of Poshivkino "for a one-year training program" under the supervision of the priest of the Odigitriev Church, Simeon (Semyon) Vasilievich Suvorov. Father Simeon had several daughters, one of whom caught Molchanov's fancy. According to Father Simeon, Molchanov was far from gifted in his studies. Thus, the scene in Musorgsky's song was drawn from real life. (See Nikolai Novikov, *U istokov velikoi zhizni* [The sources for a great life] [Leningrad: Lenizdat, 1988].)

15. See Iu. Platonova's recollections and notes, below.

16. O. Petrov died on February 28, 1878.

17. Shestakova refers to the period when she was writing "My Evenings" (at V. Stasov's suggestion). At the beginning of the manuscript is the date May 31, 1889.

18. The author of the project for the monument was the architect I. Bogomolov, and the *bas-relief* was the work of the sculptor I. Ginzburg.

19. The beginning of a letter from Musorgsky, dated January 17, 1876. It refers to Borodin's Second Symphony, in B minor, entitled *Geroicheskaia Simfoniia* [Heroic symphony] or *Bogatyrskaia Symfoniia* [The Bogatyr symphony].

20. Stasov was collecting Musorgsky's autographs for the Public Library.

21. The letter has not been found.

22. Fyodor Gridnin (1844–1917), a journalist, Leonova's common-law husband.

23. Stasov's nickname in the Balakirev circle.

N. Rimsky-Korsakov

1. *Kniaz' Kholmskii* was a tragedy written in the 1830s and 40s by the famous playwright Nestor Kukol'kin, a friend of Glinka. The latter wrote the music for this tragedy (1840); apparently that was why the Balakirev circle took interest in it.

2. On Aleksandr Arsen'ev, see above, note 2 of Unkovskaia's recollections.

3. During this period of close acquaintance with Balakirev and his studies with him, Musorgsky composed an Allegro for orchestra (not preserved), a Scherzo in B-flat major, "Alla marcia notturna," Menuetto (not preserved), and a Symphony in D major (not preserved). The music for the tragedy "Tsar' Edip" [Oedipus] has not been preserved except for the chorus in the temple scene.

4. Here, Rimsky-Korsakov repeats an accepted legend (see also Balakirev's recollections, above).

5. Musorgsky's brother was christened Filaret; the name Evgenii was often used out of superstition, to protect him from death, if death were to seek him out (his parents had lost two children before Filaret's birth).

6. "Koroleva Mab" [Queen Mab scherzo] and "Bal u Kapuletti" [The feast at the Capulets] are episodes from Berlioz' Symphony "Romeo and Juliet"; Musorgsky's arrangement has not been preserved.

7. *Kavkazskii plennik* [The prisoner of the Caucasus] and *Syn Mandarina* [The mandarin's son] are operas by Cui. The symphony is Rimsky-Korsakov's First Symphony.

8. The Scherzo in B-flat major was performed on January 11, 1860, at the concert of the Russian Musical Society under A. Rubinstein's direction. The chorus from *Oedipus* was performed on April 6, 1861, in the Mariinskii Theater, in a concert directed by K. Liadov.

9. Cf. Balakirev's letter to Stasov: "Musorgsky is almost an idiot," dated June 3, 1863. (Quoted in M. Balakirev and V. Stasov, *Perepiska* [Correspondence], [Moscow, 1970], vol. 1, p. 212.)

10. The symphonic fantasy *Noch' na Lysoi gore* (Ivanova noch' na Lysoi gore) [Night on bald mountain (St. John's night on bald mountain)] underwent a series of "transformations." The first version mentioned by Rimsky-Korsakov is unknown; it is possible that it was never even written down. According to Musorgsky himself, it was planned in 1866. In 1867, it was written for a symphony orchestra but it was rejected by Balakirev, to whom Musorgsky wrote: "I was blue not because of living in the country or because of my financial situation. It was an author's spleen . . . due to your guarded response about my "Witches" [this was what Musorgsky called "Noch' "]. I thought, I think so now, and I will think that I consider this piece a decent one, particularly because, in it, after several independent trifles, for the first time I independently came up with an important work. . . . Whether or not you agree, my friend, to perform my "Witches," i.e., whether I will hear them or not, I will change nothing in the general outline or treatment; both are closely linked with the content of the picture and executed sincerely without pretense or imitation. Every author remembers the mood he was in while conceiving and executing a project, and this feeling or the memory of a past mood greatly supports his personal criterion. I accomplished my task as well as I could—to the best of my abilities." (Letter dated September 24, 1867.) The work was not performed during Musorgsky's lifetime. In 1880 the composer included this music in "Son parobka" [Rêverie of a young peasant] in the opera *Sorochinskaia Iarmarka* [The fair at Sorochintsy], having transformed the symphonic poem into a chorus with orchestra. It is precisely this version which Rimsky-Korsakov revised and orchestrated and turned into the widely known symphonic fantasy *Noch' na Lysoi gore* [Night on bald mountain]. At the end of the 1920s Musorgsky's original manuscript was discovered in the library of the Leningrad Conservatory by the musicologist Georgii Orlov. It was performed once by the Leningrad Philharmonic Society and then forgotten. In the West, Musorgsky's symphonic poem, in the author's version, is known and performed. The conductor N. Mal'ko brought along a copy of the score when he emigrated from the USSR.

11. On the chorus of *Porazhenie Sennakheriba* [The destruction of Sennacherib], see above, note 59 of V. Stasov's recollections. The chorus of "Iisus Navin" [Joshua] (the biblical text had been rearranged by Musorgsky) was dedicated to N. Rimsky-Korsakov (the author's date on the manuscript is July 2, 1877).

12. This statement by Rimsky-Korsakov shows the biased attitude toward Musorgsky which was generally accepted at the time, when people did not understand the innovative searching of the brilliant composer.

13. During these years Musorgsky and Rimsky-Korsakov maintained a correspondence dealing particularly with problems of creativity.

14. The choice of L. Mei's drama *Pskovitianka* is characteristic of the sixties. At the time, young Russian composers such as Musorgsky, Rimsky-Korsakov, and Tchaikovsky simultaneously turned toward subjects from their own history, subjects in which moral problems played a determining role.

15. Musorgsky, following in Stasov's footsteps, also opposed marriage and family responsibilities for artists. His feelings had their origin in Glinka's unsuccessful marriage and painful divorce, which left an excruciating imprint on the composer's life.

16. Aleksandr Serov (1820–1871) was at first a friend but later a fierce enemy of the Balakirev circle. Aleksandr Famintsyn (1841–1896) was a critic and a professor at the Petersburg Conservatory. He was the enemy of the composers of the New Russian school and violently attacked the works of Musorgsky, Rimsky-Korsakov, and others. Famintsyn's criticism of the symphonic poem *Sadko* by Rimsky-Korsakov provoked Musorgsky into composing his satirical song "Klassik" [The classicist]. (Incidentally, Famintsyn is the author of an interesting but still unpublished music dictionary; it is kept in the Manuscript Section of the Leningrad Public Library.)

17. In the summer of 1871, Musorgsky did not go anywhere.

18. Rimsky-Korsakov's older brother Voin (1822–1871) was a sailor. Raised on Italian opera he was, nevertheless, from his youth able to appreciate Glinka's *Ruslan i Liudmila* [Ruslan and Ludmila], an opera which was far from understood by many contemporaries.

19. Musorgsky and Rimsky-Korsakov became roommates on September 1, 1871. Musorgsky was then working on the second version of *Boris Godunov.*

20. Aleksandr Opochinin (1805–1887) and his sister, Nadezhda (1821–1874), were close friends of Musorgsky's (about his relationship with Nadezhda see Stasov's recollections above.) Musorgsky lived at the Opochinins' while he was working on the first version of *Boris Godunov.*

21. For information about Lukashevich, see the recollections of Iu. Platonova and L. Shestakova in this volume.

22. N. Krabbe, head of the Naval Ministry, was Rimsky-Korsakov's patron.

23. The first Polish scene was also performed. The benefit was for K. Kondrat'ev.

24. Rimsky-Korsakov and Nadezhda Purgold were married on June 20, 1872. Musorgsky was their *shafer* [he held the crown].

25. The *Khovanshchina* project goes back to 1872, i.e., when the orchestration of the second version of *Boris Godunov* was on the verge of completion. It is of interest to note the following dates: June 23 when the score of the scene at Kromy was completed; and July 7, when Musorgsky finished researching the historical sources for *Khovanshchina.*

26. The author's date on the manuscript refers to a later period.

27. This passage and the following one from *Letopis' moei muzykal'noi zhizni* [My musical life] reflects Musorgsky's loneliness and the total lack of understanding of his tragic situation (see also the Preface to the present volume).

28. Rimsky-Korsakov's tone attracts one's attention. For example, when he talks about the stage history of *Boris Godunov* in *Letopis' moei muzykal'noi zhizni* [My

musical life], it is one of estrangement: "it was rumored"; "it was said that the censors did not like the subject"; "the opera, which has been performed for two or three years, was now taken out of the repertoire." At the same time, Rimsky-Korsakov was not only a witness to these events but also close to Musorgsky. And he alludes to rumors. As for the "removal from" the repertoire of *Boris Godunov*, he is mistaken: the opera was not taken out during the reign of Aleksander II; it was taken out during the next reign, after Musorgsky's death. Indeed, the opera was seldom performed, but each of its performances was a triumph for the composer. Despite the violent attacks by the critics, the public, particularly the young people, liked the opera (see above, Stasov's recollections).

29. This statement shows a lack of knowledge of the circumstances of Musorgsky's life and an even greater ignorance of his acquaintances and relationships. Malyi Iaroslavets was not simply a tavern, as Russians understood it. It was a restaurant where the avant-garde intelligentsia gathered; it was a unique club of actors, physicians, writers, and artists. Rimsky-Korsakov writes about the personnel of Malyi Iaroslavets with aristocratic arrogance. The author of the present work discovered a letter from Musorgsky addressed to P. Shemaev, the maître-d'hôtel of this tavern. It testifies to Musorgsky's democratic spirit and his respect for people, regardless of their social status.

30. Musorgsky's statements refute Rimsky-Korsakov's assertions that Musorgsky had a negative attitude—due to some personal reason—against Rimsky-Korsakov's studies in theory. Musorgsky considered Rimsky-Korsakov's academism a betrayal of the precepts of the Mighty Handful, a betrayal of the innovators' ideals. On September 19, 1875, Musorgsky wrote to Stasov: "When I think of some artists who are behind the "barrier" [*shlagbaum*], I feel some sort of anguish as well as some sort of *slushy witchcraft*. All these yearnings of theirs, *drizzling* drop by drop, in such regular, dear, little drops; they are amused, but one who looks on is bored and grieved. Cut your way through, my dear fellow, as real men would do; show us if you have claws or fins; are you a beast or an amphibian? It is beyond you! Don't you see the *barrier*? Without reasoning, these artists have unwillingly chained themselves to tradition. They corroborate the law of inertia and think they achieve something."

31. Again it is not a matter of "liking" or "disliking" but a divergence of opinions.

32. Regarding Musorgsky's relationship with Balakirev, see Balakirev's and Stasov's recollections and their notes in the present volume.

33. During the "decline" of his talent (according to Rimsky-Korsakov) Musorgsky wrote two scenes from *Khovanshchina* and *Sorochinskaia Iarmarka* [The fair at Sorochintsy], *Pesni i pliaski smerti* [Songs and dances of death], *Kartinki s vystavki* [Pictures from an exhibition], the cycle *Bez solntsa* [Sunless], and a series of songs and romances.

34. Rimsky-Korsakov himself reviewed *Pskovitianka* [The maid of Pskov] once more and wrote a new version. He made an independent one-act opera, *Vera Sheloga,* from the Prologue.

35. *Parafrazy* [Paraphrases] for piano, based on the theme of "Chopsticks," consists of eight variations and six pieces by Rimsky-Korsakov, Borodin, Cui, and Liadov.

36. The rendition of the scene in the cell from the opera *Boris Godunov*, in a concert of the Free Music School on January 16, 1879, under the direction of Rimsky-Korsakov. See also below, I. Tiumenev's recollections about this concert.

37. The opera *Maiskaia Noch'* [May night] was premièred on January 2, 1880 in the Mariinskii Theater.

38. The concert was held on November 27, 1879. See I. Tiumenev's recollections below.

39. At the concert on November 27, 1879, Leonova sang "Pesnia Marfy" [Marfa's song]. The newspaper *Voskresnyi listok muzyki i ob"iavlenii* [Sunday leaflet of music and announcements] reported: "Mrs. Leonova and . . . Musorgsky had many curtain calls." (Reprinted in A. Orlova, *Musorgsky's Days and Works* [Ann Arbor: UMI Research Press, 1983], pp. 594-595.)

40. Leonova had been Glinka's student, in itself a very solid recommendation. Furthermore, she took special voice lessons with the singer Andrei Lodi, who had studied with the Italian school. Her trip to Japan was to promulgate Russian music. The ironic attitude toward Leonova was characteristic of all the members of the circle (Balakirev, Shestakova, and, in part, Stasov).

41. See D. Leonova's and A. Demidova's memoirs, below.

42. Fyodor Gridnin was a journalist and a translator. The Balakirev circle regarded him and Leonova with contempt. "Leonova and her companion," wrote the shocked Shestakova to Stasov, suspecting that they were making a drunkard of Musorgsky.

43. The tour took place in the summer of 1879.

44. The programs of the concerts included works of both Russian composers (Glinka, Dargomyzhsky, Balakirev, Borodin, Rimsky-Korsakov, Musorgsky) and West European composers (Chopin, Gounod, and others). The programs had been thoroughly worked out: In the cities where there were no opera theaters or symphony orchestras, Musorgsky and Leonova performed excerpts from opera, including Russian operas, and so introduced the provincial audience to the new works of the composers, especially those of the New Russian school.

45. For details see I. Tiumenev's recollections, below.

P. Stasova

1. "Voldemar" is Vladimir Stasov; Aleksandr Meyer was a friend of the Stasov family.

2. Konstantin Vel'iaminov, a general, was an amateur singer with a bass voice.

3. Musorgsky's friend Victor Hartmann (1834–1873), a talented architect and artist, died suddenly in June 1873. His death was a shock to Musorgsky (coincidence or not, the first information about Musorgsky's drinking bouts goes back to the summer of 1873). The piano suite *Kartinki s vystavki* [Pictures from an exhibition] was dedicated to Hartmann's memory. The themes were based on Hartmann's drawings.

4. Vasilii Clark was married to Sofiia, the sister of Vladimir and Dmitrii Stasov. She died in 1857.

5. Vladimir Il'inskii (d. 1890s), a physician and an amateur singer (baritone), was close to the Balakirev circle.

6. See above, note 1 to Filaret Musorgsky's recollections.

E. Dianina

1. Since Borodin's mother died in the summer of 1873, this took place in the early seventies.

I. Repin

1. M. Saltykov-Shchedrin's essay "Mezhdu delom" [At odd moments], a parody on the New Russian school, depicts Stasov as the critic "Neuvazhai-Koryto" [Do-

Not-Respect-the-Pig's-Trough] and Musorgsky as the composer "Vasilii Ivanovich." Signed M.M., it was published in the November 1874 issue of the journal *Otechestvennye zapiski* [Notes of the fatherland].

2. Nikolai Rubinstein (1835–1881) was the younger brother of the composer and pianist Anton Rubinstein (1829–1894). He was a distinguished pianist and conductor and the founder of the Moscow Conservatory.

3. Stasov wrote to his daughter explaining his being delayed in Petersburg: "I postponed my trip for a whole week. . . . I kept waiting for you; besides, as if on purpose, I had to wait a long time for my money." (Letter dated July 8, 1875. In V. Stasov, *Pis'ma k rodnym* [Letters to relatives] [Moscow, 1954], vol. 1, Part 2, p. 241.)

4. During his stay in Paris in the summer of 1875, Stasov mentions Musorgsky in his letters only twice: "As for the good news, I have just received beautiful letters from Musorianin and Shcherbach" [the composer N. Shcherbachev]. (Letter to his brother Aleksandr dated August 14/26, *Letters to Relatives,* p. 267.) "I am now convinced that he [Repin], despite having several wonderful talents, lacks the talent of imagination, the talent that Hartmann and Musorgsky have in abundance." (Letter to Dmitrii Stasov, August 17/29, 1875, *Letters to Relatives,* p. 271.)

5. Stasov's letters to Musorgsky were published in M. P. Musorgskii, *Pis'ma i dokumenty* [Letters and documents] (Moscow, 1932).

6. Incorrectly quoted from first sentence of the essay "Pamiati Musorgskogo" [To the memory of Musorgsky], written for the unveiling of the monument on the composer's grave, November 27, 1885. (In V. Stasov, *Stat'i o muzyke* [Articles on music] [Moscow, 1977], Part 3, p. 267.)

7. Repin incorrectly quotes and condenses an excerpt from Musorgsky's letter to V. Stasov dated January 2, 1873.

8. The whole essay, not just the foreword, ends with these words.

9. This quote from Musorgsky's letter to Repin, dated June 13, 1873, is incomplete and incorrect. It should read: "Keep on pulling, *wheelhorse,* keep on pulling; the cart is heavy, and there are many jades." Stasov called Musorgsky, Antokol'skii, and Repin his "troika"; and Musorgsky, in order to underline Repin's significance in art called him a "wheelhorse" and himself a "trace horse" (in the same letter).

10. Repin painted Musorgsky's portrait on March 2, 3, 4, and 5, 1881. Aleksandr II was assassinated on March 1.

11. Musorgsky, as well as all his family, makes a mistake about his birthday. He was not born on March 16 but on March 9. He was baptized on March 13. V. Karatygin discovered an entry in the register of births, deaths, and marriages in the church where he was baptized (see also above, note 54 of Stasov's memoirs).

12. Repin is mistaken: Musorgsky died on March 16, but the sudden turn for the worse happened on March 6.

Iu. Platonova

1. Liudmila Ivanovna Shestakova.

2. Nikolai Alekseevich Lukashevich (1821–after 1894) was the stage manager of the Imperial Theaters. Gennadii Pavlovich Kondrat'ev (1834–1905) was the manager of the Russian opera. Fyodor Kommissarzhevskii (1838–1905), a tenor; Dar'ia Leonova (1829–1896), a contralto; and Osip Petrov (1807–1878), a bass, were artists in Russian opera.

3. See E. Napravnik's recollections, below, concerning his opinion of *Boris Godunov.*

4. See L. Shestakova's *Moi vechera* [My evenings], above, regarding the rejection of the opera by the committee.

5. Stepan Gedeonov (1815–1878) was an archeologist, a literary historian, and the director of the Imperial Theaters from 1867 to 1875.

6. Platonova's story is not entirely clear. In her contract for the 1873–1874 season there is no mention of this benefit performance. In S. Gedeonov's personal papers there is a letter from the singer, dated April 11, 1873, in which she asked that her contract include a clause about a benefit performance and requested that it be a new opera (the author's name and the title were not specified). Were there other, private letters from her to Gedeonov, which he did not put in the theater files?

7. Platonova is mistaken: the confrontation with the Grand Duke refers to the first presentation. Here is what V. Stasov wrote immediately after the episode described by Platonova, i.e., while he "was hot on the scent": "The first representation of *Boris Godunov* was most brilliant. Musorianin was given, if I am not mistaken, between eighteen and twenty curtain calls. In the entire audience, I think only Konstantin Nikolaevich was unhappy (he does not like our school, in general), and it is said that he even forbade his son's applauding, right there in the theater. Incidentally, perhaps, it was not so much the fault of the music as that of the libretto, where the 'folk scenes,' the riot, the scene where the police officer beats the people with his stick so that they cry out begging Boris to accept the throne, and so forth, were jarring to some people and infuriated them. There was no end to applause and curtain calls." (Letter to his daughter, dated February 2, 1874, in V. Stasov, *Pis'ma k rodnym* [Letters to relatives] [Moscow, 1954], vol. 1, Part 2, pp. 206–207.) The success was immense: "After each of the seven scenes the vast majority of the audience called for the performers and the author." (*SPB vedomosti* [Saint Petersburg news], no. 37, February 6, 1874.)

E. Napravnik

1. Napravnik could have heard Shaliapin's first appearance as Boris in 1896, during the tour by Mamontov's Private Russian Opera in Petersburg.

S. Kruglikov

1. Kruglikov was studying at the Free Music School, and it was through the school that he made Rimsky-Korsakov's acquaintance and became a close friend. He might have heard Musorgsky's performance in Rimsky-Korsakov's house.

A. Golenishchev-Kutuzov

1. In the draft of the manuscript, the introductory sentence reads: "Without having won for himself any particular fame or even any recognition for his obvious merits"; and this paragraph contains an additional sentence: "And these talents were undoubtedly considerable. All his life Musorgsky geared these talents toward the realization of tasks which bore in themselves the lively, healthy seeds which sooner or later will bear fruit in the field of Russian musical art."

2. In the draft of the manuscript there is an additional sentence which was deleted by the author: "Among those who accompanied him was the author of these lines." The following paragraph begins: "On one hand I am deeply convinced that the seeds I mentioned earlier, which were sown by Musorgsky in the field of Russian art, will not disappear without leaving a trace but sooner or later will bear fruit, and that the name of Musorgsky, in time, will be inscribed in the history of Russian music along with its most honorable names. On the other hand, during the last eight or nine years I enjoyed the particular favor of the deceased, and I had the right to call myself his friend, not in the general sense, but in the real meaning of this word;

immediately after Musorgsky's death, I intended to write, and eventually publish, my personal recollections about him. . . . " From here on, except for minor and unimportant differences, the draft concurs with the final manuscript, which still has some breaks and unfinished sentences.

3. Golenishchev-Kutuzov's name is mentioned for the first time by Musorgsky in a letter to Stasov dated June 19, 1873. The composer must have made his acquaintance just prior to this date.

4. See Stasov's recollections, above.

5. Unfortunately, it has been impossible to establish in whose house Golenishchev-Kutuzov and Musorgsky had met. At any rate, it could not have been in a house frequented by the members of the Balakirev circle, for Musorgsky would not have had any reason to recommend Kutuzov to Stasov, since Stasov would have met the poet in the same house (usually all the members of the Balakirev circle were in one house or another). Musorgsky's circle of acquaintances was extremely wide and spread well beyond the limits of the people known by the Balakirev group.

6. When Golenishchev-Kutuzov moved into Zaremba's house on Panteleimon Street, Musorgsky had already left. The composer moved there in August 1871; and from September 1 he shared a room with Rimsky-Korsakov. The next summer, just before his marriage, Rimsky-Korsakov moved out, and on September 1, 1872, Musorgsky moved to Shpalernaia Street, to the house where Cui was then living. Rimsky-Korsakov and his wife were living in a house nearby.

7. The song "Tsar' Saul" [King Saul], based on Byron's poem and translated by P. Kozlov, was composed in 1863. The song "Noch' " [Night], based on a much-altered text by Pushkin, was composed in 1864.

8. Obviously, the author has Stasov in mind. Although Stasov did not have a formal musical education, he was extremely well trained in music.

9. Musorgsky, an ardent lover of the Russian past, could hardly have been "enthusiastic" about Golenishchev-Kutuzov's verses in their second version, which was as pitiful as the first. A stern critic, Musorgsky was an expert in versification. For instance, his remarks on the manuscript of N. Shcherbachev's poem "Zabytyi" [Forgotten], an attempt to give a text to Musorgsky's ballad, and on the manuscript of Golenishchev-Kutuzov's drama "Smuta ili Vasilii Shuiskii" [Sedition] (Golenishchev-Kutuzov had kept all these materials in his archives) contradict the memorialist's assertion that Musorgsky sought originality for originality's sake.

10. Regarding Musorgsky's agreeing to the deletions in *Boris Godunov,* Stasov wrote: "Unfortunately this year, our poor Musorgsky is drinking more and more, and at present, he is so fogged by the wine and the fear that his opera will be taken off the stage that he blindly obeys Napravnik and all the singers, men or women, in the Mariinskii Theater . . . he deletes anything they tell him to delete." (Letter to his daughter, dated February 2, 1874, in V. Stasov, *Pis'ma k rodnym* [Letters to Relatives] [Moscow, 1954], vol. 1, Part 2, p. 209.) This explanation seems more reliable than Golenishchev-Kutuzov's comments. For Napravnik's appraisal of *Boris Godunov,* see his recollections, above.

11. After the deletion of the scene at Kromy from the presentation, Stasov wrote a sharp article "Urezki v *Borise Godunove*" [Deletions in *Boris Godunov*] (letter to the editor of *Novoe Vremia* [New time], no. 239, October 27, 1879). Although none of Musorgsky's views about the deletion of the scene at Kromy have been preserved, one readily accepts that the composer shared Stasov's opinion, otherwise he would have come forth in writing with a refutation on behalf of Napravnik and the Board of Directors immediately after the première of the opera, at least for the reason indicated by Stasov (see note 10). In 1876, the composer could have feared seeing his opera taken out of the repertoire for the same reasons as in 1874. Golenishchev-

Kutuzov's quotation of Musorgsky's alleged words, that in the scene at Kromy the composer "had lied about the Russian people," does not inspire confidence, not to mention the fact that the expressions used by Musorgsky and quoted by the poet conflict with the composer's vocabulary. We can, of course, assume that Golenishchev-Kutuzov repeated Musorgsky's thought in his own words. However, it is utterly unbelievable that the composer would disavow the scene at Kromy. For an artist, especially such a truthful one as Musorgsky, to disavow something he had written was a frightening thought. Undoubtedly it would have been reflected in his correspondence of the time. In the meantime, in 1873, the composer wrote: "I am rereading Solovyov [Sergei Solovyov's historical work] to become acquainted with this period [i.e., the period of Sof'ia's reign and the Streltsy riots], as I became acquainted in *Boris* with the origin of the 'troubled times' in the tramps." [Musorgsky called the scene at Kromy "the tramps."] (From a letter to V. Stasov, dated September 6, 1873.) Six months later the famous dedication of the opera *Boris Godunov* appeared: "I view the people as one great individual, animated by one idea. This is my task. I have attempted to resolve it in the opera (January 21, 1874)." In 1876 Musorgsky wrote: "Before *Boris* I had created some folk scenes. My present wish is to make a prediction which is the following one . . . a realistic melody and not a melodic one in the classical sense. . . . " (From a letter to V. Stasov, dated December 25, 1876.) Does this look like a disavowal of *Boris Godunov,* or was he talking about the growth he had achieved through it? Incidentally, this letter had been written after the deletion of the scene at Kromy, i.e., after the "renunciation" invented by Golenishchev-Kutuzov. On August 15, 1877 Musorgsky wrote to the poet: "The delight experienced with the musical exposition of Pushkin (in *Boris*) is renewed with the musical exposition of Gogol' (in *Sorochinskaia* [The fair at Sorochintsy])" and "Woe to those whose whim it is to use Pushkin or Gogol' only for their text!" Where is his rejection of *Boris Godunov* or, at least, of the scene at Kromy? In *Khovanshchina,* Musorgsky developed all the elements which were embryonic in *Boris Godunov.*

12. Golenishchev-Kutuzov's dramatic chronicle *Smuta* [Sedition] was dedicated to Musorgsky and obviously written under his influence.

13. During the first season, i.e., from January 27 to February 10, 1874 (the season ended at Lent), *Boris Godunov* was performed four times.

14. C. Cui and his article about *Boris Godunov.*

15. There is no evidence to ascribe to Musorgsky the opinion that the music criticism of his time was the voice of "competent judges"; quite the contrary! The quality of music criticism in Petersburg then was very low. Except for the talented and intelligent Laroche—by principle a fiery enemy of the New Russian school—the music criticism of that era astonishes by its dismal mediocrity. (Serov—also an enemy—died in 1871; Stasov at that time rarely voiced his opinion; his article in defense of *Boris Godunov* was his first article about Musorgsky.)

16. This entire passage is a testimony to the total misunderstanding of *Boris Godunov.* One is absolutely at a loss to see how Golenishchev-Kutuzov could have said that the Balakirev circle neither appreciated nor understood the great poet. In their works, the composers of the New Russian school demonstrated exactly the opposite. In referring to the "additional rubbish" supposedly included by Musorgsky in the libretto, Golenishchev-Kutuzov seems to be talking about the movement of history, about everyday occurrences, about reality. Musorgsky found material for his opera not only in Pushkin's tragedy but also in historical works, primarily in *Istoriia Gosudarstva Rossiiskogo* [History of the Russian state] by Karamzin.

17. The piano suite *Kartinki s vystavki* [Pictures from an exhibition] is one of Musorgsky's greatest works. It is far from being a simple "illustration" of Hartmann's drawings. It is a profoundly philosophical work, a meditation on life and

death, on history, on the people, and on man in general. In short, it is much more than Golenishchev-Kutuzov's perception of this suite. (Incidentally, there are no "kittens" in the suite; the memoirist obviously mistook "Tanets nevylupivshikhsia ptentsov" [Ballet of the unhatched chicks] for "kittens.")

18. Letter to Stasov, dated November 23, 1875.

19. The piano score of *Khovanshchina* was published in 1884.

20. Musorgsky lived with Golenishchev-Kutuzov for a very short time: On November 7, 1874, the poet had not yet moved to Shpalernaia Street, since on that date, Musorgsky wrote him a letter in which he regretted being unable to come to see him. On December 29 and on March 7, 1875, the composer wrote letters to Golenishchev-Kutuzov in the country. In February, Golenishchev-Kutuzov left for the country after receiving a telegram from his mother. Therefore, he was in Petersburg in January (the exact day is unknown) and part of February. It is only at that time that he could have moved to Shpalernaia Street. An undated letter from the poet to his mother is believed to date from that time: "I want to find an apartment. At Musorgsky's it is cramped and cold. I hope to drag him along with me." (Quoted in M. P. Musorgskii, *Pis'ma k Golenishchevu-Kutuzovu* [Letters to Golenishchev-Kutuzov] [Moscow, 1939], p. 33.) After returning from the country, not earlier than March 10, Golenishchev-Kutuzov moved to Galernaia Street. But on May 11, 22, and 25, Musorgsky wrote to him in Tver'. In the first half of June, Golenishchev-Kutuzov was in Petersburg (Musorgsky mentioned him in his letter to Stasov dated June 13, 1875); and on June 27, Musorgsky announced to Shestakova that he was going to move from Shpalernaia Street. Apprently about July 1, he did move to Golenishchev-Kutuzov's apartment on Galernaia Street. Near the end of July the poet left, and Musorgsky moved in with P. Naumov; he did not live with Golenishchev-Kutuzov after this. Therefore, Musorgsky lived with Golenishchev-Kutuzov on Shpalernaia Street a little bit longer than a month, and they lived together for about another month on Galernaia Street. The cycle *Bez solntsa* [Sunless] (six and not five songs) was composed between May 7 and August 25, 1874; the ballad "Zabytyi" [Forgotten] was composed in May of the same year. On September 2, 1874, "Vstuplenie (Rassvet na Moskve-reke)" [Introduction. Dawn on the Moscow River] was written for *Khovanshchina*. Musorgsky wrote the first scene (the scene of the clerk with the recently arrived newcomers) on January 2, 1875; the first act was completed on July 30; between August and December, he wrote the beginning of the second act; and on December 31, the beginning of the third act. In other words, while living with Golenishchev-Kutuzov, Musorgsky wrote almost nothing for *Khovanshchina* (of course, this does not preclude his thinking about the opera).

21. Among Musorgsky's unfinished works, there are outlines for a song "Krapivnaia gora" ("Rak") [The hill of nettles (The crab)], based on Golenishchev-Kutuzov's words. It dates from 1874.

22. Golenishchev-Kutuzov carefully kept not only all the letters from Musorgsky but even notes of no importance and other autographs by him. The letters from which the poet quotes these words are not in his archives.

23. No trace of these scenes can be found in the manuscript of *Khovanshchina*.

24. It is unknown what nonprogrammatic piano pieces the poet is talking about.

25. The opera *Sorochinskaia Iarmarka* [The fair at Sorochintsy], based on Gogol's novel, was begun during the summer of 1874 and was being created simultaneously with *Khovanshchina*; it was not completed. Golenishchev-Kutuzov collaborated on the libretto; in his archives there is an outline in verse for "Rasskaz o krasnoi svitke" [Story of the red *svitka* (a Ukranian garment)] (*Muzykal'noe nasledstvo* [Musical heritage] [Moscow, 1935], p. 48).

26. There is no information about Musorgsky's intention to write an opera on the

seventeenth-century "Povest' o Savve Grudtsyne" [Tale of Savva Grudtsyn] or on "Vii" by Gogol'. Except for their being mentioned by Golenishchev-Kutuzov, there is no trace of these projects.

27. In 1872 S. Gedeonov, the Director of the Imperial Theaters, commissioned Borodin, Musorgsky, Cui, and Rimsky-Korsakov to write an opera-ballet called "Mlada." This project was never completed, although all the composers worked on it. "Marsh kniazei" [The march of the princes] and "Sluzhenie chyornomu kozlu" [Worship of the black he-goat] are from Musorgsky's pen. It is at a later date that Rimsky-Korsakov composed an opera-ballet *Mlada*.

28. The sudden change for the worse in Musorgsky's condition began after March 6; three days prior to his death paralysis struck him.

29. The brothers Matvei (1794–1866) and Mikhail Viel'gorskii (1788–1856)—a cellist and a composer—were enlightened patrons of art. They played a great role in the musical life of Russia in the first half of the nineteenth century.

N. Cherepnin

1. The father of the composer N. Cherepnin was Nikolai Cherepnin, a well-known physician and journalist who wrote for the radical press. Evgraf Golovin, also a physician, was Borodin's pupil.

2. Musorgsky lived in Oranienbaum in Leonova's *dacha* during the last summer of his life (1880) and while there he worked on *Khovanshchina*.

3. Musorgsky regarded Gorbunov highly. After listening to Gorbunov in a folk scene, the composer wrote to him: "Keep on the same artistic path; stay with the same force for truth, love, and spontaneity" (letter written during the night of January 4–5, 1880). Musorgsky wrote the musical piece, "Privet Gorbunovu" [Greetings to Gorbunov] for the twenty-first anniversary of "the *national* Russian artist." (*Polnoe sobraniie sochinenii Musorgskogo* [Musorgsky's complete works], vol. 5, Part 10, p. 43.)

D. Stakheev

1. Sergei Maksimov (1831–1901) was an ethnographer and a writer.
2. The famous playwright Aleksandr Ostrovskii (1823–1886).

N. Bruni

1. Mikhail Valuev (1823–1897) was an employee in the Harbor Customs Office; his wife was named Mariia, née Iudina (d. 1901). They had two sons—Pavel and Fyodor (d. 1917), both communications engineers—and a daughter, Elizaveta.

2. Musorgsky apparently moved to the Valuevs' toward the end of 1879 and lived there a short time, but the length of his stay has not been established. Most likely he lived there during the winter and moved to furnished rooms in the spring. From a letter Rimsky-Korsakov wrote to Stasov about Musorgsky's visit of May 10 dated May 11, 1880, we can conclude that Musorgsky lived by himself, i.e., in furnished rooms. (See N. Rimskii-Korsakov, *Polnoe sobranie sochinenii, Literaturnye proizvedeniia i perepiska* [Complete Works, Literary works and correspondence] [Moscow, 1963], vol. 5, p. 370.

A. Vrubel'

1. This episode can be dated to the summer of 1879 or 1880.

Aleksandr Molas

1. Aleksandr's brother Nikolai (1843–1917), a painter, was the husband of A[leksandra] Purgold.
2. Aleksandr Molas errs; the Free Music School had no ties with the Conservatory.
3. This concert of the Free Music School was held on March 23, 1876, under the direction of Rimsky-Korsakov (see also the memoirs of A. Molas [née] Purgold and Tiumenev, below).
4. The first public performance of "Sirotka" [The orphan] took place on March 3, 1874 with A. Kruglikova as soloist. At the second performance, on April 23, 1875, the soloist was Makhina. There is no information about the "failure" of this song, nor can it be assumed that the singers did not perform it in the declamatory manner that was intrinsic to A. Molas, but in an academic one. The shattering impression left by A. Petrova-Vorobyova's rendition of "The Orphan" is described by the author himself, by Shestakova, and by Turgenev (in a letter to Pauline Viardot). (See also the recollections of V. Stasov and of Shestakova, above.)
5. See note 2.
6. Molas errs: Vasil'ev the Second was a tenor. Pimen's part was sung by Vasil'ev the First, a bass.
7. Musorgsky began to compose *The Fair at Sorochintsy* in 1875.
8. See Repin's memoirs, above.

Aleksandra Molas

1. This statement is inaccurate: The Purgold sisters met Musorgsky on March 5, 1868; the idea of *Boris Godunov* dates from the fall of the same year.
2. Aleksandra Purgold married Nikolai Molas on November 11, 1872.
3. Glazunov began to visit the Molases soon after Musorgsky's death.
4. Compare with N. Purgold's entry in her diary for April 30, 1870: "I am convinced that some of Musorgsky's pieces would never have been written were it not for Sasha. Without realizing it himself he wrote his 'kids' (*Detskaia* [The nursery]) only because of her and for her, because he knew very well that she was the only one who could perform them as they should be performed. By her performance, she inspires the others." (A. Rimskii-Korsakov, *N. A. Rimskii-Korsakov, Zhizn' i tvorchestvo* [N. A. Rimsky-Korsakov, life and work] [Moscow, 1935], Part 2, p. 96.)

V. Bessel'

1. Dargomyzhsky's piano score for *Kamennyi gost'* [The stone guest] is kept in the Tsentral'nyi muzei muzykal'noi kultury imeni Glinki [Central Museum of Musical Culture named for Glinka] in Moscow. The dedication is by V. Bessel': "To Modest Petrovich Musorgsky from the Publisher. January 22, 1872." On the same sheet Musorgsky had written the date of the première and the names of the performers. Underneath he added: "German text according to Bodenstedt [Alexander Puschkin Dramatische Werke, Berlin, 1855], copied by me in June, 1872. M. Musorgsky." In this copy Musorgsky added the German text in pencil (A. Orlova, *Musorgsky's Days and Works*, pp. 255 and 271). Apparently the German text for Listz had been included in a different piano score.

N. Lavrov

1. Musorgsky's copyright was given to Tertii Filippov, who gave Bessel' the right to publish Musorgsky's works without any royalties. If Stasov paid Musorgsky's

debts, he did it out of his own pocket. It is Stasov again who made the largest contribution for the monument.

2. This statement is inaccurate: Musorgsky was dismissed from the Government Control on January 1, 1880, as he was no longer able to work.

A. Leont'ev

1. "Plyvyot, plyvyot lebyodushka" [The swan glides on the water] is the chorus honoring Khovanskii in Scene 1, Act 4 (Khovanskii's chambers), of the opera *Kovanshchina*.

I. Lapshin

1. Rozhdestvenskii was a professor at Petersburg University.

2. Druri's identity has not been established.

3. See recollections by A. A. Vrubel', above.

4. Larin is mentioned by Musorgsky in a list of people who were to receive tickets for the opera *Boris Godunov*. He is also mentioned in a letter to Golen-ishchev-Kutuzov, dated August 17, 1875. Musorgsky includes Larin among the people who visited the Naumov family, with whom the composer lived after Golenishchev-Kutuzov's departure for the country. Since no additional information about this person is available, it is difficult to establish the exact time span mentioned later.

5. Iakov Polonskii (1819–1898) was a famous poet.

6. "Kol' slaven nash Gospod' v Sione" is an Orthodox hymn.

7. The memorial concert for Dostoevsky was held on February 4. This was not the next to the last appearance by Musorgsky. He appeared twice more as accompanist, both times on February 9: in a concert in the editorial office of the newspaper *Novoe vremia* [New time], and in a musical evening for the benefit of needy students of the Art Academy.

V. Bertenson

1. The concert was held on April 6, 1880.

D. Leonova

1. Leonova refers to the performance on February 5, 1873, of three scenes. She had the role of the hostess of the inn (see below). Neither *Khovanshchina* nor *Sorochinskaia Iarmarka* [The fair at Sorochintsy] was completed.

2. The two scenes (in the inn and in Marina's boudoir) scheduled for Leonova's farewell benefit performance were not performed because Kommissarzhevskii was ill (he was to perform the role of the Pretender).

3. Leonova had made a worldwide concert tour.

4. The Naumov family.

5. The concert tour of the summer of 1879. In the spring of 1880, Leonova and Musorgsky went to Tver'.

6. Three-part exercises without words have been preserved: *Andante cantabile, Largo,* and *Andante giusto.* Also preserved are arrangements of two Russian folk songs for male chorus in four voices: "U vorot, vorot batiushkinykh" [By father's gates] and "Ty vzoidi, vzoidi, solntse krasnoe" [Rise, beautiful sun]; a rearrangement for two tenor voices (soli) and male chorus of the song "Uzh ty, volia, moia volia" [O! Thou, my freedom]; and a rearrangement for four male voices of the song "Skazhi, devitsa molodaia" [Tell me, young girl].

7. February 10, 1881.

8. Musorgsky was admitted to the hospital on February 12, 1881.

A. Demidova

1. The translation has not been preserved.

2. For details about Musorgsky's funeral see Tiumenev's recollections, below.

L. Bertenson

1. See M. Ivanov's obituary, above.

2. A monograph by K. Wolfurt, Musorgsky's German biographer, provides additional information. The author reports that after Filaret Musorgsky, the composer's brother, visited him in the hospital, " 'Something sad happened,' the then-75-year-old Leningrad physician Dr. Bertenson told me personally in 1926. Filaret had left the composer some money; the composer, without knowledge of the hospital administration, sent for wine and drank himself to oblivion. This immediately provoked a terrible catastrophe. Musorgsky became mortally ill with erysipelas. True, on March 15 he felt better, and he and all his friends hoped for the best. But this was only a spark from his last vital forces. On March 16, at five o'clock in the morning, he twice uttered a loud cry and then died. His adipose heart refused to keep on working. None of his relatives or friends were with him at the end. Two hospital attendants paid him the last respects and closed his eyes." (K. Wolfurt, *Mussorgskij* [Stuttgart, 1927], p. 128; translated from the German.)

M. Ippolitov-Ivanov

1. Glazunov "appeared on the horizon" the year of Musorgsky's death.

2. Ippolitov-Ivanov is mistaken; in 1881, Musorgsky was already dead, so this story must refer to the winter of 1879–1880. It is possible that that was when Ippolitov-Ivanov met Musorgsky.

3. This statement is inaccurate: Glazunov's friendship with Laroche came later. At the time of this incident, Glazunov had not yet appeared on the musical scene.

4. The actual date was December 11, 1881. Napravnik wrote in his notebook: "*Boris Godunov* was resumed with great success." (A. Orlova, *M. P. Musorgsky's Days and Works,* p. 664.)

M. Ivanov

1. Nikolai Rubinstein died on March 11, 1881.

2. See L. Bertenson's recollections, above.

3. Musorgsky's copyrights were officially given to T. Filippov on March 14.

4. The description of Musorgsky's funeral has been deleted from Ivanov's obituary. For additional details, see I. Tiumenev's recollections, below.

5. Musorgsky's portrait by Repin was exhibited during the Ninth Traveling Exhibit in Petersburg on March 17, 1881. After this, the portrait was acquired by P. Tret'iakov; it is now located in the Tret'iakov Gallery in Moscow.

6. Nothing is known about this intention.

7. Musorgsky's participation in the musical morning of February 9.

8. It is obvious that Ivanov got his information from someone else. Musorgsky's drinking bouts began much earlier.

9. In Ivanov's assertions one sees his animosity toward Stasov.

10. Stasov was outraged that Ivanov made Musorgsky's alcoholism public. Stasov's obituary states that Musorgsky died of erysipelas. It is interesting to notice

that this version is still repeated today. Thus, Mikhail Goldstein (Hamburg) categorically proclaims in his article "Inakomysliashchii Modest Musorgskii" [Modest Musorgsky, the heretic]: "He died . . . of erysipelas of the leg and not of any of the other illnesses which were ascribed to the composer" (*Novoe russkoe slovo* [New Russian word], April 26, 1981). But Musorgsky's contemporaries thought that concealing his illness was senseless. "An unfortunate weakness for alcohol," according to Repin, "was the main reason for his early death." "Remember how many times you saved him from this poisoning," Repin wrote to Stasov, on June 14, 1881, "how you sobered him up, how you took care of him and how with all sorts of remedies you brought him back to his previous human, artistic creativity—this man who had become a half-idiot with shaking hands. . . . Why should one hide this distressing fact? It was known to almost everybody who knew him." (I. Repin, *Izbrannye pis'ma* [Selected letters], 2 vols. (Moscow, 1969), vol. 1, p. 258.)

I. Tiumenev

1. Rimsky-Korsakov was then head of the Free Music School, which had been founded in 1862 by Balakirev and Gavriil Lomakin, the famous choir conductor.

2. The scene in the cell was not performed in the theater. The censors had forbidden its staging.

3. Borodin was writing the opera *Kniaz' Igor'* [Prince Igor]. He died without completing it.

4. Rimsky-Korsakov completed the opera *Maiskaia Noch'* [May night] in 1879.

5. V. Vasil'ev the First, a bass, was a soloist in the Mariinskii Theater.

6. V. Vasil'ev the Second, a tenor, was a soloist at the same theater.

7. During the concert at the Free Music School, on November 13, 1879, the following were performed: excerpts from the new version of *Pskovitianka* [The maid of Pskov]; excerpts from *Kniaz' Igor'* [Prince Igor]; Beethoven's Sixth Symphony, Berlioz' overture *Benvenuto Cellini*, and Liszt's fantasy on Verdi's *Rigoletto*.

8. The second concert of the season at the Free Music School was held on November 27, 1879. For this event, Rimsky-Korsakov orchestrated "Pliaska persidok" [The Persian dance] by Musorgsky.

9. A friend of Tiumenev's whose identity has not been established.

10. Mikhail Berman, a choir conductor and leader of the Dumskii Circle.

11. All these prominent figures died about the same time. Dostoevsky and Pisemskii were writers; N. Rubinstein was a pianist and a conductor; and Azanchevskii was at one time Director of the Petersburg Conservatory.

12. Filaret Musorgsky.

13. It was not S. Botkin who took care of Musorgsky but L. Bertenson, then a young physician.

14. Musorgsky was paid for composing *Khovanshchina*.

15. A choir conductor.

16. Nadezhda Nikolaevna Rimskaia-Korsakova, the composer's wife.

17. Karl Davydov (1838–1889) was a famous cellist, a conductor, and a composer. At one time he was Director of the Petersburg Conservatory.

18. I. Mel'nikov (bass), M. Kamenskaia (mezzo-soprano), and I. Prianishnikov (baritone) were artists at the Mariinskii Theater.

19. Aleksandr, Vladimir, and Dmitrii Stasov.

20. N. Solovyov was a music critic, a composer, and a professor at the Petersburg Conservatory. He was the sworn enemy of the New Russian school.

21. Slonovaia was the former name of Suvorov Prospekt.

22. A singer.

23. These ribbons had been embroidered by Musorgsky's admirers for the première of *Boris Godunov*.

24. Aleksandr II had been assassinated on March 1.

25. Tiumenev was studying in the Art Academy.

26. Musorgsky regularly participated in concerts for the benefit of the students of the Art Academy. His last public appearance was for the students of the Academy.

27. F. Stravinskii (bass), F. Velinskaia (soprano), and O. Shreder (Napravnik's wife, a mezzo-soprano) were artists at the Mariinskii Theater.

28. Vasilii Maksimov was a painter.

29. The Bestuzhev Courses was the name of an institution of higher education for women. Musorgsky participated in concerts for the benefit of the Courses. Borodin was their active organizer.

30. Grigorii Lishin was a composer and a translator.

31. These leaves are pasted in Tiumenev's diary.

ALEXANDRA ORLOVA is a musicologist and historian specializing in chronicles of the lives and works of Russian composers. Among her subjects are Tchaikovsky, Glinka, and Rimsky-Korsakov. From 1944 to 1978, when she emigrated to the United States, she was a member of the Union of Soviet Composers.

.   .   .

VÉRONIQUE ZAYTZEFF and FREDERICK MORRISON are professors in the Department of Foreign Languages and Literature at Southern Illinois University at Edwardsville. Zaytzeff is in French and Russian, and Morrison is in Spanish. Both are active as translators, and they have collaborated on a translation of Simone de Beauvoir's lengthy article "Merleau-Ponty and Pseudo-Sartreanism."